spirited

spirited

AFFIRMING THE SOUL AND BLACK GAY/LESBIAN IDENTITY

Edited by
G.WINSTON JAMES
LISA C. MOORE

⊕REDBONE PRESS

NEW ORLEANS, LA
www.redbonepress.com

For my father, John E. Moore; he shows me how to love.
And to Eunice, who gives me flight lessons.
Thank you both for continuing to teach me.
—LCM

Acknowledgments

G. Winston James: Heartfelt thanks to Lisa C. Moore and RedBone Press for embracing and shepherding the vision of this project, and my sincere appreciation to Curu Necos-Bloice, a friend and angel who reminds me almost daily to shed judgment and strive to do better. Special thanks to Ronald K. Brown for helping to instill in me spiritual principles by which I continually endeavor to live.

Lisa C. Moore: Thank you to LaShonda Barnett and G. Winston James for bringing your ideas for the book to RedBone Press; thank you to Carolyn Adams for continual encouragement and support. Thanks to Jane Troxell for the extra pairs of eyes. Thanks to Anthony Hardaway for your patience. Thank you to everyone who sent love and light after the fire on Sept. 10, 2002. And many, many thanks to co-editor extraordinaire G. Winston James.

Publisher's note: RedBone Press is grateful for the kind contributions of the following:

Adelina Anthony
Emily Bernard
Lynn Bolton
Terri L. Carver
Imani Davis
Staci Haines
Tsehaye G. Hebert
Sarah B. Stewart
Teri Lynn Varner
Michelle Wilkinson and L. Pepper Heusner

Contents

Lifting Our Voices

By Rev. Irene Monroe

Finding our spiritual voice has been an arduous journey until this collection of spiritual narratives, *Spirited: Affirming the Soul and Black Gay/Lesbian Identity*. As black lesbian, gay, bisexual, transgender and queer (LGBTQ) people, we have had no language that adequately articulates the unique embodiment of our spirituality.

However, these spiritual narratives do articulate that very thing, and they function as our talking book, speaking to our social realities. These narratives construct a spiritual vernacular and theology that helps speak for and to black LGBTQ spiritual sensibility. They are representative as a mode of speaking about our personal stories that reinforces spiritual identity, and are also representative as a mode of speaking that affirms our everyday lived experience as LGBTQ people of the African diaspora.

For too long many of us black LGBTQ people have been looking for ways to express the ethos of our spirituality. In so doing, many of us have borrowed language from both white queer and black religious cultures that, at best, have muffled our spiritual reality, and, at worst, extinguished it. With one of the roots of racism planted in American Christianity, LGBTQ Christian activists have an uphill battle when it comes to eradicating the stain of racism from the LGBTQ movement. The inherent racism in both Christianity and in the LGBTQ movement challenges all LGBTQ people, but for LGBTQ people of the African diaspora, racism leaves no space for uncompromised expressions of faith.

The black church muffles our queer spirituality by applauding us in its choir pews on the one hand, yet excoriating us from its pulpits on the other. Our connections and contributions to the larger black religious cosmos are desecrated every time homophobic pronouncements go unchecked in these holy places of worship.

For us, as we straddle both black and LGBTQ cultures, the task has always been to develop a theological language that speaks truth to our unique spirituality. However, housing our spirituality in both religious cultures—white queer, and black—has been one of tenuous residency, that of spiritual wanderers and resident aliens.

As spiritual wanderers in white queer religious culture, we navigate through the dominant queer spiritual lexicon for words to speak truth to our reality. However, we as black LGBTQ people in white churches find that their control and dominance of the lexicon erodes our power and deletes our spiritual expressions. We have found that being subsumed by a queer universality not only renders us invisible, but also renders us speechless.

As resident aliens in black religious culture, we black LGBTQ people speak of a God we know about through heterosexist theological language because sexuality has never been a comfortable topic of discussion in the black community. With the embrace of fundamentalist Christianity that has an asexual theology embedded in its tenets, African-American bodies and sexualities that were once systematically usurped by white slave masters are now ritualistically restrained by the black church and violently policed in the black community. With the Black Church's theological qualifier to love the "sinner" (us), but to hate the "sin" (our sexual orientation), we are permanent souls of the Black Church, but we are never fully permanent souls in it. Consequently some of us have left.

Earthlyn Marselean Manuel, in "Still Waters Run Deep," left not only the Black Church, but also Christianity, for Nichiren Buddhism because it offered a different kind of liberation. Mona de Vestel in "Buddha on the Land" embraced Buddhism because through it she experienced a profound and wondrous connection to the universe.

Natasha Tinsley in "summers & the seven paths of yemaya," and Steven G. Fullwood in "I Hate God," returned to the religions of our ancestors. For Fullwood spirituality began to make sense when he started practicing in the Oshun tradition. And sharon bridgforth in "interlude #21: the road to Higher Power," writes about her deep longing for a oneness with God, and how she was found and was reborn by her spiritual mother, Yemonja.

Some of the contributors found their spirituality by standing alone on their own faith. Tracee Ford, in "Why I Am a Heathen," is a bisexual who speaks her mind and doesn't adhere to conventional religious and moral codes. Tonda S. Clarke, in "The Journey to Myself," chronicles her spiritual path home to herself and how she got sidetracked by religion. Tawanna Sullivan, in "Sufficient As I Am," warns her readers, "you can't let other people dictate what your relationship with God is going to be." And Marvin K. White, in "Who Say Amen Over Me?," makes it clear that he'll have the last word.

However, for those LGBTQ people of faith who have stayed connected to the Black Church but have left its homophobic baggage behind, they have done so in a variety of ways, and their stories also speak of a defiant faith. Linda Villarosa found solace worshipping at the Unity Fellowship Church, the only African-American LGBTQ denomination in the country. The Rev. Jim Webb states in his essay, "In Broad Daylight," that we engage in internalized homophobia and undermine our self-esteem as LGBTQ people when we embrace and financially support churches that don't embrace us. He encourages us to actively seek solutions within our churches, and assures us that "with every passing day, there are many more courageous spirits" in our church communities who are there to embrace us on our journey toward spiritual and self-acceptance.

In the tradition of many of our Christian ancestors and present-day ministers who discarded all damning and damaging racial references and interpretations of scripture, so, too, do a number of contributors when it comes to homosexuality. In "Regardless of or Despite the Church I Love Myself: One Lesbian's Opinion," Diane Foster finds her connectedness to God through the scripture passage John 4:8 that states God is love. In "Spirituality and Sexuality," Dyan McCray is guided by the scripture passage Mark 12:31 that states "Love thy neighbor as thyself." And the Rev. Wanda Y. Floyd, in "Fearfully and Wonderfully Made," is affirmed every day as a black Christian lesbian minister by the scripture passage Psalm 139:14 that reads, "I praise you, for I am fearfully and wonderfully made."

The stories in this collection are rich and numerous—all of them a must-read. These black LGBTQ spiritual narratives are a way to be visible and to be heard.

For our African ancestors, writing became a subversive tool, particularly in a Western culture that did not value the veracity of their lives, much less their oral tradition. Writing allowed our ancestors to tell and to compile the stories of their lives as a sacred text. Writing makes visible, at least in print, those lives that are too often intentionally omitted. Writing is a political necessity.

For LGBTQ people of African descent, our writings create a counter voice, text and knowledge that become a tool that not only gives us a voice and visibility, but also power.

As LGBTQ people of African descent we write these spiritual narratives because not to write them would cause us to participate in our own spiritual death. We write these spiritual narratives because those who come after us will need them. We write these spiritual narratives and our texts become a canon for survival, our Holy Bible, in spite of the claims that our sexual orientation is both an abomination to our community and God. And we write these spiritual narratives because we know that the holiness of our lives is sacred.

Rev. Irene Monroe is a professor of religion and associate director of multicultural and spiritual programming at Pine Manor College. She is a Ford Fellow completing her doctorate in the Religion, Gender and Culture Program at Harvard Divinity School. Monroe is a religion columnist who writes "Queer Take" for the online publication The Witness, *a progressive Episcopal magazine, and "The Religion Thang" for* In Newsweekly, *the largest lesbian, gay, bisexual and transgender newspaper in New England.*

I heard God's voice very distinctly tell me that I am to be a minister. Of course, even though I had no doubt that I'd heard what I heard, I did not believe that God could possibly mean me. "It must be some mistake," I thought… Not me — I am a lesbian! — and not one who lived quietly in the closet either.

Answering the Call

By Rev. Beverly Saunders Biddle

I am an out African-American lesbian who serves God and God's people as an ordained minister. Yes, I, who very seriously considered taking my own life when I came out in 1974. Yes, I, who believed I was unworthy of living. Yes, I, who endured fourteen years of serial monogamy, in relationships with one woman after another, before I found my life partner. Yes, I, who was a professional lesbian working in the LGBT and HIV/AIDS arenas for ten years. I, a woman who loves women — a woman who has no shame, no regrets, and, no guilt about it either.

The Holy Spirit chose me to be a vessel and vehicle for world transformation and healing. I have been called by God to minister to His/Her children. I have been called as a Minister of Spiritual Consciousness, as a Spiritual Life Coach, and as a Master Teacher of Universal Law and Spiritual Principles. And I have said "yes." I have answered the call.

Wait a minute. I am way ahead of myself. How is it that someone like me, who would be considered an abomination before God by people in so many churches, has "inclined her ear" to hear God's voice and has exercised her free will to surrender her entire life to Divine Will? How is it that I have found peace within my mind, my heart, and my soul and determined that I am, indeed, worthy of this sacred and awesome honor and responsibility?

My Journey to Spirit

In many ways, it seems unlikely that I would have become a minister. I mean, despite the obvious challenges that any gay, lesbian, bisexual, transgender or questioning person faces within traditional spiritual communities, I did not always have what I would call a relationship with God. I was not "raised in the church." Even though my grandfather was a Baptist minister and my parents were certainly God-fearing, I don't remember church being a dominant factor in my early development. Since we lived far from my grandfather and my father was estranged from his family I never knew my grandparents and was never really influenced early in life by the Black church experience. As an Army brat, I went to whatever church was nearby. Going to church was just something that I did because "my mother made me do it." I never saw it as the cornerstone of our family structure, and no one in my immediate family even belonged to a church. I certainly never felt that I had a direct connection to God. That came much later in my life. Ironically, it was not until I began to get in touch with my sexuality and began to define who I was as an individual separate from my parents, my brother, and, at that time, my husband, that I even thought about joining a church. I had done what many adolescents and young adults do in terms of going to church: I only went when I was forced to, and when I got old enough to make my own choices, chose not to go. Yet, when I was coming out, I found I was in search of something more in my life, though I was not exactly clear what that something was.

It was a time of great despair for me. I felt that I was an embarrassment to my family, that I would be shunned by the people I considered friends, and, most importantly, that I would be damned to hell. The first woman I loved thought our being intimate was so shameful that she left New York for two years without telling me where she'd gone. I remember sitting in the dark a lot and having thoughts of throwing myself from the balcony of our ninth floor apartment in Brooklyn. Were it not for the love and intervention of a friend and co-worker, I might have followed through on those thoughts. She was a psychiatric social worker in the community mental health clinic where we worked. I was blessed that she cared enough about me that she broke her own rule about seeing friends as clients. I went into therapy with her. In hindsight, I can see that she was an angel that God sent to literally save my life.

It was at that time, during perhaps the darkest period in my life, that the same dear friend encouraged me to go to church with her. It's amazing that when we have dropped all of our defenses and pretenses we become most open to God. So it was for me. I opened my heart and mind to receive the message, accepted Christ and joined the church. I was baptized, became active in the church choir, and was a faithful member of a missionary Baptist church.

I was twenty-six and my new involvement with the church was in many ways my saving grace. My new church home provided a refuge in a time of trouble, a safe port in a storm. Alas, all was not as pretty as it appeared. My involvement in the church was clouded by a veil of guilt and shame. I began seeing one of the other female choir members. I hid who I was from my fellow choir members and from the other congregants. After separating from my husband, I even started having intermittent encounters with men, almost as if to prove that I wasn't really "that way."

Even though I was in intensive therapy, and, after a couple of years, was getting to a point where I was ready to accept who I was, the message I was receiving at church was that I was an abomination. I believed that I was not worthy of God's love because I was living in sin. As with many lesbian, gay, bisexual and transgender (LGBT) people attempting to find solace in African-American congregations, I absorbed the mental, emotional, and spiritual brutalization into my being and accepted it as a testament of who I was. I did what so many "family" members within so-called Christian congregations do—I hid my real self and played the shame game. I denied who I was when I was in church or in the presence of church members. I was bombarded by derogatory remarks about homosexuality from the pulpit and from other "Christians." I was not even aware how much I had internalized the insidious homophobia that was all around me. The message that I was not good, not lovable, not worthy had touched the very essence of who I thought I was.

I lived this lie of being someone else while at church for five years until I moved away to graduate school. By that time, I was completely disillusioned and had no interest in finding another church home. Fortunately, I eventually came to see that a lot of what I had believed about myself and about God was a lie. At the time, however, I felt betrayed and my faith had been shattered.

I know now that even though I had given up on God, God had not given up on me. At that point in my life, I believed that I directed the steps that I took in my life. I believed that I was in control. In spite of my beliefs, God found a way to reach me when I least expected it and when I certainly wasn't looking to be reached — at least not consciously. I had finished graduate school and was living and working in Washington, D.C. I was in pain, even though I didn't realize it at the time. I was still searching for myself, yet I was still hiding who I was in major ways. I was one person on my "good government job" and another person in my private life. You know the drill — using those acceptable pronouns, lying about what I did over the weekend, and avoiding certain business functions because I wasn't in a relationship with a man.

So, this is where God showed up in the form of personal growth seminars. I was indeed desirous of knowing who I was at a very deep level. At the time, I did not have the awareness to understand that I was seeking some external validation for my life. I needed to know that I was "okay." I needed to know that I was lovable. I needed to find a sense of self-worth and acceptance. I found all of this in Insight Seminars. Unbeknownst to me, I also found Spirit. It was in those seminars, despite the organizers' efforts to disguise the spiritual foundations of the teachings, that I opened myself to Spirit. I learned to meditate and to do what they called spiritual exercises — using a mantra to facilitate going within. I learned Spiritual Principles, cleverly disguised as tools for productive living. Perhaps most importantly, I learned that the very core of my being is good, that I am indeed worthy of love, and that I have many desirable qualities. I found myself — or so I thought at the time.

But God was not through with me. I still felt this inner pull to know more, and more. I began a quest to discover the truth, which led me to the Truth. I was searching to understand the mysteries of life and to understand why I am here. I received a glimpse of my purpose through the seminars. I discovered that I was put here to lovingly facilitate change, in myself and in others. I accepted this, though, on a very superficial level, or should I say on the level of appearances. In accordance with the focus of the seminars to which I became almost addicted, my focus was on changing outer effects in my life (e.g., car, house, job). The spiritual depths of my life's purpose still remained undiscovered. I did not accept my purpose as a Divine gift or as an appointment, and certainly not as a calling. I looked at my purpose only as an indication of what I was to do professionally. For that reason, I pursued becoming a facilitator of personal growth seminars. When I allowed fear to derail that pursuit, I began to examine organizational development as a career. Then, it was massage therapy and then, and then… The search for my true self continued.

I was looking in all the wrong places. I was focused on the outer, not looking within myself for the answers. I did not know at that point that the kingdom of heaven is within. I did not realize that the answers I was seeking and my connection to God were deep within my being. An active relationship with God or Spirit was still not a part of my conscious awareness. I did not recognize myself as a spiritual being; therefore, I did not know that my quest was really a spiritual one. I did not realize that I would not be fulfilled until I made conscious contact with the

One Power and One Presence we know as God.

Again, God reached me when I was not looking. Another friend invited me to attend Unity of Washington, D.C. on the pretext that its services and teachings were very similar to what I had learned and loved about Insight Seminars. Even though I was not actively searching for a church home, I went, and home is exactly what I found. I finally discovered a place where I was accepted for who and what I am. I found a spiritual community where the teachings are based not so much on what we have been told about Jesus, but what Jesus actually taught — unconditional love and acceptance. I found something that I had never encountered before or even heard of — Practical Christianity — utilizing Jesus' teachings and spiritual principles in an active way in one's life and affairs.

At Unity I got in touch with the Spirit within me. I had never considered that I was indeed a spiritual being. I came to know that the true essence of each of us is just that, spiritual — that we are spiritual beings having a human experience, not human beings having occasional spiritual experiences. I began to look beyond the world of appearances to the metaphysical (beyond the physical). I came to accept that things happen in our lives for a reason: that all things are in Divine Order. Though we often may not understand the purpose, there is a meaning to all things.

I came to know God in a different way, as well. Until then, my concept of God had been that of the old man in the sky with the long white beard passing out judgments and keeping record of our slightest transgressions. Instead, I came to know a God whose Will for me is absolute good. I came to accept the indwelling Presence of God. I came to develop a relationship with a God who sees me as a beloved daughter in whom S/He is well pleased — a God who has prepared a table before me. All I have to do is avail myself of the good that awaits me. As it says in Luke, Chapter 12, "It is the Father's good pleasure to give [me] the kingdom." I know this as the Truth now. My life before that realization was evidence of that lack of awareness and spiritual understanding.

For much of my life, I thought I was the one in control. I thought that I had what I had and achieved what I did solely on the basis of my own will and hard work, or lack thereof. I had no concept of God's Will for me. I had no understanding that it is the Creator who is in control of all things. Now, though, I have come to accept that I am but a co-creator with God and that it is only by surrendering to His/Her Will for my life and operating in accordance with Spiritual Principles and Universal Law that I will have the life that I truly desire. I have come to understand that I desire what I do because my desires have already been ordained by God ("desire" can be interpreted spiritually to mean "of the Father" — de=of; sire=Father or heavenly body).

Little did I know, at the time that I joined Unity fifteen years ago and began a study of metaphysics and Practical Christianity, that God was still preparing me for His/Her Divine purpose. You see, I had not completely surrendered my will to Divine Will. I studied for several years and thought I knew the Truth. I had "learned" many Truth principles. I knew the teachings of Charles and Myrtle Fillmore, the co-founders of Unity; and I had studied several metaphysicians and other proponents of New Thought (e.g., Ernest Holmes, H. Emily Cady, Joel Goldsmith, Rev. Dr. Johnnie Colemon, Rev. Dr. Michael Beckwith, and Rev. Dr. Barbara King). My personal library reflected my voracious appetite for Truth teachings. I still didn't know that I was only being primed.

In fact, I did not realize that in preparing to become a Licensed Unity Teacher, I was opening myself to participate in a larger plan. I continued to believe that I was in control. Yes, I thought I had learned the principles, but I was still not consistently using them in my life (my beloved teacher, Rev. Dr. Iyanla Vanzant says that learning has not occurred until the behavior changes). I understood the Truth on an intellectual level, but I had not taken it into my soul, into the depths of who I was — my "beingness." I had not surrendered to allow Spirit to move in me, through me and as me. I was continuing to follow my plan, not God's plan.

The Call

So, God decided to send me a message I couldn't pretend I didn't hear. Even though I was moving along with my life, actively participating in Unity, I was still in denial. I was in the choir, on the sound team, on the Board of Directors, had even been Board President. I had studied enough that I had been invited by the minister to lead the service on occasion, to deliver the message during mid-week services and to teach new member orientations. I was having a grand old time, but was still oblivious to God's plan for my life.

On some level, I knew that there was still more for me to "do" and that I had more to offer, so I *thought* it would be a good idea to become a pastoral counselor. I started looking into programs in the Washington area and went to the Howard University School of Divinity to get some information. It was there that something completely unexpected occurred: I heard God's voice very distinctly tell me that I am to be a minister.

Of course, even though I had no doubt that I'd heard what I heard; I did not believe that God could possibly mean me. "It must be some mistake," I thought. What arrogance! Me assuming that God had made a mistake. Yet, I could not fathom that God would want me to be a minister. Not me — I am a lesbian! — and not one who lived quietly in the closet either. By this time, I was out in all areas of my life. I had advocated on behalf of lesbians and other GBTQ communities for equal access to health care. I had worked for several LGBTQ organizations and headed one, becoming a sought after speaker addressing national conferences, Congressional hearings, and participating in Cabinet level meetings. I was marching in the streets, and had even been featured on CNN as a lesbian health advocate. I had been a member of a congregation that completely affirmed who I am in all of my "outness," and my minister had even performed a commitment ceremony for me and my life partner. Yet, at the core of my being, I was harboring that old stuff. Those old tapes were still running. I *still* thought I was "not good enough" to do God's work. I still believed that I was unacceptable for this task.

I saw it as something else to "do" — something that I was not worthy to even consider.

But what do you do when you know that you have been called? What do you do when you know at the depths of your being that God does not make mistakes and that you can't really argue with God? In essence, what you do is run — you make it so difficult to be obedient that you feel justified in saying "no." What I did was to allow deceptive intelligence to convince me that I must become a Unity minister; that there was no alternative. I had not realized at that point that I had been called to ministry by God, not Unity. That would mean that I'd have to enter into the program at Unity Village in Kansas City, Mo. That would mean that I would have to prepare myself to be "acceptable" to enter this program, and that I would need to save enough money for tuition, books, and relocation expenses. That would mean that I would have to convince my partner to move to Kansas City even though I knew she was quite content being in Washington, D.C.

Again, I *thought* I was in control and I began "preparing." I met with my minister and I took the Unity courses that I knew were the requirements for admission into the Ministerial Education Program. I talked to my partner about moving to Kansas City and she was very supportive. I then began to focus on the money and having to leave Washington. What I was really doing, though, was stalling and avoiding — running and hiding, slipping and sliding.

There was something unsettled within my being. In my mind, there was still something about being an out African-American lesbian that was not quite congruent with entering a predominately white ministerial program — New Thought or not. I had been the chocolate in the milk during both undergraduate and graduate studies. I was unwilling to blaze that trail again. I began to investigate other programs in which I would be among a majority, at least as an African-American. Yet, I was still avoiding the issue.

Bigger questions remained to be answered. The question of my sexuality loomed as big and bold as ever. I had been out and what I call a "professional lesbian" for almost ten years (I got paid to talk to women all day). I had my partner's picture on my desk at work, even when I worked at another good government job. So, being out was not the issue. Or was it? I was still conflicted about being out in the larger community versus being out in my own community. I was out at my church, which is a predominantly African-American congregation. I know it's safe there, familiar, but did I dare venture into Howard University's School of Divinity or the Interdenominational Theological Center in Atlanta? Or even Rev. Dr. Johnnie Colemon's or Rev. Dr. Barbara King's programs, two New Thought ministerial programs?

What I finally realized was that I was trying to tell God just how I was going to answer His/Her call. I was still trying to be in charge. In the end, I acknowledged that I was attempting to do God's work and I did something novel (for me): I prayed. I surrendered it all to the Holy Spirit. I asked that I be shown how to be obedient and to be in integrity with who I am as an out African-American lesbian.

As always, my answer came in a form that I hadn't expected. In March of 2000, I was attending a workshop at Inner Visions in Silver Spring, Md., when I learned about a program that was beginning that July that would prepare me to be a Spiritual Life Coach and ultimately an ordained minister. The program was described as being based on Universal Law and Spiritual Principles, and would involve two to three years of intensive study. The Inner Visions Institute of Spiritual Development became the answer to my prayer. At the time, all I knew about the program was what I read in the brochure, and that the program was founded and directed by Rev. Dr. Iyanla Vanzant. I knew nothing else except that I was being directed to enroll as a member of the inaugural class.

How unlike me — the control freak. How uncharacteristic of me who usually needed to have all the details, who needed to see all the fine print, who needed to know about accreditation, curricula, certification, etc. For the first time in my life, I allowed my path to be directed by the Holy Spirit. I trusted in God, stepped out completely on faith and met the application deadline of April 15th. I didn't even know how I was going to pay the tuition. I just knew all that I needed to know: God had ordained me to be a minister before I became flesh.

Okay, so I didn't exactly know that when I enrolled. I did know that my life had taken a turn that was totally unexpected and unpredicted. I knew that it was time that I put my faith and trust in something beyond what I could see, feel, smell, hear and taste. I allowed the Presence of God to fill me and I allowed my thoughts and actions to be Divinely guided. Over the next two years, I dug down into the depths of my being and unearthed all the wretched stuff that had kept me in bondage to core beliefs, race consciousness, and "the way things had always been." I forgave myself for the judgments that I had held and was still holding against myself. I forgave myself for all the judgments that I had held against others. I acknowledged my fears and my doubts. I replaced them with love, integrity, faith, commitment and grace.

I released myself from the stranglehold that my core beliefs had upon my life: that I was unworthy and unlovable. I surrendered the thought and the belief that because I love women I am a sinner and an abomination — I mean really surrendered it; not just giving lip service to it. I made another choice: I chose love over self-brutalization. I chose peace over inner turmoil. I chose the joy that comes of a Spirit-filled life over superficial happiness based on external effects.

Then, I went even deeper. I surrendered further and entered the Inner Visions ministerial program. I accepted the calling that God placed on my life. I accepted that God had chosen me to be a vessel and vehicle for world transformation and healing — that I am to serve through spiritual education and the elevation of consciousness. I accepted the call to be a channel through which the illusion of separation from God, from each other, and from disowned aspects of ourselves may be brought into the Light to be transmuted. I took a deep breath and surrendered the limiting thoughts that surfaced when I considered how phenomenal that is.

Okay, so I'm still surrendering. I am living daily in a state of surrender. I am trusting and relying on the Presence and Power of God that I know is within me. I take each step forward knowing that I am not the one "doing" the work. I have learned the meaning of obedience. I listen for each new direction, and I allow God to be God in me. I don't have to "do" — I just have to "be." I don't have to have all the answers — I just have to "be." I don't have to know the how, the why, or the when — I just have to "be." I just have to surrender my need to know, my need to be in charge, my need to do it right. I just have to surrender my will to God's Divine Will to know that I am loved just as I am, and to know that I am being rightly guided on the path. I just have to stay on the path.

I just have to be willing. I just have to say "yes" and trust that I will be guided each day, each hour, and each moment. I just have to believe that everything I need as a minister, as a coach, as a master teacher is being and will be provided — before I can even ask. I just need to completely surrender — not to give up (yes, give up the illusion of being in control), but as my minister says, "open up" to the indwelling Spirit of a loving God.

All I have to do is say "Thank you, God" and "Here I am Lord, send me." I am answering the call — even me, an out African-American lesbian. God has deemed me perfect in His/Her sight. And I accept!

As I have spent time studying the book of Esther, I have found that this book speaks to us as lesbian, gay, bisexual and transgendered people like no other book in the Bible. … It seems to be pointing its finger right at us. It seems to be up in our face.

It's Time! Esther 4:14 (Sermon)

By Amina M. Binta

I come from kind of a high church background. So if you're lookin' for someone to make you shout and turn over benches, wrong preacher, wrong preacher. But I assure you, there is a word from the Lord today. Amen? As a young person growing up, my mother took me to the African Methodist Episcopal Church. At that time, if you heard someone shout, everybody looked around to see who it was. The only person who shouted on a regular basis was one of the women ministers in the pulpit. Many years later, as I found myself a minister in that same church, I got to know her and began to understand why they couldn't "hold her mule."

As I have continued on my spiritual journey, God has led me to experience many different kinds of worship. I remember when, as a teenager in college, a friend took me to her church where they spoke in tongues. Never having experienced this before, I was scared to death! Later, as a young adult, living in Oklahoma, in a section of the country commonly called the Bible Belt, I became accustomed to seeing the outpouring of God's spirit being manifested in spectacular ways. I began to shout myself and wouldn't let anybody "hold my mule!"

But I have to admit both high church and low church, as some would call them, have caused me a lot of pain. It is the church that excluded me—first as a woman, and then as a same gender loving person—from full participation in the house of God. It is the church, which we love so much, that led us here to this place, to the Gay and Lesbian Center, to this makeshift house of worship, at this time. But even though the church has caused me, has caused you, so much pain, it is during this time that I am most aware of my "high church roots."

It is during this time that I remember that it was the early church that began to observe the season that we call Lent. Lent is a time when the liturgical color worn in the church is the color purple. The color purple, the color purple, the color purple. Purple is a sign of passion. The Lenten story is a passionate story. Lent is the time when many Christians all over the world observe a time of deep prayer and fasting. It is a time of reflection, it is a time when, in the words of Howard Thurman, we go on "the inward journey." It is a time when we examine ourselves, we take stock of ourselves. It is a time when we look in the mirror to find God. It is a time when we retreat from the hustle and bustle of life, to observe the newness of life, in the budding of the leaves and the flowers and the trees.

Lent is the time when we remember the cost of Christ's earthly journey. It is the time when many Christians choose to remember and to enter into the Christ experience by purposefully deciding to deny themselves worldly pleasures. It is a time when some abstain from anything that would prevent them from a closer relationship with Christ. The question could be asked, what is it that's keeping you from a closer relationship with Christ? Is it your bed? Or who it is that's in your bed? Lent coincides with spring. Is it time for you to do some spring cleaning? What do you need to get rid of? Maybe I need to clean that up.

I thank God for a church, for a movement that doesn't tell me who I can or cannot date, sleep with or marry. Amen? If you've been with this movement for more than a day, you know that this church, Unity Fellowship Baltimore, this movement, Unity Fellowship, has come about because someone decided to follow Jesus. Someone, Archbishop Carl Bean, someone, Bishop Kwabena Rainey Cheeks, someone, Rev. Harris Thomas and Bro.

Willie Hinton, someone, Minister Kevin Taylor, someone. I know it's Womyn's Herstory month, and we're gonna get to the sistahs don't worry, someone, Elder Jacqueline Holland, someone, Rev. Gwendolyn Hall, someone, Rev. Tonyia Rawls, someone, Rev. Nadine Rawls and Sis. Rochelle Ross-Mays, someone, Deacon Harrison, someone. All of you within the sound of my voice decided to follow Jesus. And I'm glad about it, I'm glad about! If you're glad about it say hallelujah, say glory, say glory hallelujah, amen!

There's a song I used to sing in the old church: *"I have decided to follow Jesus,"* (sing) *"I have decided to follow Jesus, I have decided, to follow Jesus, no turning back, no turning back."* And then what about that second verse? (sing)

"Though no one follow, still I will follow, though no one follow, still I will follow. Though no one follow, still I will follow, no turning back, no turning back." And that brings us to our text for the day.

The book of Esther is about a woman who decided it was time. She decided one day that it was time to step up to the plate. She decided one day that come what may, come hell or high water, death or destruction, she was going on with and for God. I don't know about you, but every day I appreciate more and more what it means to go on with the Lord. To go on with God is a decision. To decide to go with God involves taking some risks. To go on with God means going against popular opinion. To go on with God may mean to go against the prevailing culture. To go on with God may even mean to break the law.

As I have spent time studying the book of Esther, I have found that this book speaks to us as lesbian, gay, bisexual and transgendered people like no other book in the Bible. It seems to speak to us and our situation. It seems to speak to us and to some heterosexual folks, too. It seems to be pointing its finger right at us. It seems to be up in our face.

The book of Esther is a book that almost did not find its way into the Hebrew canon. There was a lot of controversy about including the book in the Bible because it failed to mention the name of God. Check it out sometime; not once is the name of

God mentioned. I don't know about you, but that doesn't bother me at all. Everybody talkin' about God ain't about God. Some folks who say God or Jesus in every other sentence make me nervous.

While Esther is often seen as the principal character in the book, which is named for her, actually there are at least two other characters worth mentioning. The book opens up with a party going on. Queen Vashti's husband, the King, is having a party for those on his staff. Everybody is invited. Vashti, on the other hand, is having a party for the women. Sounds like a lesbian thing going on! Anyhow, the King, after drinking and partying for seven days (now that was a party, don't act like you don't know nothin' about that!)... Anyhow, after seven days, the King wanted to see his Queen. But he didn't just want to see her, he wanted to parade her around for all to see. But Vashti had a mind of her own. Vashti wasn't about to be used and abused. Vashti wasn't gonna jump just because her husband told her to jump.

Someone here may be in an abusive relationship. Someone here may be feeling like you have to submit to abuse. That's a lie from the pit of hell. The Holy Spirit has led me today to say this to someone. I've already said this but you need to hear it again. You don't have to let anyone in your bed that you don't want there. You don't have to take abuse from your partner. It's time to call a spade a spade. I don't care who's beating who. I don't care if it's men beating men, or women beating women. And all the time it ain't beating. Sometimes it's just wearing a person down mentally. Sometimes it's using somebody for a booty call. If you can't say amen, say...

As we continue to explore the book of Esther, we find that because Queen Vashti refused to be abused, Vashti lost her place in the palace. We don't hear anymore about Vashti, but I believe that God took care of Vashti. And God will take care of you if you decide that enough is enough.

Now that Vashti had been removed from the throne, the King quickly sought a replacement. Isn't it amazing how quickly some folk replace their mates? Some folks change mates quicker than they change their shoes! If you can't say amen, say... Anyhow, the King asked that all the young virgins in each province be brought to Susa so he could look them over and decide who he wanted as his new queen.

In Susa, there was a man, a Jew, whose name was Mordecai. Mordecai had raised a child named Hadassah, whose name was also Esther. The child was an orphan, and had neither father nor mother. Mordecai was Esther's cousin, but he raised this child as his own. Esther was very beautiful, so she was taken away at the King's command. When Esther, a Jew, arrived at the palace she found favor in the sight of the King. And the King loved her more than all of the other virgins. Esther did not reveal her identity to anyone because it wasn't time. Mordecai had her best interests at heart and he knew that timing was everything.

That brings us to the first point of our sermon: Timing is everything. In the book of Ecclesiastes, which belongs to the wisdom genre, the writer tells us that there is a time and a season for everything under heaven. "For everything there is a season, and a time for every matter under heaven: a time to be born, and a time to die; a time to plant, and a time to pluck up what is planted... A time to keep silent and a time to speak."

As I continue on my spiritual journey, I continue to learn that everything really does happen in its own time, not my time, but God's time. Anyone who has known me for a reasonable length of time knows that I can be rather impatient. I've also learned that if you need patience, God has a way of giving it to ya. God has a way of slowin' your tail down. God has a way of making you look around in order to smell the roses. It's really true that trials and tribulations will give you patience. Amen?

Sometimes we're less concerned about people, and more interested in how many ticks on a clock go by while doing something. How many of us spend time on the telephone while loved ones are starved for companionship? It's all about timing. Ever known people who just always seem to have something to say at the wrong time? It's all about timing. Nothing happens before the time. Someone here may wonder why certain things have not happened for you yet. Nothing happens before the time. Rosa Parks did not give up her seat before it was time. Nobody knew about that preacher named Martin Luther King before Rosa Parks, the mother of Civil Rights, decided that one day she was tired. Rosa Parks had no idea that she would become the mother of the Montgomery, Alabama bus boycott. That's when Martin Luther King became famous. That's when they began to march. You hadn't heard about no Ralph Abernathy until this one black woman said, "No! I'm tired. I've worked all day. I ain't gettin' off this bus." They drug her off the bus. One had one arm, one had another. They booked her, fingerprinted her, the whole nine yards, because it was time. Bail was going to be ten dollars for violation of the civil rights law. But she said "No!" She said no because it was time. Time for black folks to be free. Check the time. Nothin' happens before the time.

Back to our text. Because Mordecai cared about Esther, he checked on her during her time in the palace. He checked on her to make sure that she was OK. In time, Esther became the new queen. As it was not time, Esther continued to keep her identity a secret. As time continued on Esther became quite an asset in the King's household. When her cousin Mordecai discovered a plot to assassinate her husband, he told Esther and Esther told her husband.

As time continued on, the King promoted his minister Haman above all the officials in his household. All the King's servants were to bow down to Haman. But Mordecai would not bow down because he was a Jew. So Haman decided that he would kill all the Jews. Haman told the King that the Jews were different, he told the King that the Jews were a threat. Sound familiar? Whenever you're different, whenever you decide that you're not going to bend your back so folks can ride it, whenever you decide that you're not going to compromise, whenever you decide that I'm a child of God, whenever you decide that you're going to live up to your divinity, you're a threat. So Haman felt threatened by Mordecai because he was a Jew. And because Mordecai was a Jew Haman wanted to kill all the Jews. You know

SPIRITED 19

how some white folk are? When you won't bow down, when you
won't do things the way they want you to do them, when you act
like and know that you got it goin' on, they can't stand you or
anybody like you.

The King decided to go along with what Haman was asking
him to do. Mordecai became so upset that he tore his clothes and
began to cry. Finally, Esther found out what was going on.
Mordecai sent one of the King's officials to Esther to ask her to
beg the King to change his mind. Esther's response was that she
had not been called to go to the King in thirty days. It was against
the law to go in unto the King unless one was summoned. So
Esther felt that it was not time to move.

This brings us to our second point: What time is it? When we
think about time, we can think about chronos and kairos time.
Kairos time is about when it's the right time to speak or be silent.
Chronos time means the quantity of time, the duration of time,
the length of time. Chronos time is a reflection on our mortality.
The doctor gives the patient a terminal diagnosis, then the patient
asks the doctor, how long do I have? One thing I always hear my
mother say is the obvious, if you live long enough you'll get old.
But life is not how long you make it, it's how you make it long.

This brings us to our third point and the focus of our
sermon this afternoon. Remember that Esther had hidden her
identity. Up until this point Esther had been passing. Esther had
been pretending to be someone else. I don't know about you, but
it seems to me, that if ever there was a time to come out of the
closet it was then. If ever there was a time to step up to the plate,
it's now. Up until now, Esther had remained in the closet. Up until
now, Esther had kept her identity secret. Up until now, Esther had
played by the book. Up until now, Esther had chosen to maintain
her security in the palace.

When I read the story of Esther, I hear our own story. When
I hear the story of Esther, I think about what it means to be black
and proud. To be black and proud has come at a price. I think
about what it means to be gay, to be lesbian and proud. I think
about Governor Parris Glendenning, and Maryland State Senator

Leo Green, both going out on a limb for our community, willing to fight regardless of the consequences.

A couple of months ago, one of the deacons at Inner Light gave me a pride sticker. I looked at it, and said, I guess it's time to come out a little more! I told him I would put it on my bumper just as soon as I got my car washed. Later, I told myself that I really should get my bumper fixed first. The bumper is cracked from having been hit in the rear. Mind you the bumper has been cracked for some time and the car is almost nine years old. Finally I began to ask myself, are you procrastinating? It's time! What time is it? It's time to come out, time to come out and get real about who we are. It's time to deal with our stuff. Time to let folk know that gay, lesbian, bisexual, transgendered folk know God. It's time to break the silence. Somebody say, "It's time!"

Only when we reveal our vulnerabilities can we heal. The truly spiritual person understands his role in the Universe as having everything to do with his relationships with others.

I Can't Make It Without You: A Conversation on Spirituality and Relationships

By Alaric Wendell Blair

Someone once told me that homosexuals (lesbians, bisexuals and transgendered persons included) are more spiritual than other (not-so-gay or lesbian) people. At the time, I was convinced. Of course, I was involved in several "spiritual" endeavors like hanging out and having coffee with some of the deep brothers and eschewing everything that seemed to distance me from my Source. In essence, I was a typical neophyte of "New Thought Theology." I couldn't speak two complete sentences without slipping in the words "Consciousness" or "Universe." So involved was I in the *practicum* of spirituality that I totally negated my personal growth and the growth of my brothers and sisters who weren't as "enlightened" as I. I soon came to realize that all the chanting and burning of incense would mean nothing without people. I'd become so deep, in fact, that I fasted from intimacy and refused to associate with old friends—especially the ones who still frequented the clubs. I had fashioned an exclusive cult where I was the only member and where there was no room for any sort of relationships. Was I in for an awakening! What I discovered was that our most effective vehicles for the journey to spirituality are our relationships with others. The hope of a viable relationship is perhaps one of the most prevalent cultural motivations in a person's life—as is the quest for a spiritual and halcyon life.

Spiritual Profile:

What does the gay brother do to obtain spiritual awareness and what does he look like?

1) He changes gods because the God of his youth has proven insufficient to support his pseudo-intellectualism. Emotionalism in traditional ecumenical services now seems unnecessary and primitive. He, rather conveniently, forgets the Sundays when the ushers at Mt. Zion Missionary Baptist Church would have to revive him after he would have nearly destroyed the choir stand. Now, as an enlightened creature, he prefers quiet worship and meditations/affirmations (two words he has recently come to know the meanings of).

2) He changes his wardrobe because everyone knows that a new consciousness requires a new closet of clothes and shoes. How can he represent a prosperous God dressed in last year's fashions? So he seizes every opportunity to sport his assumed prosperity in the face of "unbelievers."

3) He changes his lexicon. When he talks to people, he uses words and phraseologies that would stymie the most profound theologian. We'll call them "buzz" words. Suddenly, he has stopped swearing and makes every conversation a lesson in *A Course in Miracles*. He wears a smug look of confidence on his face when he knows that he has spoken over your head.

4) He changes his diet. This is probably the most obvious evidence that someone is en route to becoming a spiritual giant. He no longer eats meat, sugar, chocolate or any of the good stuff. He has forgotten that it isn't what goes *in* a person that defiles him; it is what comes out. But there he is, sitting across from you on a date, ordering a dry salad with tofu and "lite" vinaigrette dressing (on the side, of course). He drinks bottle after bottle of spring water. Won't he be surprised to find that some company in an underdeveloped country has been filling those bottles with

plain tap water?

5) He's joined a gym. Of course he protests that he hasn't joined the gym to admire the sinewy specimens of male pulchritude that parade naked through the showers and locker rooms. He's there to release physical energy and to build his temple into a monument of praise to God/Universe. It also is no mistake that most of his new wardrobe is one size too small. After all, what good is there in having a great-looking temple and no admirers? Advertise. Advertise. Advertise.

The above hyperbole is by no means an attempt to belittle those who strive to lead healthy lifestyles. It is, however, important to know the motivation for a lifestyle change. Clearly, the character mentioned does exist on some level and at varying degrees. Many of us have had life-altering experiences, which have caused us to behave differently. The missing link, however, for many of us is the fostering of healthy spiritual relationships. *A Course in Miracles* says that we enter relationships to heal and be healed. Spiritual partners help to buffer us and to call us on our "stuff."

For years, we have seen couples meet, marry, procreate, divorce and reconcile. Sociologically, the significance of family plays out in most every cultural message, particularly the media. Even (as most are painfully aware) in the face of an ever-shifting paradigm for relationships and family structure, most people hold fast to the idea that they will find the one person with whom they can build a "life."

Quixotic "spirituality" that negates the spiritual is a formula for what I will call *socio-pathology*. This pathology has caused many to enter into illusory bonds with others in an attempt to quench the thirst of loneliness, replicate themselves on earth, and to address the ineffable axiom that says "There is someone for everyone." Whereas we herald the strides the gay and lesbian community has made in matters of the spirit, we also want to remind ourselves that relationships are essential to spiritual growth.

If there is only Love and Fear in the Universe, what causes us to occlude channels for spiritual growth and happiness? Fear. A provocative follow-up question would be: What are we afraid of? There isn't enough room in this work to go into all of the possible responses. I will, however, address a few. Needless to say, we would have to examine certain cultural ramifications in order to really undress the issue of fear.

Some purport that an over-emphasis on the physical is the major suspect. We have become a culture of the "body," with the body functioning as the "new narrative" from which we decode the spirit of the possessor. The gay community (in particular) hasn't been immune to this myopic view of the "other." We have juxtaposed compatibility with physical attractiveness. Apparently, looks *are* everything. We are a population of mortally wounded people who have yet to do the personal work necessary to heal; that work is done in spiritual relationships.

We flit from one bad relationship to the next, hoping to find the sanctuary of family and belonging. We are all looking for love and we don't find it until we "become" love. We attract who and what we are. When there is too much focus on the external, the challenges of any relationship are no longer holy but temporal. What really rings true is that many of us in the gay and lesbian community are left to our own devices when it comes to discovering our spiritual selves. No one has taught us, in laymen's terms, the way of spiritual development. It is no small wonder, therefore, that many of us falter along the way.

What happens when we let love happen—when we really let go of our egos and past experiences? For one, we feel vulnerable and surprisingly alive. Through the annals of modernity, many have tried to pen rules of love and even more have their own personal rules. Unfortunately, "rules" reduce people to commodities or "subjects"/applicants. We often forget that we are dealing with other humans just as random and arbitrary as ourselves.

Let's say that we meet someone (wherever) and they are exactly what we have been praying/looking for. What are the typical reactions?

1) This is some sort of joke. What's wrong with him? 2) He's too much like me, so it would never work. 3) What's the catch; what does he want from me? It's true that our experiences inform our responses, particularly when we stand in disbelief at our dream come true. What is also true is that to *not* believe that *what we want also wants us* is to act outside of faith. Whatever isn't of faith is of sin (sin = error in thinking). Consequently, we repel more people than we attract.

Let's look at each response.

1) "What's wrong with him?"

Our nitpickiness forfeits healthy relationships. We have built labyrinths of standards so high and twisted that when we see their manifestations, we don't often believe it. The "wrong" we're searching for is, more than likely, in us, not in the other person. We think that we're too flawed for a seemingly flawless person and have written ourselves out of our own system of standards. No one can measure up because *we* can't measure up. It's similar to the student who has performed poorly in his studies and has applied for admission to a school with an extraordinarily high academic standard. He knows that he won't be admitted, but he needs the rejection to justify his cynicism toward the academic system.

2) "He's too much like me, so it would never work."

Any novice student of psychology can field this response. The fact that we disqualify another person because of too many similarities could be the result of deep-seated self-hatred. There could also be a manifestation of the age-old expression "opposites attract." No one can say, unequivocally, that they (opposites) do not attract, but we can note the duration of said attraction. For how long will the differences *not* matter? Whenever I thought of dating an opposite, I always thought of the reasons my parents divorced or my mother's constant complaining that her husband was insufferable and insensitive—her opposite qualities.

3) "What does he want from me?"

This reason stems from a sordid past of others taking

advantage of us—with our permission, of course. Because our first "lovers" were chosen in ignorance or for the wrong reasons, we assume that everyone is out to get us. And since we already have a lowered opinion of ourselves, we don't feel as though anyone would want us for us. There has to be a catch. The more pressing question might be: "What do I want from him?" Naturally, we want total disclosure, loyalty, security, adventure, someone with a great body and great sex. In short, we want perfection. Perfection is a good place to start, but very often what we end up with is someone just south of perfection. How close to what we want are we? Like attracts like.

Spiritual perfection does exist, but it exists outside our standards. It is the perfection within you that draws the perfection that is in others—to the point where we see what's "right" with another and not what's "wrong." We then begin to celebrate similarities and differences and we lower our defenses to allow love to happen. Only when we reveal our vulnerabilities can we heal. The truly spiritual person understands his role in the Universe as having everything to do with his relationships with others. There may be outward expressions of a more "healthy" lifestyle, but they are direct reflections of a healthy consciousness. The wonderful thing about being co-creators with God is that we get to redefine ourselves as many times as we need. We have the uncanny ability to change in a single moment. In light of that, we can change from isolationists to being inclusivists *right now*. All we need do is be willing; God/Universe will do the rest.

We need each other. As trite as that may sound, it is a truism that peals even louder in a world of technological, cultural and social ambiguity. A mechanistic approach to spirituality that is based on competing for external power is the long way home.

If we truly are the shamans of our generation, it's time we stepped up to the plate and walked worthy of the vocation wherein we are called. Aché!

frustration replaced joy discipline replaced Prayer. the
woman who came to inhabit my body was mean contrite
controlling spiritually ugly/ and i did not like her.
so i decided to kick that bitch to the curb and walk away.

interlude #21: the road to Higher Power

by sharon bridgforth

1.
i come from delta people/from
laughter
the blues
remembering
knowing
finger popping/right on
migrations
bid whist ray charles hard living/good timing
and attitude.

i am country in the big city
Hope made flesh/the Ancestral Prayer incarnate
the what was and should be
i am how we got here/and why

i am You.

2.
i could taste the soil.
i remember the smell the flavor of the air.
over and over stories repeated repeated so often
they filled my head with a thickness/a tonal mantra that

colored and shaped my sensibilities
over and over repeated repeated/lessons given history
passed on
life explained.

3.
i almost became a minister.
when i was 21 i applied, visited and prepared to study
religion at a school in san francisco.
i had not yet been baptized but loved the ritual of church.
driven by a deep longing for Oneness/for preparation/for
God
i began to cleanse myself of "unChristian" conversation
and deeds.
however
during this process i lost my easygoing nature to rigidity and
regiment. i became so completely focused on human
behavior that i let go of Spiritual practice. judgment
replaced compassion
frustration replaced joy discipline replaced Prayer. the
woman who came to inhabit my body was mean contrite
controlling spiritually ugly/and i did not like her.
so i decided to kick that bitch to the curb and walk away.

being the extreme person that i am
i walked a little too far away.
i took up cussing drinking drugs and partying with more
vigor than i ever had in the past.
up and down/through and around california/like a kid
doing the four corners at her first
sock-hop/i
partied!
in the place i grew up/los angeles
i danced, drank, laughed and pee'd/all over them streets
from south central to Hollywood—from east l.a. to
westwood

shiiit
baybay
l.a. was
my
city!

4.
some years later i decided to settle down
i married a nice Christian man   who liked to party as
much as i did.
i started going to church again
and soon found out i was pregnant.
during pregnancy i experienced an astounding series of
revelations and a desire to change that was similar to my
earlier feeling of being "born again." the real gift of it all
was that i gave birth to a beautiful and perfect baby girl.
feeling that the most important gift that i could give her
was the understanding that she had the power to create her
own reality and to make her dreams come true/i decided
that i first had to give by example.
i dug deeply/worked hard to understand and create a reality
that uncovered and reflected my own dreams (which until
then had centered around the next good party).
eventually i emerged with the truth
and
of course it was dramatic.
i realized that i was a lesbian (although i did not yet
embrace that word. after all lesbians were white women.
sisters/well sisters were just women lovers)
i had a burning desire to be a writer
and i needed a divorce. i had been masking for far too long.
chile

fire and brimstone came to visit
her name was mother.

we entered into a ten-year battle
we fought till we just wore one the other down/got too
tired to continue the fight.

5.
the first time i went to The Catch
i found Jesus/fo real though.
in the flashing of lights the pounding of house the jacking
of Black bodies/sweat pouring down women on women
men on men other and all and everyone grinding against the
pillars against the walls against each other/dancing till
sunrise   it was church.
better than any catholic ritual or baptist Spirit rising i'd ever
experienced
and
me there in my Black multi-gendered body/queer
was holy
was safe
was wanted
was free.

6.
i felt like i was dying in los angeles
like it was impossible for me to afford to dream there.
i had to get out
it didn't much matter where to.
i moved to austin, texas.

when my daughter was eight she went to live with her
father.
that was the hardest most unselfish decision that i have ever
made in my Life.
yet i had no choice 'cause deep down i knew she would be
better off/safer/happier there/'cause
deep down i knew i had a drinking problem.

7.
for the first time in years being a mother did not define
every movement during the course of my day. once again
it was necessary to articulate to myself who i was and what
kind of reality i needed to create to bring my dreams to
life/to teach my daughter.
by this time i had earned a bachelor's degree in creative
writing
but i didn't know how to BE a writer.
then i met marsha.
a Red-Cajun from a tiny town in louisiana/a sculptor-
environmental & human rights activist—a wildass—older
than me—geechee queen
marsha ann gomez
she became my best friend/teacher/past Life
connection/running buddy/sometimes Lover.
it was with marsha that i first paid attention to the
polyrhythms of my everyday Life
dreaming/Spirit talking/party loving /meditative/
baddgurl/queen/past life knowing/artist/liberation
working/multi-ethnic/courageous/flamboyant/macha/
shit-talking
marsha.
she taught me how to conjure myself/an artist
how to use art as a vehicle for social justice
how to serve the Divine by serving humanity
and how to make a little juju   with herbs incense candles
and Prayers
offerings
for the Spirits.
marsha revealed sacred Native American traditions to
me/ showed me how
through Sweats honoring Mother Earth the Ancestors the
Elements and elders
i could find parallels of African traditions/that i could Live
a Spiritual practice

and
channel it all into my writing and artistic vision/Praise.
yessuh i had a Geechee for a mentor
volatile passionate Ancestrally inspired monumentally
talented cigarette in hand cussn fussn pot smoking
beer drinking partying brilliant crazy marsha.
yeah/na
i was running with the big dogs fo real.

8.
it started with lent one year.
i decided to give up drinking/for lent
an offering of thanks
a sacrifice
in honor of the Gift of the stories.
i fasted
and prayed
got a colonic/started exercising and consistently taking
herbs and vitamins
i had already given up red meat and poultry/so i went the
extra mile and gave up fried foods.
it was all good. i wrote and wrote and wrote/felt connected
to Vision
received guidance. i felt full of Light and joy and
determination.

the day after lent
i drank and drank and partied
to celebrate.
for the first time i felt that first drink douse my inner light
for the first time i felt ashamed by my fourth drink
for the first time it occurred to me that the Angels must be
protecting me and those around me because i was driving
drunk
for the first time i wanted to stop drinking for good.
for the first time i realized that one of my best friends

talked about being a recovering alcoholic all the time. and
that i had once told her that i wasn't no gotdamn alcoholic/
i was Spiritually challenged. to which she replied,
"i'm sure you are fucka."
i became mindful that although this woman went to the bar
with us every week-end
she never drank
i began to ask her over and over/again and again how she
did it.
how could she refuse to drink/a phenomenon to me
because this woman
was a baddass foul-mouthed old school butch bull-dagga/
who we lovingly said was a grumpy old man trapped in a
young woman's body.
she told stories that had to be the truth 'cause they were too
funny for anybody to make up
she hooted at women (which she claimed to have learned
from me)
and she
had given up the liquor   for the first time i thought
maybe i could too.

it took four years.
i fasted, prayed/stayed off the grease and on the
vitamins/got more colonics exercised
had a church sister to come to my house and lay hands on
me
"make her get sick lawd, make her afraid lawd, punish her
lawd
if she
EVER
touches the drink again/lawdlawdlawd
help her na/lawd!" BAM! she popped me upside the head
and yes/i feared the power of that woman's prayer/still
reflect on it from time to time.
but ultimately

it was the many long nights sitting at the bar
lusting after women with/watching and talking with
my friend the grumpy Angel
that led me to walk down the road to sobriety.

after i stopped drinking/got clear/i realized that
some people did not want to see me sober
some people in my life were fools/some of my ideas and
actions were real fucked up/and i knew i had to clean
house/again.

9.
marsha was killed. her son
a schizophrenic—off his medication
brutally
murdered her.
marsha and i had become estranged a couple of years
before her death
but the loss of this sister
caused a deep and shocking grief for me
and for her loved ones around the globe.

10.
sober/i realized that i kept picking the same kind of
unavailable wrong-for-me women/over and over and that i
kept blaming them for my misery.
i figured i needed a time-out from women
so i focused
rediscovered the adventure of reading
conversation and work.

my time-out didn't last too long
but it did clear my head/which was good for my heart.
i entered into a partnership with a woman/a poet who used

her community organizing experience nationally to educate
adults and train professional facilitators in dismantling
oppression techniques.
her laser wit/the fire in her eyes/the whirl of her neck/and
her hands on hips attitude
was so exciting to me that i just loved to comply to her "i'm
not having it" calling me out on my bullshit. in that
relationship i learned that feeling my feelings talking
processing and compromising
is an all the time thing. she taught me that we had to
choose each day/to stay together that we had to do the
self-reflection and work necessary to keep staying together
in a good way
which was hard work yo.

11.
my partner of seven years and i broke up.
my life fell apart.
my heart was broken.

12.
time passed
i Healed/learned to be happy alone/to take good care of
myself.
became kinda vegetarian/i still didn't drink do drugs or
smoke
still loved a good party though.

one day the Sun shone and a friend/collaborator of ten
years and i looked at each other as if we had never said
hello. i Praise Divine Order 'cause a minute sooner and i
would have been too ignorant to have known what to do.
she is my partner now/my old friend/collaborator
she is a Yoruba Priest/a child of Osun.
my Life has come full circle. a little juju here Earth Praise
there through poetry rituals and dreaming/my Ancestors

taught me about the Orisa a long time ago. i called this
moment/this perfect Love this woman/this opportunity to
be in community with a practicing Yoruba family
to me with every choice every step along the way/Here.

13.
blues
circles
sinning
jazz
spinning
rituals
carnal
human
love.
art
Sacred/Destiny.

14.
the Orisa called me.

15.
i was diagnosed with cervical cancer.

16.
i was feeling great/work was going wonderfully
my daughter and i were closer than i ever could have
dreamt/she a working artist living in new york city. my
partner and i were happier than ever. i had health insurance
for the first time in 9 years. i went for a physical
and BAM!
CANCER.
things started moving fast/and in unexpected directions.

17.
i had a radical hysterectomy
was laid up for two months
had to re-imagine Life.
had to surrender.
discovered new definitions of gratitude.
was changed.

18.
during surgery and recovery i was lavished with Love and
support from family and community.
my Yoruba family Worked and Prayed hard for me.

19.
feathers
colors
light.
singing
dancing
voices.
whispers
warmth
knowing.
Ancestors
Dreams
Awake.
the hairs on my neck stand up
i see them
Africans Indians Geechees kiss my face/rumble when not
happy
tell me the stories
My Ancestors
save me from myself.
when i was drunk
        they kept dancing
when i was running

       they kept guiding
when i was broken
       they kept singing
when i gave up
       they didn't.
my mother's people
from arkansas mississippi memphis chicago
my father's people from
louisiana Geechee/Black Indians
made remembering wake.

all my Life
i've been recording it all
in my writing/it is
my Spiritual Practice
making Words shaped by Blood.

20.
i am Yoruba now.
my mother is Yemonja.

Yemonja is Big Mama/She governs wo'mn-business/
wombs belong to Her.
Osun brings people together/makes things happen/brings
Joy/carries the Tradition.
Osun saved my Life. Yemonja Rebirthed me.

21.

i am cancer free.
i do not have to have further treatment.

Life is a Blessing/yeah ummmhummm
sho nuff/indeed!

You remember that it no longer mattered that you taught Bible School, or Gospel Aerobics… [T]he minute the parishioners saw you walk in the door with your butch lover of three years, after doing all of God's work, church work, you were a leper, cast out of the valley, and those who looked at you were destined to turn into a pillar of salt.

At the End of My Suffering...

By C. C. Carter

So it's the week after your thirty-sixth birthday, and finally you're sober enough to remember how you got home at 5 a.m. without crashing your car. You're lying on the floor of your unfurnished apartment (don't even have a bed yet) with the same clothes on from last night. You're trying to figure out where things went wrong, and feeling hopeless that there's nowhere else to go because you've hit rock bottom—and from where you're looking there are no more signs of the good life you once had.

That's when you begin to remember the foreshadowing of the fall. You remember November '99, and the first call about the casting of a movie, the accolades and praises for winning the title role, the taping with famous actors, the producer and the director telling you that you were going to be a star. You remember your spouse being supportive and sticking by your side.

You remember January, the newspapers plastering your face all over the city, writing columns and predicting your rise to fame. You remember the endless calls asking for interviews and being gracious and humble enough to wonder why all the fuss. You remember your spouse making remarks about becoming lonely, remarks that you only take as her being selfish.

You remember February, reading and performing all around the country promoting your new poetry book, and taking advance orders because the publisher and the editor are constantly arguing about the typesetting and the look of the collection, and that's why you don't have a final copy yet. You remember your spouse and her daughter, who has just had a son, playing with the newborn and you not having enough time to savor and relish the moment because you have a deadline. You also remember feeling jealous because wasn't this the year you were supposed to get pregnant and the daughter beat you to it?

You remember March, writing a column about needing a moment to yourself, a break to slow down and be still. But you can't because the momentum is in your favor and you only have fifteen minutes of fame before someone else lurking in the shadows with more talent, more anything, comes and steals your thunder and then you become the "used to be" of the past. Isn't that how it happened to you? You remember the fatal mistake on a road trip that ultimately severs your relationship, one week before your fifth year of partnership and first year as spouses.

You remember April, organizing the event of your life and the pressure from it all, but the thrill of seeing it come to fruition, despite the poor turnout; the arguing with your spouse; the constant demand to keep your own performing career in the spotlight. You remember your spouse sticking through it with you until the end and then dissolving into her own depression, your road trip secret found out.

You remember May, coming back from a trip to see your mother, whose last words before your fall were, "Are you going to church?" You remember responding, "For what, ain't nothing there but hypocrites." And she replying, "But God is good all the time, all the time God is good, even amongst hypocrites. That shouldn't be what keeps you from the Lord." You say, "Whatever, Ma." You return to your home to find the beginning of the end.

The movie was cut because of funding and then thrown out

during the edit, despite rave reviews about your performance from the critics who saw the trailer. You remember your publisher vanishing off the earth, no contact, no forwarding address, and your manuscript that took five years to write along with her. You remember the final talk of the "This isn't working and I've found somebody else. I still love you, but I don't trust you" speech. You remember waking your friends up at twelve and two in the morning because you felt like you had no place to go and you're too embarrassed and ashamed to surface in public while you're going through this.

You remember taking every last dime in your savings account and moving into a condominium in the middle of Bronzeville because you can't stand staying in the same house with your spouse who has now become just your friend. You remember a friend of a friend of a friend knows somebody who knows somebody that owns a building. You take it without asking what the surrounding environment is like. For the next three days you lock yourself in the house afraid to walk too close to the window after 10 p.m. because every night the neighborhood residents think it's the Fourth of July, shooting guns in the air. You remember friends taking turns inviting you to dinner because you have no money and no job (because you were going to be an actress and writer, and your ex-spouse wanted that to happen for you so she supported your dreams financially while you both lived in her mother's house).

And in all of this remembering you finally understand how you came to be here. But you don't understand why. And one day in June, after your thirty-sixth birthday, you begin to question faith and God and why this happened to you of all people. You remember when you first lost faith, in college after a minister quoted from the Bible about your lifestyle being a sin. And that the one place you felt safe throughout your whole coming out experience was suddenly enemy territory. You remember that it no longer mattered that you taught Bible School, or Gospel Aerobics, or organized a praise dance team, or sang in the choir, or spent every spare moment of your time giving back and loving

God. But that the minute the parishioners saw you walk in the door with your butch lover of three years after doing all of God's work, church work, you were a leper, cast out of the valley, and those who looked at you were destined to turn into a pillar of salt. You never turned around once you walked out. You accepted your fate that maybe this and you are against God's rules, but know intrinsically in your heart that your father, a minister, did not condone the other minister's sermon so you are not to believe this either. But the pain from the people in the church cause you to turn your back on them, the church, and ultimately on God for ten years. And you begin to believe that all the good in your life has been because you made it happen, with hard work and dedication, and with determination to one day throw back in the "so-called" saints' faces that you are not a leper. All the time you were thinking, God has nothing to do with this.

So eighteen years later you look around the empty apartment and watch for any living thing that might reveal itself as a sign, but everything looks distorted when you're lying on the floor face up. You hear the residents begin their long night's ritual, look at the clock and confirm your suspicion that it must be 10 p.m. You've blacked in and out all day and can't remember where the time went. You hear the gunfire, and the first time you've prayed in over eighteen years is tonight, and you still do it with anger in your heart and accusation coming from your mouth.

And as you accuse God for giving you everything and then taking it all away, you hear the residents decide that down the block is too far away to make you feel scared, so they bring their fighting ritual through the alley on your side of the building. And between you cursing out God and them cursing out each other, gunfire overshadows the words, and a window breaks, a car alarm goes off, chaos erupts in the street, people run and yell, tears pour down your face as you put the pillow over your ears and rock back and forth on the floor, because you can't understand, "HOW DID I GET HERE, HOW DID I GET TO THIS POINT?" And right when you are about to lose it and go join the crowd because you feel that things can't get any worse, a mother's scream brings you back to the moment and everything goes silent. You are still, the residents are gone, and the mother's screams get louder while ambulance sirens grow closer.

You look up as if expecting the woman to be standing right there, and instead you see all of the self-help books that you haven't read on a shelf: *One Day My Soul Just Opened Up, Don't Sweat the Small Stuff, The Celestine Prophecy, The Greatest Miracle in the World, Affirmations of Faith for African American GLBT, The Grateful Journal, The Holy Bible...* but you only use them for show. You stand up, letting the screams keep you in the moment as a reminder that losing a child is worse, pick a book off the shelf at random, open to any page, and read the words in black on white, "...at the end of my suffering there was a door."

That's when you see the flashing lights from the ambulance blazing through your window, you hear the woman's screams turn to wails, you look up to the ceiling and mouth "thank you," promise to stay faithful from now on, and learn in that moment that lessons come in disguises that you may not want but always need. You begin to understand old familiar sayings such as "Always count your blessings," "That which doesn't kill you makes you stronger," and your mother's favorite, "God is good all the time, all the time God is good." You begin crying for acting like a fool and forgetting that you were made in the image of the great I AM, and failure is only a word, not a destiny.

You remember that when you were little, God lived in your house and that you had a personal connection with God through your father who was a minister. And that every Sunday morning was a celebration when you got dressed to go to church, gospel music blaring from the stereo, and each of your family members danced and sang along while getting ready. You remember your father's sermons and your mother's smile, and the Bible teacher's scriptures, and the choir singing, and the feeling that you got when you stood up to lead your first devotion. And that it didn't matter what other people thought or said because God was in your soul back then.

You remember first communion, and becoming saved and

how people looked at you because there was something in your spirit that drew them to you. And never once did you take for granted all that was given to you without thanking God for the blessings first.

And now reading the life-changing phrase, "at the end of my suffering..." you can feel that warmth again, and you understand that this is what was missing; this is what you forgot. That with all of the blessings, you forgot to give God the glory.

You accept that you must have faith and that even if church is still not the venue for you to express it, that having faith is a necessity, and worshipping God in whatever form—Goddess, Spirit, Allah or Jehovah—gives your life meaning, and purpose, and power. You stand up in your empty apartment, go to the window, face your fears, and know that life is about to change for the better as you know it.

During my first two years of high school, I tried to purge my feelings of unworthiness, as well as my attraction to girls and the gradual deconstruction of my home life, by devoting myself to church six days a week.… But even under the weight of guilt that had been placed on me by early indoctrination into religion, there was a place inside that kept saying that I was all right.

The Journey to Myself

By Tonda S. Clarke

This story chronicles my journey on the path to spirit, which got sidetracked by religion, took a turn to goddess and resulted in my coming home to myself.

My earliest memories of Spirit, God and church were a mixture of anticipation, curiosity and utter terror. I grew up in a matriarchy and the women who governed the family were not overly religious. I was never forced to attend vacation Bible school in the summer or wake up early on Sunday mornings for service. Sometimes my grandmother would take me with her when she occasionally attended the Mt. Herman Missionary Baptist Church on the south side of Chicago. I never remembered my mother, who was a serious party girl back in the day, attending church when I was a little girl; she reserved her conversion for the second half of her life. My great-grandmother was the only one that I can remember actually maintaining a channel of communication with the Lord. I know this was true because she would confirm it by telling me that "Jesus was on the main line." Although she regularly attended church, the same one that my grandmother would periodically grace with her presence, I was convinced that it wasn't the place where she actually met with God.

I vividly remember Sunday mornings in the kitchen, windows

fogged with steam from a stove full of dinner pots already on the boil, my great-grandmother listening and humming to a choir blaring from her small transistor radio. Sometimes she would cry and sometimes she would sing. Sometimes she gave affirmations of "Well!" "Yes, suh!" or "Amen, choir." Other times, she would shake her head and moan like a painful recollection had visited and cut her soul. But every Sunday, without fail, a divine mystery would occur. My great-grandmother would get "happy." It would come from nowhere that I could fathom; she would throw her head back, shout, jump, fall out, knock over chairs and release whatever might have been in her hand into the air. The first time that I witnessed this, I was mortified. I thought that she was having some kind of seizure. I remember running from the kitchen screaming for my great-aunt to come and see what was wrong with "Precious." I also remember the calm in my great-aunt's voice when she told me that nothing was wrong with my great-grandmother, that she was just full of the Spirit.

Then, there were the women that I would watch in church when I went with my grandmother. These women would parade in early for service strutting from one end of the church to the other, flitting here, perching there, giving anyone who cared to observe the opportunity to be enchanted by their regal entrances. I remember thinking that they resembled peacocks in their colorful array of fancy suits, high-heeled shoes with matching purses and ornately designed hats.

I would watch curiously as these creatures would methodically come undone. It could be a testimony. It could be a song. It could be a passage of scripture. No matter what it was that would take them from their place of feigned piousness to a place of purse-slinging, wig-tossing rapture, I was beginning to recognize that it all emanated from Spirit. After early years of witnessing this both in my great-grandmother's kitchen and at the various Baptist churches I'd attended, I knew only this: That Spirit was real, ancient and a powerful ally to women. It was reserved for adults. And that I had never felt it. Or so I thought.

When I was eleven years old, my mother enrolled me in a

Lutheran school. To this day, I don't really know why. I suspect that it was because of the school's reputed practice of issuing out discipline to unmanageable children, and, while I was not would you call "bad," I was different. By this time, I had already experienced my first love affair with another girl. I had skipped two grades in school and was curious about spirits, white people and what was really out there in the universe. I was aggressive, outspoken, rebellious and highly imaginative. I guess these types of characteristics in a young girl some adults felt needed to be tamed. So, I found myself at St. Paul's Lutheran under the strong hand of an ex-nun with a crew cut. It was at St. Paul's that I was formally introduced to religion. As part of the curriculum, we were required to learn the tenets of the church through the study of catechism. Unlike other classes, which were held in regular classrooms, catechism class took place in the church's sanctuary. What I remember most about this weekly requirement was the feeling of dread that would embrace me whenever our class prepared to walk through the long, dark hallway that joined the school to the church.

We were to think about our sins in prayerful meditation and solemn remorse before entering this sacred space. There was no talking, laughing or playing allowed; only silence, guilt and fear were permitted. When we arrived at the sanctuary, the pastor would be standing in the pulpit, submerged in flowing robes and self-righteousness. We would take our seats, heads bowed by the unbearable weight of sin, and wait for class to begin. It was always the same: lots of dogma, lots of empty prayers and repetition with an abundance of persecution. We were told that we were the product of sin, were evil by nature and design, destined to an eternity of burning torment just for having been born and constantly susceptible to the wiles of the devil. We were horrible, wretched, gullible beings, destined to a fiery hell all because of our weak, pathetic, disobedient flesh.

But there was no discussion about Spirit. There was acknowledgment of the Holy Spirit but only in the context of something that served in the role of translator—an intercessor, whose job was to carry our requests for pardon from our childish sins to a God who, although having created us, could not understand the words of our prayers. When I questioned the Spirit that I'd witnessed working through my great-grandmother and the women of the church, I was told that it wasn't really the spirit of God but ignorance and emotion that caused them to behave that way. We learned about Mary, a white woman with blonde hair and blue eyes who was so special that God visited her personally, gave her a baby who would save the world and sent angels to cater to her every need. We learned about the life of Christ, his sacrifice, his blood, his betrayals, his beatings and his murder but not of his love. It was a weekly torture that lasted for years in my head.

Sometimes I would sneak into the sanctuary by myself between classes and walk up to the altar, hoping to uncover a different perspective, another truth in the silence. I would stare curiously at the golden man with the chiseled features and flowing hair who hung from the large crucifix at the center of the altar. I would imagine his loneliness, just hanging there by himself all the time. I'd talk to him, share my empathy for his plight, offer him a sympathetic ear for all of the rage and disappointment that he must have felt and hoped that maybe, just once, he would speak to me. He never did. I remember feeling sad and rejected. I remember thinking that, maybe if I looked more like Mary, he would talk to me.

I left St. Paul's school after only one year. My family could no longer afford the tuition. I continued to attend services at the church for maybe another year, not because I felt that I was becoming closer to God but because I was mystified by the image of the golden man who hung from the cross and never said a word.

As I was growing up, I continued to search for a place where I could find Spirit, the Spirit that had touched my great-grandmother. That Spirit that was a friend of women and girls who looked like me and loved making us "happy."

One day, my best friend invited me to attend church with her and her family. They had the kind of family that I'd always dreamed of having. Both the mother and the father lived in the same house; each of the two children had their own bedroom; and they did family things, like eating dinner and going to the movies, together. They were also the only black Catholics that I'd ever known.

The first time that I stepped into the massive stone structure of St. Philip Catholic Church, I was overwhelmed. The ceilings appeared to be miles away from the floor. There were candles everywhere. The air was thick with smoke that emanated from the incense burner that swung in the priest's hand. There were large basins of water located just inside the three doorways that led into the sanctuary, and the parishioners would stop, dip their fingers into the water and then replicate a symbolic cross over their bodies.

Before entering the pews, they would stop again, bend one knee and with the same hand that had been dipped in the water, replicate the cross again. Finally, before actually taking their seats, they would pull out small, padded ledges from beneath the pews in front of them and kneel there. Some of them would kneel with mysterious strands of beads between their palms, whispering prayers. Others would kneel and look morosely toward the altar, from which hung a life-sized cross with the body of Christ affixed. This crucifix was very different from the one at St. Paul's. It wasn't golden; it was flesh-colored. It didn't blend in with the other altar fare; it was the focus. The expression of pain depicted on the twisted face of the icon was realistic and horrifying. I could see the holes in the palms and the feet. Red paint that represented blood streaked the face from wounds created by an actual crown of thorns. I had never been so intrigued or more afraid in my entire life. I just knew something spiritually huge and magical had to be going on here and I excitedly anticipated what I might feel.

There was no choir; instead there was a call and response, first done in Latin and then repeated in English. I tried to follow along with the small book that I was given, but it was no use. Not wanting to appear as an outsider, I watched the actions of my friend and faked it. The priest was quiet and reverent as he delivered the message. I don't remember what he said. Unlike the Baptist and Lutheran churches I'd attended, the sermon was over in about fifteen minutes. I remember thinking there had to be more to it than that, what with all that we'd gone through before even getting a chance to sit down.

Then came communion. It wasn't as if I'd never participated in communion before. I sat there waiting for the ushers to bring the plate of crushed crackers and grape juice around. I was not prepared for what happened next. My girlfriend leaned over and nudged me, telling me to get up and follow her to the altar. What? I knew she didn't expect me to walk up there, through all that smoke in the midst of all those people, and be exposed as a fraud. I asked her, "Why do we have to go up there?" She told me that we had to go before the altar to receive the sacrament. My earlier excitement was replaced by panic. As I walked up the aisle, looking from side to side at all the perfect, polished families seated in the pews, I felt small and foreign, as if I didn't belong. Not me, who was attending church with someone else's ideal little family. Not me, who had been labeled strange and different from the day I was born. Not me, a little bastard child, who had crushes on girls. When I finally knelt at the altar to receive the sacrament, I looked up at the priest and then beyond him to the white Christ that was hanging there and felt something deep inside. Something that, in my child's mind, I mistook for Spirit. I felt unworthy, undeserving and ashamed.

These feelings were reinforced throughout the next few years of my spiritual journey. During my first two years of high school, I tried to purge my feelings of unworthiness, as well as my attraction to girls and the gradual deconstruction of my home life, by devoting myself to church six days a week. I was a member of the choir, the young women's missionary society, the junior Rose of Sharon circle, the pastor's guild and any other auxiliary that I could join. I became a part of the Cavaliers for Christ group at my high school, meeting with other confused, convicted and condemned kids once a week to pray out our queerness and be admonished for all of our other incidental sins. But even under the weight of guilt that had been placed on me by early indoctrination into religion, there was a place inside that kept saying that I was all right. That I was good and loved and cherished no matter what anyone said to the contrary. This was the true Spirit of Divinity that dwelled within me. The Spirit that sustained me and provided for me even before I was aware that it was there.

Toward the end of my sophomore year of high school, my mother and stepfather's marriage began to fall apart. My home life was in complete shambles and my grades were starting to slip. The matriarchs held a meeting and decided that it was best that I be removed from the home during this time because the emotional turmoil was interfering with my academics. I pleaded with God not to let this happen. I begged him to restore my family. The response I received, as usual, was silence. Soon I was shipped off to Ohio to live with my biological father.

I'd never really had a relationship with him and only remembered him through sporadic visits that he'd made every other birthday to drop off presents. I was alone in a strange city, with no friends, a new family and a broken heart. My biological father turned out to be a tyrannical monster who handed out beatings to the point of welts, cuts and bruises at the slightest sign of disobedience. To deal with this new hell, I quickly found a church to attend and became as busy with activities there as I had been before I left Chicago. When the pain, loneliness and abuse became unbearable, I used the church and days of fasting and prayer as sedatives. But one day I grew tired. I grew tired of praying and receiving no answers. I grew tired of the abuse and the disappointments. I grew tired of God.

After graduation, I went back to Chicago, leaving Ohio and God behind. When I entered college, my mind was fertile ground for any religious experience that was different from that which I had known. Although I had rejected the traditional white male god that I had believed in for so many years, I still believed that there was a creative energy, a life-sustaining force at work in all of humankind. I simply had not found it.

I came out as a political lesbian with a bunch of feminist, white dykes that I'd met on the north side of Chicago. These women were separatists. They wanted absolutely nothing to do with the patriarchy or its male god. After living under the iron hand of my father and years of praying to a mute male god, it was easy for me to accept this philosophy.

I started to become more involved with women's, feminist and lesbian issues. I spent more and more time with my new friends and was eventually invited to participate in a gathering to honor the arrival of the Winter Solstice. During this celebration, I was introduced to the idea of recognizing a feminine principle of divinity. It had never occurred to me that God or Spirit could be female. As I further explored the traditions of this way of worship, I embraced the accepting nature of the deity; the image of the goddess looked more like the women that I knew. She was large and welcoming and had body fat. Her hair wasn't blond and flawless. She possessed great humor and great wrath. She was sensuous and earthy. She was nurturing, resilient and wise. She wasn't a victim and she wasn't a fragile virgin in need of angels to protect her.

I secretly lived and worshiped this way for a while, and although my Amazonian lifestyle was empowering and served as a balm to soothe some of my childhood anger and disappointment, it was also debilitating. Instead of feeling the peace that comes with healing and letting go, my feminist and separatist beliefs caused me to begin accumulating new wounds of resentment toward men. Eventually, I realized that this was not the path for me. I was still looking for the Spirit that my great-grandmother knew. The Spirit that seemed to have love for everybody, men included. That Spirit that made folks happy.

Over the years, I dabbled in many different "nontraditional" forms of worship. I tried everything from Buddhism to Ifa, gave it all up and found myself back at the place of my beginnings: the black Baptist church. It felt comfortable and familiar. The singing, preaching and exhortation reminded me of the love of black women in peacock suits and steaming kitchens. But there was a problem. According to the church, I could not be a lesbian and loved by God. I discussed this issue with my brother-in-law, a black Baptist minister. He listened to me with genuine respect and concern. After I finished explaining that, although I missed the church and wanted to come back, I could not accept the notion that God didn't love me because I was a lesbian. He told me that he felt that I had tremendous talents to contribute to the church and expressed the need for my gifts. He then tried to convince me that who I thought I was wasn't real. He told me that my being a lesbian was the manifestation of a demonic spirit and my self-acceptance was the result of God turning me over to a reprobate mind. He then proceeded to suggest that I pray, read the New Testament book of Romans and continue to attend church regularly. He was certain that the more involved and educated I became about what God was really about, the less I would believe that my entire life had held any legitimacy in God's eyes.

I went back to church, intent on showing my brother-in-law the error of his thinking. I read the Bible, I hung out in the Bible bookstore, I volunteered to work church functions, I took advanced classes, I convinced myself that I had truly found my calling. I wanted to become a deacon, enter Divinity school and provide ministerial therapy for women who were survivors of sexual and domestic abuse. That was until one night during adult Bible class when I was informed that women had absolutely no authority in the church. Oh yes, I could have a ministry and I could even go to Divinity school and become a therapist. But a deacon? Never. Not in our denomination.

I had been studying the Gospel and really getting to know Jesus as more than an icon hanging at an altar. I had learned about his tolerance and love for all people. I also learned about his stance on women as equals. I read about Mary Magdalene and her important role as an apostle. I debated the people in class about this archaic, denominational tenet. My brother-in-law, the pastor, ended the debate by stating his father's position on the matter: "Jesus had twelve Disciples and one of them was a traitor but none of them was a woman." All the men in class laughed, and I felt the heat of shame that I thought I'd long ago buried resurface, cover my face and crawl down the back of my neck.

After many years of traveling down the spiritual paths of others, I found myself again tired and coming up short. Although I'd gained something beautiful from each experience, I still hadn't connected with the Spirit that I had chased all of my life. The Spirit of my great-grandmother, who was also the Spirit of my grandmother and my mother. The Spirit that was a friend of dark women and always made them happy. The Spirit that I thought that I had never known.

Then I remembered the voice that had always been with me. The One that told me that I was an extension of the Creator and cherished more than heaven or earth. The One that reassured me that I was beautiful and good when others rejected and condemned me. The One that comforted me when the eviction notice or the pink slip came and let me know that I would be provided for. The One that set my belly on fire and caused me to stand as a warrior in the face of injustice. The One that allowed me to take another step when fear would have left me paralyzed. The One that knew that my love for a woman was as real as the heartache I felt when she left. It was the voice of the one true Spirit that had always been with me. The Spirit that is nothing but love and has nothing but love for me. The One that bears all things, fears nothing and walks in peace.

This is the Spirit that I finally learned to revere. Sometimes I call It God, Father, Jesus, Brother. Sometimes I call It Goddess, Mother, Mary, Sister. I always call It Love. This is the religion that I follow. It has only one commandment: that is to love everybody. It has many holy books of reference, the biblical teachings of Christ being the ones closest to my heart. Although I have no frightening images of bleeding, silent icons in my home, I have practiced the ritual of maintaining an altar for several years now.

There is no golden man hanging above it, or angry woman

sitting below. There are only reminders of the Creative Spirit's many divine embodiments in this plane of existence. There are candles that represent the purifying and rejuvenating power of fire. There are flowers, leaves and stones that remind me of the simplistic beauty that exists in everything. There is a fountain that shows me the ever flowing and constantly replenishing abundance of life. And there is incense that, with each spiral of smoke, reminds me to be grateful for the air I take into my lungs. This is the place I go to for encouragement, wisdom, solace and joy. This is my spiritual home, the place where I get "happy." And the Voice there is never silent.

As a Black Gay Christian I realized that, as a community, GLBT people cannot afford the luxury of running and becoming members of the one or two Black GLBT inclusive churches in our cities. ...Every church should be a safe haven for God's children, GLBT or Straight.

Standing Up to the Black Church
By Herndon L. Davis

On Sunday, January 12, 2003, I sat through a fiery, homophobic sermon authored by my brilliantly dynamic and highly admired pastor. The title of the sermon was "When God Gives Up on You." His text was taken from Romans 1:21 and Matthew 12:31-32. During his delivery, however, the text expanded to include verses on up to Romans 1:31, and as far back as the eighteenth and nineteenth chapters of Genesis.

Most of the sermon dealt with the concept of homosexuality being a sin that is so great that God will finally give up on you if you continue to commit it with full knowledge of its iniquity. He preached that for this sin God would eventually turn his back on a sinner—giving one over, as a consequence, to a reprobate (evil, demonic) mind. Although he also preached against adultery, fornication, idolatry and pride, it was homosexuality that he railed against most. In fact, he came dangerously close to saying that homosexuality was an unforgivable sin, but stopped just short of that by referencing Matthew 12:31-32, in which Jesus clearly states that all sins can be forgiven with the exception of blasphemy against the Holy Spirit.

I have been in church my entire life and have heard numerous anti-gay sermons before, but this one was a bit different. At that point in my life, as a Gay, Black, Christian man, I had been out of the closet for many years, lived in gay neighborhoods, dated, and had grown very comfortable not just with my sexuality, but foremost with my relationship with God. For this reason, my pastor's sermon seemed to appear out of nowhere and really took me by surprise, especially given his over-the-top pulpit theatrics and the congregation's sensational participation in his performance.

With powerful intensity, blatant insensitivity, and a fire-in-the belly passion, my pastor rabidly and scornfully preached against homosexuals. His vitriolic pronouncements were quickly accentuated by the bloodcurdling screams of women and the football-sounding cheers of men, who were wholly in agreement. The entire spectacle was topped off by thunderous applause and a partial standing ovation by the almost 1,500 people in attendance at the 7:30 a.m. service. The entire outrageous experience motivated me to do the following:

• Re-evaluate, one last time, as a Black Gay man my entire spiritual and emotional relationship with God through his son Jesus.
• Decide whether I should remain a member of that church, or instead find another church home with a kinder, gentler stance toward GLBT Christians.

I went to God in complete, humble submission, intense prayer and continual meditation, taking all of my feelings out of the mix in order to hear a clear and decisive word from him. As a result, God answered and not only encouraged me to remain a member of this 13,000+ congregation for another year, despite its non-affirming views, but also inspired me to write the GLBT affirming book entitled *Black, Gay and Christian: An Inspirational Guidebook to Daily Living*, which speaks directly to my experience of Black GLBT Spirituality.

As a Black Gay Christian I realized that, as a community, GLBT people cannot afford the luxury of running and becoming members of the one or two Black GLBT inclusive churches in our cities. We are too dynamic, complex, creative, and colorful a people to be relegated to serving God within the confines of only "safe havens." **Every church should be a safe haven for God's children, GLBT or Straight.**

The upfront reality is that Black GLBT Christians are alive and well, and often thriving beyond belief within the Black Church, though many are still deeply closeted, afraid of the retribution awaiting them from their congregations, fellow clergy, co-workers, family and friends. Contrary to popular belief, Black GLBT Christians do far more than just sing, shout and direct church choirs. We also serve as church pastors, preside as bishops, work as deacons, minister to the sick-and-shut-in, preach, teach, feed the homeless, and manage church finances in the accounting and budgeting of church member tithes and offerings.

An encouraging and growing number of us are actually beginning to step out of the dark, cold, lonely closet in order to live, breathe and thrive in the bright sunshine as the holistic, spiritual beings God created and meant for us to be. Daily, more of us are realizing that we should neither expect, nor resign ourselves to, pulpit rantings and disrespectful spiritual talk directed toward us. We should never view these instances of oppression as part of a reality that simply cannot or will not ever be changed. Had Dr. Martin Luther King, Jr. accepted his fellow Black clergy's discouragement and ridicule in the face of racial oppression, we all just might still be living under Jim Crow laws today!

Hence, the major reason I remained a member of this non-affirming church was because I decided that I finally had to personally stand up and speak out on the issue of homophobia in my church. I believe that we ALL must individually and collectively begin to think along these lines in terms of strategizing, facilitating change and lobbying in support of our demands for GLBT inclusion within the Black Church.

I fully realize that standing up to the Black Church on the issue of homosexuality is no easy feat. On top of being notoriously fundamentalist concerning scripture, the Black

Church eagerly foists an extra heaping of cultural and ethnic shame on GLBT people. Further, we, as Black people, still face energetic racism and a myriad of other social issues, making the mere thought of Black men tiptoeing their way through the swishy waters of homosexuality enough to motivate some congregants to hurl their Bibles at the nearest suspected gay "threat." Yet through it all, Black GLBT Christians must withstand and endure, much like we withstood and endured as a race during the civil rights struggle of the 1960s and today. We need a plan of action and very brave soldiers to march into battle.

For those who are seriously up to the task, I believe there are six crucial steps we must take in standing up to the Black Church:

1. Pray for direction on your specific approach and methods. Remember that the GLBT inclusion strategy used at Mt. Liberal White Methodist Church across town probably will not fly at Greater Conservative Black Baptist Church in downtown. Get to know your congregation, pastor or bishop. It helps to know the political dynamics of your church before initiating a dialogue. You must know your church congregation, pastor/bishop, etc., before you begin to strategize a plan of action.

My church environment at the time, for example, was very traditional, with a demographic slant more toward the fifty-plus crowd. The youngest deacon was probably in his late forties. The song service was less of the newer praise and worship style of music of today, but more of the soul-stirring hymns and traditional gospel songs from generations past. In fact, the church still had a thirty-minute mournful sounding devotion. My pastor held a very high position within the Black community and was known for his long-winded and often comical parable-driven sermons that eventually whooped up to a fever pitch toward the end.

Based on prayer and my familiarity with my church I chose a quiet, grassroots approach, which meant coming out to individuals in my church who I believed were gay and growing the level of support from there, rather than trying to rush the pulpit directly. From there I gained assistance and support from some very well-connected people.

First, I came out to a church friend who I thought was gay, though we had never confirmed it to one another. His mother was extremely supportive of him and she also liked me. She was also very connected within the church. She was friends with a few of the senior ushers next to whom we often sat. These senior ushers happened to be founding members of the church and knew the pastor directly.

Everyone involved liked me and, despite their conflicting feelings, were more inclined to assist me than block me. Hence, the old saying is true: blood (true connection with others) is thicker than water—no matter how much the pastor shouts "Adam and Eve not Adam and Steve" on Sunday morning.

2.   As a collective group of parishioners, we Black GLBT Christians must peacefully speak directly to our pastors, bishops and ministry staff about our concerns. Believe it or not, a calm, intelligent and articulate conversation about the issue is far more effective than a fire and brimstone debate over homosexuality and its inclusion in the church. Remember Proverbs 15:1—"A soft answer turneth away wrath, but grievous words stir up anger."

Further, make sure that everyone in your group agrees and is on the SAME page. You do NOT want a GLBT person on your team who still thinks homosexuality is inherently a sin and could be easily swayed by the intimidating presence of your church pastor, bishop or ministers.

My pastor, although very kind-hearted and genuine, still has an intimidating presence. In his over thirty years of pastoring, he's heard and seen just about everything. He has a prepared answer for every topic known to man. He definitely knows the word and can easily run circles around most people he encounters. Hence it took someone like myself, and others who are not only confident in their knowledge and understanding of the word, but who are even more confident in their heart relationship with God, to calmly convey to him the need for a re-look, re-study and re-assessment of the topic of homosexuality and Christianity.

For a long time I saw my pastor not as a man, but as this untouchable lieutenant of God. I had to overcome that fearful mindset and come to the realization that he puts his pants on one leg at a time, too! Although God may use him differently than me, my pastor still doesn't have special privileges or access to God that I do not. We both have Jesus as our conduit and access to our heavenly Father.

3. If you are not able to find other GLBT church members to join you in your quest, then you must summon up the courage to go it alone. Be fully prepared to be outed and even preached against by name. No one ever likes being the pioneer on this journey of gay inclusion in the Black Church, but it must be done. We must recognize that our efforts are not just about us, but about the many generations to follow. There comes a point in life when we must stand, walk and eventually run our faith.

Although my pastor hasn't gone to this point in terms of outing and name-calling from the pulpit, I believe that I was indeed the inspiration for at least one of his gay-bashing sermons that was preached three days after I met with him for a conference on an unrelated matter.

We just have to face the facts. It could happen to any one of us. If you're not prepared for the outing or the name-calling from the pulpit, then don't even go down this path.

4. During your dialogue with your church clergy, DO NOT debate scripture or the interpretation of scripture. Provide them with literature from your local gay bookstore that speaks to this issue. Speak to your own personal experience, path and growth with God as a Black GLBT Christian. Speak to how you are no

different in your beliefs, understanding and spiritual walk and that your personhood in part is a reflection of your sexual orientation.

Be very clear in expressing to them that you did not choose to be gay/lesbian, but you are proud to be what God created you to be. **Do not say this unless you really mean it.** If an argument or debate does indeed start, please allow the clergy to attack you and NOT the other way around. If they are indeed godly individuals, sooner or later, their consciences will catch up with their actions.

My pastor is a GREAT listener. I thank God for that. Although he already had his mind made up about homosexuality, he was still open to listen and to learn. This is a bright point in my experience. In the past, he was once against women preaching, but today his pulpit is filled with women ministers. In fact, his current wife is an evangelist. I am praying that my ongoing dialogue with him and the release of my book will over time enter into his heart and spirit, allowing him to go to God for his direction on the issue, rather than following personal bias.

5. Recruit heterosexuals in your church to broaden your base of support. It may seem like an impossible task, but think again: There are too many gays in the Black Church, along with their family members and friends, for there not to be some straight people to take a stand for what's right. We cannot make the mistake of automatically assuming that absolutely no straight Black Christians will join us in our quest.

In my case, I really didn't know anyone who would do this. However, this does NOT mean there weren't heterosexuals in my church who would join in such an alliance; I just didn't know of any who I felt would be willing to take the chance.

6. Continue to pray and have lots of patience. Don't give up if you are denied or even given fierce treatment by your pastor, bishop, ministers or staff. There are many ways to skin a cat, and

prayer is the chief of these. Prayer does indeed move and turn the hearts and minds of others. So don't give up, but allow God to work through this situation in his own time and in his own fashion.

God can do the impossible and we must have the faith that he will indeed move the mountain of homophobia within the Black Church. In the interim, we must continue to witness to other GLBT individuals. Actively seek out those closeted men and women who need to hear an encouraging word. Finally, remember that we must reach out and spiritually empower each other, because no one else is going to!

I know that the journey to acceptance in our churches can be long and frustrating, but it's a route that has to be traveled. We will never overcome if we are too afraid, too timid or too reactive to rise up and finally stand up to the Black Church!

It was as if the forces in the universe had magnetically drawn me to this place so that I could be faced with the same opportunity I had avoided the year before. … The message was clear: I was supposed to attend this workshop and explore my own confusion and pain in relation to my legacy.

Buddha on the Land
By Mona de Vestel

The Chinese character for crisis is made up of elements signifying danger and opportunity. Danger first began manifesting in my life as a child. It was present in the hands of my father, and the violence of his ways. It was present in the strange confusion of my identity somewhere between my brown mother born in the Belgian Congo and my white father who came from Belgium. It was present in the void left in the heart of Ani—my sister's child abandoned when she was two. And it was, without a doubt, present in the years I spent mourning my sister Maisha, who later disappeared—vanished completely.

Danger had always existed outside—but with time, it had been passed on to me, transferred symbolically into my bloodstream until I'd learned to manifest it on my own. By the time my life had reached a breaking point, I began making strides toward a spiritual practice. It all first began on "the land" at the Womyn's Michigan Music Festival. These were the days when danger (and opportunity) sometimes manifested in the form of tears.

I rarely cried in those days but when I did, it felt like

erosion—like a dam breaking. I remember crying quietly at the foot of a willow tree planted in the arid soil of a Michigan summer. I was holding a smooth stone in my clutched fingers, holding on to a piece of "the land" tightly—urgently—cradling it. It was my first summer at the Womyn's Michigan Music Festival. Just after finishing loading up the car in the parking lot, I'd slipped away from the crowds of women getting ready to travel home, and I sat at the foot of the tree trying to hold on to myself. These were my last few minutes on the land before I had to ride "home" with the ex-girlfriend I'd taken with me out of fear of being alone. If I could carry the experience of the festival all back home with me, I could contain the darkness and the pain.

My life was everything I hated: boring, drab, like the brown carpeting of my Connecticut apartment; empty and lonely. A void existed inside—a vacuous hole I desperately tried to fill. But the emptiness came from within. In the course of the week at the festival, I'd caught a glimpse of my new self. A self larger, so much larger than my tiny, innocuous life of days spent working in a cubicle as a technical writer – a position destabilizing by its name: It evoked a semblance of creativity with the word "writer" only to be offset by "technical" which meant a comfortable salary. Now I was leaving this land—thousands of women gathering together each summer around ideals of community, empowerment and music. The desire to begin to face myself honestly and to move toward the power I'd witnessed on the land had been planted in my life.

These were the days of containment, when I held on to everything, storing every experience in the many compartments of my psyche. There was a place for the pain of my childhood, an open cesspool of buried feelings where I kept it all intact; and there was another place for keepsakes: objects that reminded me of the presence of beauty because I wasn't able to experience it firsthand. I contained it all. When Maisha was finally declared missing after ten years of silence, I secretly wished I could have found a way to preserve her.

Through the years, I'd tried to make sense of Maisha's

absence and I realized that as the oldest child in our family, Maisha had suffered the brunt of my father's abuse. By the time my parents had split up when I was five and a half years old, Maisha was nearly fourteen—bruised and cracked by the damage of my father's incestuous ways. When she disappeared years after the separation, Maisha simply cut herself off from everything that connected her to the darkness of our family's karma.

I took the small, smooth rock and placed it in my pocket; it would be a reminder of the vows of wholeness and truth that I'd made with myself in the past week. Like vows of chastity or vows of any nature, it would require a renewed faith and daily challenges of overhauling, dismantling and, later still, rebuilding my life piece by piece. But for this to happen, I'd need to build a strong spiritual foundation, a solid ground onto which I could construct and rebuild myself.

Opportunity: Six years after that first festival, I returned to the same arid land in Michigan in the month of August. I showed up for my work shift in the Womyn of Color tent. The festival operates on a community-based model where each participant contributes two four-hour work shifts of their choice to help run the festival. I was immediately comforted by the familiar feeling this tent evoked: the bright red carpeting, taped down onto dry, uneven earth, the rudimentary folding chairs that could be arranged quickly in a circle for workshops in the afternoon or alongside the long rectangular table at night for parties, dinners or games. I liked the smell of bales of hay where women sat listening to the sound of the flapping "tarped" door on windy days. This was a home, a womyn-constructed home that existed a few weeks out of the year.

I wrote my name on a tag as was the custom, plastered it on my chest and picked up a broom to sweep an already perfectly clean tent. As I'd discovered the year before, this work shift was an incredible find. It was an excuse to hang out for four hours with powerful women in a nurturing setting. If five minutes of sweeping and two trips to the water spigot counted as work, then this experience qualified as a work shift. As I finished sweeping the tent, a workshop was just beginning. "Coincidentally," I'd signed up to work during the same workshop I'd opted out at the last minute the year before. This was a workshop for women of mixed ancestry and consisted of a two-day exploration of ways to embrace the whole of our legacy. The workshop culminated in a three-hour sweat in a lodge on the second day. It was the idea of the sweat that had me walking out of the workshop the year before. But this year, I knew that I had to confront my fear. I knew that everything had been put on my path for me to choose to take on the journey.

I recognized Akiba—a Sundancer who led the ceremony in the sweat lodge and the workshop the year before. She noticed me, and invited me into the circle. I told her I was on a work shift and she smiled and said:

"Well sit down anyway, and if you have to go, you go."

I was busted. It was as if the forces in the universe had magnetically drawn me to this place so that I could be faced with the same opportunity I had avoided the year before. Women introduced themselves candidly, revealing conflicted emotions about their mixed ancestry. Some women cried about their legacy of oppressed/oppressor existing within; others talked about their emotional connection to one set of ancestors versus another. The message was clear: I was supposed to attend this workshop and explore my own confusion and pain in relation to my legacy.

Childhood memories came pouring in as we collectively began peeling back the layers.

Danger: I remembered holding out my caramel-colored hand in the dusty roads of Kinshasa where we lived for a year with my family. I was only five years old and my father's best friend, and CEO of a Belgian airline company in Zaire, had just found a dead black man on his property. This man, a thief, had tried breaking into the house, only to be met by "Chewy" the German shepherd. Now the thief was dead. My father's friend, who explained to me that Chewy had never "liked black people," just tossed the body in the river. I held out my arm, wondering how light is light enough to stay alive in colonial Africa.

Opportunity: A recently shaven, bald woman walked into the workshop as we were a third of the way through the introductions; she sat down and frankly apologized for being late. I couldn't have known that this bald, abrasive, sometimes crude woman, wearing black leather boots without socks, would actually change my life.

As she introduced herself, Aleana said that she was a practicing Nichiren Buddhist. She spoke of her childhood growing up in an abusive household. I could relate. She shared her fears with the group—not only fears due to the residues of her abusive childhood but also fears of the spirit world, and of the other dimensions around us. As she spoke, I felt as though we were strangely related, like sisters, or old relatives who hadn't seen each other in a long time. But Aleana was also uncompromising: She spent quite a bit of time arguing with Akiba about not being able to use any drugs or alcohol for twenty-four hours before the sweat. Usually, Aleana's attitude would have irked me, maybe even have pushed some serious buttons. I came from a family where alcohol was a back door to abusive behavior. But nothing Aleana did seemed to bother me. I could see right through her in her simplest form: She was a beautiful and powerful spirit, embodied in a wounded and guarded woman. And as I listened to her argue and get angry about being told not to smoke pot prior to the ceremony, I felt complete compassion for her.

On the second day of the workshop, we walked up past the showers where dozens of naked women were washing. I heard the chatter of their voices slipping away into the distance as we made our way deeper into the fern-lined path toward the lodge. The fire keeper, a young apprentice, was working hard heating the lava rocks we would later take inside with us. The morning air was cool; I felt hopeful that this was a good sign. For the past twenty-four hours, I'd focused on Akiba's words of warning about the intense heat in the lodge and the need to hydrate constantly before the sweat. I had since become obsessed, sipping water every ten minutes until it was time for us to step into the lodge. I could feel the fear creeping inside me again with worries crowding my head: What if I had to pee? Would I succumb to a heart attack in the lodge? After all, I was in my mid-thirties. Each thought became more and more absurd. Danger…opportunity.

The lodge seemed small, innocuous even, with its small and round structure made of pliable branches and covered with thick layers of wool blankets. Why was I afraid of such a tiny little place? My fears seemed ridiculous, in the bright morning light. We finished making our tobacco ties—offerings to the spirits. As we wrapped tiny pieces of colored cloth around small bundles of tobacco, Akiba warned us that the darker colors would bring out darker energies in the lodge. I carefully picked my favorite blues, purple and white to ward off the darkness.

Akiba asked if any of us had an issue with tight spaces, and all of a sudden I decided that I was claustrophobic. This had never been a problem up to this point, but every fear I'd ever had, small or large, was now surfacing. Akiba told me to sit down in the spot closest to the door. The rocks in the pit would bring the temperature well into the hundreds. The rocks were brought inside and the thick layers of blanket framing the door were dropped. Suddenly, we were plunged into complete darkness. I wasn't prepared for this sudden change. Something snapped; my body began to shake uncontrollably. I had always thought of myself as a very controlled person, someone who didn't break easily under pressure. I'd lived and survived harrowing experiences and I thought of myself as a strong woman, but all of a sudden, in this dark and warm womb, I'd become a baby once again.

Danger: In the lodge, I thought of my sister Maisha. She had been gone longer than I had known her. In my memories, Maisha was always calling out my name, like a wounded animal caught in a trap: "Monina!" With remembering came the fear of not being able to remember. I had spent years wishing I had a recording of her voice, like a preserved corpse, embalmed in fluid. Instead, I kept the purple frog she had sewn for me as a child. It was in this velvet pouch of old rice that I found comfort. I would hold the frog in my hand thinking that this was the same rice my sister had touched years ago.

In the darkness of the lodge, I began to cry. Akiba handed me a feather. She told me this was the feather of a powerful white female owl; holding it would give me power, she said. In some remote place, I sensed the honor of what she had just bestowed upon me, but the little girl in me remained terrified. I thought of my father—the shadow of his presence in our room at night. Now I was sobbing. Akiba poured some water on the rocks. Intense wet heat was released into the pitch-black lodge. All sense of time and space had disappeared. I couldn't identify where I was or how long I'd been there. I felt trapped and I wanted to flee. I knew I could leave if I really wanted but I remembered Akiba's words earlier: "Ride through the discomfort; the lodge is not about being comfortable." I forced myself to stay put. As I continued to cry, Akiba asked me to express what I was feeling. I had no words. I felt I was inside my mama's womb but I was terrified.

Opportunity: We honored our ancestors and began singing. Aleana offered a song: Nam-Myoho-Renge-Kyo—her Buddhist chant of the Lotus Sutra. These strange syllables were released one by one into the scorching air of the lodge. Later I found out that Nam-Myoho-Renge-Kyo is the mystic law of cause and effect that governs our universe. Immediately, the little girl inside me became connected to the powerful adult woman I'd become. Just as fast as the fear had taken hold of me, it suddenly lifted out of my body. We continued to chant Nam-Myoho-Renge-Kyo for a few minutes: In the perfect stillness of this absence of light, I heard my own voice rising. I felt calm, strong and endowed with an absolute strength that always existed inside me.

We continued our spiritual journey in the dark. The sweat was divided into four cycles—like the four seasons in nature, the four cycles and inevitable sufferings of life in Buddhism: birth, sickness, old age and death. Between each cycle, Akiba opened the lodge and allowed us to breathe cool air. We didn't drink. For three hours, I peeled back the layers of my life. I allowed the image of my father's face to drift away into the invisible moisture around us; I let go of Maisha, and the echoes of her voice. I let go of the weight of her absence filling me like lead. I let go of eternity in the darkness; death and absence vanished, loss and tears. From now on, I would no longer need amulets to carry me. I would no longer be afraid of the dark. Suddenly I thought of Maisha's now teenage daughter Ani whom I had adopted a couple of years earlier. I felt myself confronting the challenge of loving someone who wasn't held at birth. In the darkness of the lodge, I felt the arid soil, moist and warm under my folded body. I remembered the dry feel of dust rising around my ankles. I tried to remember the discoloration of my skin under the caked layers of earth after a day on the land. Loving the unloved is a fertile place of opportunity… and danger.

After the workshop, I felt as light as a feather. I couldn't remember ever having felt so light and alive as I did on that day. As I sat at night stage—an open-air concert under the stars—with my beautiful partner, I knew something had changed but I couldn't name it. I watched the sunset holding Celia's hand while the night air cooled around us. This was the first time I'd acknowledged the danger in my life without trying to run away. It was in the cool night air of this Michigan summer, while holding my lover's hand, that I began to move toward opportunity.

At the end of the festival, Aleana and I vowed we'd stay in touch but, caught up in all of the festivities, we somehow didn't exchange addresses. I left the festival not knowing when or where I'd see Aleana again.

In the months that followed, I quickly became immersed in the challenges of my own life once again. By the following winter, the resonance of my spiritual journey in the lodge seemed like a distant dream. After two years of parenting my niece Ani, things were beginning to unravel between us. I was also facing some challenges in my professional life. I had somehow managed to finish a draft of a memoir I'd written in stolen moments before and after work, and I'd transitioned from working as a technical writer to doing web design for the same company. Though closer to being where I wanted to be professionally, I still felt that something was off. Worse yet, the position was both unfulfilling and financially comfortable. I was more than making ends meet and paying off debt, but I was miserably unhappy confined in a cubicle, making web sites for a company, when all I wanted to do was teach and write.

My partner Celia and I were also facing challenges of a legal nature. She was a French national, and we didn't know how she would be able to legally stay in the country once she finished her MBA the following May. As an American lesbian, I didn't exactly enjoy the same rights as my American heterosexual counterparts. I couldn't just marry the woman I loved and have her benefit from my legal status.

On a day when I was feeling particularly sorry for myself, I played hooky from work and attended a free poetry workshop at Syracuse University. The workshop felt like home. Eileen Myles, a wonderful poet, talked about the art of writing. For a few short hours, I pretended that I hadn't stepped out of my life to be in this place. As we were introducing ourselves to the group, the door opened and who walked in but Aleana!

I hadn't seen her since the festival and I had no idea she was even in Syracuse. We screamed and yelled and hugged for a long time as the people in the workshop watched us, partly annoyed and partly intrigued. As it turns out, Aleana had family in Syracuse, she was staying there for a few weeks. After the workshop, we exchanged information. I told Aleana about all of the obstacles that I was facing and she suggested we chant Nam-Myoho-Renge-Kyo together. I agreed.

A few days later, in the midst of conflicts with Ani, I attended my first Nichiren Buddhist meeting and chanted Nam-Myoho-Renge-Kyo.

Like the feeling of release I had felt while chanting in the lodge, my life unexpectedly opened up. I felt connected to the universe and inside the thread of this connection existed Ani, my lover, the trees outside of the room, my father, mother, sister and brother; we were all one. The heavy burden I'd always felt was simply lifted. Up to this point in my life, my place of worship had always been nature. Whenever I felt drained or down, I'd go hiking into the woods, surrounding myself with natural beauty, reconnecting with a deeper and higher consciousness inside myself. Chanting gave me a similar feeling. It wasn't that my problems had been removed from my life or even from my sight. In fact, I could see them more clearly than ever before. I saw all of my strengths, my weaknesses, my sorrows and my joys in full light. And for the first time, I could feel compassion for myself, for Ani and for every member of my family. As I chanted, I experienced the profound connection between us all so clearly.

Opportunity: As soon as I began chanting, I moved mountains. The results were not always pleasant. I received Gohonzon on May 15—a few weeks after my first meeting with Aleana. The Gohonzon is a scroll inscribed with Nam-Myoho-Renge-Kyo, the law of cause and effect that governs our lives and everything in the universe. Contrary to other religions, Nichiren Buddhism does not believe in devotion outside of the self. The Gohonzon is not an object of worship, but rather a point of focus. The practice of chanting has the sole purpose of developing one's own inherent Buddha nature. I enshrined my Gohonzon in a wooden cabinet called the Butsudan and I began chanting twice a day. For years up until that point, I'd been living my life with the attitude that my "real life" hadn't yet started. I'd always felt like what I was experiencing didn't really count and that my real life would soon begin. And then I understood that life is in the here and now. If I had dreams and a mission I wanted to realize, I'd have to start realizing them now.

Little did I know that the law of cause and effect operates in mysterious ways: Six days after receiving Gohonzon, I was laid off from my job as a web designer due to downsizing. With the news of the layoff came a series of mixed emotions. This was the job I'd disliked, but which had felt so comfortable. For years, I'd wanted to earn a living by writing and teaching; I wanted to get my work published. Now, I'd been kicked out of the nest and I was forced to confront my life full on. Luckily, I collected unemployment, which allowed me to continue to pay my basic bills. Ani moved out and I continued to support her until she decided to drop out of high school. The life lessons were coming hard and fast. I needed to let go of my super-hero syndrome and the idea that I could simply "save" Ani from her troubled past.

As a child, I had always wanted to make sense of my world. I remember watching the movie *The Holocaust* when I was eleven years old. I walked into the kitchen where my mother was cooking and told her that I was Jewish. My mother, who was used to my emotional eccentricities, just laughed it off. But deep inside I felt a kind of remembrance from a time past. I yearned with my entire being to understand how something that heinous could be possible. I wanted to be able to comprehend the nature of evil. Years later, when I stepped into a synagogue for the first time with an ex-girlfriend—the same girlfriend I'd traveled to Michigan for the first time—I burst into tears after hearing the Rabbi speak in Hebrew. It had ignited an ancient memory—a kind of remembrance I could feel inside every fiber of my being. And yet, in the present day, the Judaic faith felt completely disconnected from my life. The sermons and the traditions were oppressively patriarchal and I had absolutely no ties to the religion anywhere in my life—at least not in this lifetime. If I wanted to answer these greater questions, I needed a spiritual foundation. Up until this point, I had turned to various religions and, like a child in a bank, I'd fallen despondent, terribly bored and a little cranky. As a lesbian of color, none of the religious institutions I'd explored so far felt embracing. Finally, after years of searching, I'd found a pathway into clear understanding.

Each day, as I practiced, I experienced clarity. I knew exactly what I wanted and I knew what I needed to do in order to get it. Even though I was surrounded by difficult circumstances, my own Buddha nature within led me fearlessly. My partner Celia had obtained her MBA, and was beginning to look for a job with a visa sponsorship. In the next few months, I restructured and overhauled my entire life. I edited my memoir manuscript; I wrote a screenplay and the first three chapters of a novel. I applied for jobs teaching writing and was hired to teach at a small local college. I was slowly beginning to construct the life I'd always wanted. But I was in no way prepared for the surprise of a lifetime ahead.

Opportunity: In the fall, Celia and I flew to Europe to see our families. It is difficult for me to see my mother regularly, as she now lives in Brussels. Celia's generous parents had paid for our trip, allowing us to visit them and for me to see my wonderful mother, whom I missed dearly. Celia's family was kind and loving, even if they sometimes still struggled with the idea of their daughter's homosexuality. I spent three magnificent days visiting my mother. The trip was a gift.

On our way home, we stopped in Paris to visit Celia's brother and his girlfriend. This was the last day of our trip before we were scheduled to fly home to Syracuse. As we were all chatting in the living room, I decided to quickly check my e-mail. Among the long list of correspondence I noticed a message from someone with the same first initial and last name as mine. I was accustomed to receiving hundreds of junk e-mails a day and I was convinced that this was yet another marketing ploy to get my attention. As I was getting ready to delete the message, I decided to click on it at the last second. The message read: "Are you Mona de Vestel? If you have a long lost sister, please contact me as soon as possible, if not, I apologize." The message wasn't signed.

My heart was racing; my entire body began to shake uncontrollably. Was this a sick joke? Who would do such a thing and why? Could this be Maisha? But why was the message written in English when French was my family's native language?

I looked at the e-mail address; it contained a reference to Japan, the last known place where Maisha had lived before disappearing. The e-mail address also contained Maisha's birth year! Who would know her exact birth year? I was on the verge of being sick. I cautiously but immediately replied to the message, and as a safety measure, to get rid of any possible imposter, I asked the person on the other end to give me the nicknames we used to give each other as children. Then I clicked "send."

I have never waited so long for anything in my life. I shared the news with Celia's family and began talking a mile a minute, confused and drunk with adrenalin. I called a close friend in Paris. She thought the message had to come from Maisha. I wanted to believe her more than anything in the world, but the part of me that wanted to stay protected from the biggest disappointment of my life still had a doubt. I'd spent the last few years of my life mourning Maisha as dead. And since the beginning of my Buddhist practice, I'd been including her in my daily prayers for the dead. But could she be alive?

The rest of the afternoon passed at a snail's pace; so did the evening. I checked my e-mail a dozen times; nothing. That evening we packed our last few belongings, got ready for our trip home the next day and went to bed. We were scheduled to leave for the airport by 9:30 the next morning. The second my eyes opened, I jumped out of bed and pounced on the computer. There was a new message from M. de Vestel. My heart was pounding. I knew this message would change the rest of my life. I clicked on it without thinking and read the few lines as fast as I could: "I am Maisha de Vestel ..." The message continued on with a list of undeniable facts about our family. The nicknames we gave each other as children, games we used to play together, the birth names of our parents. For ten years I'd thought my sister to be dead. One day she had disappeared leaving us with nothing more than outdated addresses and phone numbers. Even when I'd adopted Ani years earlier, the authorities had performed a search finding nothing more than dead-end trails and deafening silence. But she was alive and living in Japan!

I collapsed on the ground and began to wail. I cried so hard every muscle in my body hurt the next day. All of these years I'd been mourning my sister's death, and now she had just written to me! I sat at the computer again, with my runny nose and swollen eyes, and I e-mailed Maisha back. I typed quickly, not thinking about what to say. I knew that e-mail couldn't possibly convey the emotions I was feeling. I focused on the tangible elements in my life. I told her that I was on my way home to the United States where I now lived and that I would e-mail her back very soon. I told her I'd adopted her daughter.

Before leaving for the airport, I checked my messages one more time and noticed a message containing a cell phone number in Japan. I dialed the number. My sister answered the phone! In one moment, I was carried back to the memory of Maisha's wounded voice. Never did I think in a million years that I would ever get to hear that voice again. Every year on Maisha's birthday, I had cried because of her absence. In those days of debilitating pain, I'd tried to make a quiet peace. This is what letting go of the dead was about: facing, over and over again, the insurmountable pain that we will never see, touch, smell or hear our loved one ever again. I had defied this sacred law somehow. I felt like a strange Houdini who had transgressed the laws of life and death. I wasn't yet in touch with the reality that I was talking to a living person; I was speaking to a ghost.

Maisha's voice hadn't changed except that she had more of a smoker's voice now, raspier, as if she'd been smoking for the last decade. Later, she told me she smoked too much.

Maisha and I didn't speak long; she simply thanked me for adopting Ani. I told her I was living in the United States, that I was a writer and that Maman was alive and well, living in Belgium. She told me little about her life and I didn't ask. I asked her if she wanted to be in touch with Ani and her voice hesitated, then said: "Let's start with e-mail first. Maybe we can e-mail each other." I hadn't expected that second of hesitation. When I hung up, my mind was reeling. I thought about the reality from her end. The two-year-old daughter she had left behind was now eighteen years old. Her daughter's face committed to memory no longer matched the real-life Ani. As I flew home, across the Atlantic, I thought about Ani and the task ahead of having to tell her that her mother was alive.

When I got home, I called Ani, who was no longer living with us, and told her to come home so I could tell her something important. When she arrived, we sat down on the couch in the living room and I said: "I just received an e-mail from Maisha. She is alive." I sat and waited for the information to sink in to

Ani's mind and heart. She was in shock, and kept repeating: "Oh my God! Oh my God!" over and over again. Slowly, the emotions began surfacing; her eyes filled with tears and she began to cry. I held Ani in my arms while we cried together. All along this journey, I'd reconnected with my emotions again, allowing my tears to be more than just a signal of danger. I was crying for Ani, for the pain and confusion she felt; I was crying for the loss we had all been feeling all of these years. I was crying for Maisha, who didn't know her child.

And then, just as I thought we had run through all possible surprises, one more revelation came my way. I was "talking" to Maisha via instant messaging when I told her I was a Buddhist. It was one of the many facts I was sharing with her in order to fill in the gaps left by the long years we'd spent apart. I read Maisha's reply on the screen. "I am a Buddhist too!" And Maisha typed the words: Nam-Myoho-Renge-Kyo. Of all the possible faiths my sister could have chosen, she'd decided, like me, to become a Nichiren Buddhist! At first I thought this faith was a common occurrence in Japan, but I later found out that it only represents 8 percent of the population.

There are no coincidences in life. The dangers that have risen to the surface in my life have brought absolute opportunity. Choosing a Buddhist path has been synonymous with naming something I have always known existed in my life. On the day I began chanting Nam-Myoho-Renge-Kyo, I suddenly turned on the light in my own house. Prior to my practice, I'd known of the contours of every room of my existence. I'd been familiar with the shapes and textures of its content, but I'd never been able to really see it. Now that I practice Nichiren Buddhism I exist in broad daylight.

Today, I do more than embrace my complex Tutsi/Belgian identity. I now understand that I have chosen my incarnation as a woman of color, a lesbian, a writer, a mother and a lover of women. I am a bridge, planks of wood where others will walk— traverse the dual abysses of our society. Reality is a concentric circle: cause and effect—ripples pushing out into the universe.

This is the secret of the world: Our interconnectedness makes the happiness of others our own.

Now that I practice Buddhism, I am a pathway into the circular journey of human emotion. I have created a space of healing through my voice and my work—a space of healing for myself and for others. I now have all of the tools to develop the life I have always wanted. Although the years of loss and devastation behind me will take a long time to sort out, I express daily gratitude for the many blessings in my life: gifts like my sister's return, my courage and ability to walk in the shoes of a writer, and the love I have for my daughter Ani, my partner Celia, my loving mother and my siblings. It is too soon to know what the future holds for all of us, but one thing is clear: With Nam-Myoho-Renge-Kyo at the center of my life, tomorrow is rich and infinite in love, reconstruction and opportunity.

I was nine when she told me, "God's going to use you. He's gonna really do something special with you." What would God choose me to do? Maybe God would have me speak, to tell the truth and shame the devil.

Love Lessons

By Elisa Durrette

Church is the place where I first received my education about desire, heartbreak and loneliness. From the stories of bad-assed Bathsheba to the scintillating Song of Solomon I learned these lessons, right down to those appropriately programmed fans—cardboard numbers with tongue depressor handles, showing pictures of clean-cut, black nuclear families sitting around dinner tables, never eating fried chicken, only respectable roasts.

These fans were fluttering suggestions of the life I suspect most of the members of my church wanted.

The fact that the families in the pictures didn't resemble the families in the pews didn't seem to matter. In fact, I think this discrepancy was planned, because Sunday after Sunday, Pastor Locke promised us that the panorama displayed on the fans could become our reality with a little steadfast prayer.

So what, if you didn't know who your daddy was or if your husband or wife had left you? Just keep praying and they would be back in time for dinner; back in time to be a family again. And if they never came back, well… Jesus could be your all.

Back then, church was about a *love thang*.

In the church I attended, black women, if not virgins, were still holy and worthy of protection. Likewise, black men were not sexual predators, perpetrators of rape, but rather fathers, sons and men of God. Women who had lost their *natural* homes because of an out-of-wedlock pregnancy, adultery or abuse could find a new home in the church. Each member of the church family was called to be her witness without judgment.

So you would think that of all the places black gays and lesbians would find a home, it would be in the black church. Even still, when asked by a friend to recall any gay people in the church I grew up in, I was at a loss. This seemed odd to me, since it is common knowledge that the one gay person in every black church is the choir director. Not so at Lighthouse Church of God in Christ. Our choir director was a married man that neither swooshed nor let his eyes stray.

After giving it some more thought, maybe the reason I couldn't remember who that secret sister or brother might have been was because I was that sister. This is not to say I was secretly seducing girls behind the basement steps after Sunday School. After all, I didn't come to understand that I was gay until my sophomore year of college, let alone admit it to anyone else until my senior year. Still, even though I was unaware of my sexuality, in church I always felt different, set apart from the other girls for reasons I did not understand.

One of my earliest memories of church was Christmas, 1983. That year Christmas fell on a Sunday. A major snowstorm the night before had cancelled most church services in the city. My mother woke me up early that morning because she had to go into the hospital to work. Thinking that my aunt and I would probably spend the day at home, she packed a pink and purple pants outfit in my kiddie bag and loaded me in the car.

This was fine with me since, even as a little girl, I hated skirts and dresses. They added a sense of "can't do" to what was generally a "can do" wardrobe. Regardless of how I may have felt about skirts and dresses, on Sundays I had no choice in the matter. In the Pentecostal church I grew up in it was considered a sin for women and girls to wear pants.

Once I arrived at my Aunt Eleanor's house, I spent most of the morning quietly amusing myself with copies of *Popular Mechanics* and the 1978, 1979 and 1980 *Guinness Books of World Records*. I enjoyed all the entries with pictures; the really tall, the really small and the really fat. The weirder the distinction the better. I needed some type of entertainment since I wasn't allowed to turn on the TV until my aunt woke up. When I did turn on the television, I usually watched a program produced by a Lutheran church in town that featured an older white woman named Miss Shirley who, along with her sock-puppet sidekick, read Bible verses and showed children's crayon drawings of Bible scenes.

Several hours passed that morning before I heard my aunt moving about. She was getting ready for church, humming her usual hymns, opening a fresh pair of stockings, and trying to find the perfectly hung slip. I got ready too: took my bath, stuck one little, last-minute roller in my bangs, and pulled on my pink and purple pants. I emerged from the bathroom looking sporty and fresh.

"You're not wearing that, are you?! Where's your dress?" my aunt said, slightly annoyed.

I must have just stood there looking clueless. "Didn't your mother send a dress with you?"

"No. My Mom said we weren't going to have church."

"Oh, we're having church! …Guess you'll just have to wear what you got on," my aunt said, taking one final look at me before wrinkling her nose.

What? Was I going to church with pants on? Once I'd seen a girl wear pants to church. She was a visitor, somebody's cousin or something, and she got to stay in the church office the entire service and color on paper. Maybe that's what I would get to do, too, since girls and women weren't allowed to wear pants in the sanctuary.

It was slow going to our little church on the north side of town, the area of town where most of the black people and poor whites lived. I noticed that the salt trucks didn't seem to come over to the north side like they did on the west side where we lived. There were some streets that were still impassable. After about an hour my aunt and I pulled into the church parking lot. As I got ready to jump out, I turned and asked my aunt, "Do I need my crayons?"

"You can take them out if you want to, but you're staying in the car. Service won't be that long, 'bout an hour."

"Can't I sit in the office?"

"The office is locked. Plus, you know you're not supposed to have on pants in church. I don't know why your mother didn't give you a dress. She knows it's Sunday."

My aunt grabbed her purse and opened the car door. It was below zero, some man had said on the radio that morning.

"I'm going to leave the heater on. The engine is running, so don't touch anything."

She shut the door and disappeared in the snow.

Most Sundays, I did at least make it inside the church. Lighthouse Church of God in Christ was not one of those storefront churches, nor was it one of those large A.M.E. congregations. It was somewhere in between. The church grounds were comprised of a middling little white sanctuary with a companion church house, surrounded by asphalt and a whiff of grass, in the middle of a neighborhood that was bordered by the freeway. On a good Sunday, Lighthouse might have had anywhere from seventy to eighty people in attendance, all of whom had known each other for years, generations after generations of parishioners.

Lighthouse was Pentecostal in the strictest sense. The church had a list of what seemed to be gender-specific no-no's, like wearing make-up and pants or cutting one's hair. And, to be fair, there were also equally restrictive general rules that applied to both sexes: no going to movie theaters, no secular music, no card playing and no alcohol. None of these transgressions, however, were watched with the same interest as other juicier sins. Sexual sins were the ones that passed from mouth to mouth, and, if serious enough, sometimes hung in the air.

According to the lessons we were taught in Sunday School, the world is littered with fallen women and men, the descendants of those who had dined on forbidden fruit and gotten caught. This is exactly why extra special attention needed to be paid to everybody's business no matter how insignificant. *Because sin was waiting at the door.*

This was an idea that was not lost on the younger members of my congregation. There was a type of moral policing that went on among them. I could wear pants and listen to pop music on Sweet 98 with abandon, without so much as a thought given to who might see me. This was both because my Mom didn't care about such strictures, being more interested that I obey the spirit of the law rather the letter of the law, and because the boundaries of that hyper-religious world didn't extend past 65th Street and I lived on 120th. My cousins, on the other hand, were right in the thick of the spying because the church was their world. They lived right next door to the sanctuary and their father mowed its lawn once a week.

My cousins kept tabs on an amazing amount of improprieties. Did I know that Tasha kept a pair of jeans in her locker or that Sophie was fooling around with boys back behind the church house? Had anyone told me that Sister Rose and Brother Daniel were married two months before their actual wedding so they could start having *relations?*

No misdeed went unnoticed.

The so-called saints were the ones that needed to be watched especially close. The saints were the men and women who had publicly proclaimed Jesus Christ as their savior and renounced all of their worldly ways. Usually these renunciations came in dramatic fashion with these newly formed saints catching the Spirit, crying and speaking in tongues. The men were usually much more reserved than the women, often choosing to stomp their feet or clap their hands to avoid shedding tears.

But when the women caught the Spirit—baby, watch out!

An all-woman team of ushers would rush to surround the Spirit-filled woman with sheets in what looked like a loose group hug. This had the effect of creating a screen so the congregation wouldn't catch glimpses of the woman in the throes of religious ecstasy. This was a practice, I was told by an older member of the church, that had started after a woman's undergarments had been exposed while she was *getting happy*. I remember how those white sheets would billow like wings around the women as they fell to the ground and began rolling on the floor. The ushers never looked down at the women on the floor. They always averted their eyes or closed them in silence. If the woman was exceptionally noisy, they sometimes hummed a few bars of a spiritual to cover her moans and cries.

I never felt entirely comfortable with this aspect of church. To witness it was to watch something intensely personal and unseemly. It was like being lifted out of the sanctuary, dropped into a stranger's bedroom and forced to watch what went on. The women who caught the Spirit were emotionally naked in ways I had never seen.

For this reason, I found altar calls, the events that were often the catalysts for these displays, totally excruciating. Even though everyone in the congregation was technically invited up to the altar to receive the spirit and become a Christian, I always feared that I somehow was not good enough. Most of the time I worried that I wasn't sincere enough or didn't want to get saved badly enough. And on the days that I did feel sincere, I didn't want to feel out of control. I didn't want to wind up on the floor like the other women I had seen come to Jesus. After a while I became defiant. I wasn't going up to the front of the church even if I had to walk out of the service to resist the urge. It really was like an urge. The pastor's voice was persistent.

Don't you wanna come?

Please come.

Don't you wanna just give your life over to Jesus?

Let go…

Say yes to Jesus! Say yes to Jesus!
And let go....

His pleading voice, along with the beat of the tambourines like drums, pushed mere mortals forward to the front of the sanctuary where they could be transformed. Despite the seductive pull of his voice, my mind was made up. If I ever caught the Spirit, it was going to be something that happened in private, not in front of a bunch of onlookers.

☙☙☙

My cousin Carol was not nearly as determined as I was to make her religious ecstasy a private ecstasy. One Sunday during altar call, she got "saved," rising from the pew and walking up to the front of the church.

"Do you accept Christ into your heart?" Pastor Locke asked.

Carol nodded and repeated the affirmation of faith in Romans 10:9. She began to cry, stutter and suddenly speak in tongues. Or maybe she was crying so hard we thought she was speaking in tongues. Maybe she was just asking for some tissue and couldn't get the words out.

After that Sunday, my cousin didn't join us, the unsaved kids, in the back pew anymore to pass notes. She sat in the front row next to Sister Williams, so she could learn up close how to be a saint. One by one all of my little playmates disappeared from the back pew, as one or two would volunteer to be "saved" each week. Saved from what, I didn't know. At one point the front row got so full, the saved children spilled over to the second row.

I didn't need to worry. Eventually, someone would backslide and be sent back to the last row. And there I was to greet them like a long lost friend with my miniature white patent leather purse stuffed with tissue, paper, a pen and sometimes Chapstick. The same as what all the other girls carried, although some had peppermints and lotion as well.

Despite my aversion to the altar call, I used to wonder what it felt like to be "saved," to feel as if you were somehow going to be spared the misery that might befall the rest of the world. I didn't even feel completely loved. I couldn't comprehend feeling "saved."

I think this desire to be saved, to be loved really, was part of the reason I found myself in Jerome Treadwell's basement one Sunday evening after church.

As usual, his mother was upstairs cooking supper for a bunch of single women and their children. Jerome and I were left alone when all the other kids abandoned us to camp out in front of the television for an episode of *Ripley's Believe It or Not*. Being alone with Jerome was not unusual. He and I had known each other since birth and Jerome was good fun, always willing to *pour the tea*. It was common knowledge among the church children that if you didn't have something nice to say about somebody then you should sit next to Jerome. He was the world's biggest gossip; worse than a girl. Jerome and I usually didn't waste our time talking about those whom he referred to as "the little people." Instead, we talked about the fabulous hair shows his Uncle Glen had gone to and browsed through old copies of *Ebony* and *Vogue* to pick out hairstyles and clothes we (well, actually he) liked.

This Sunday was different, though. It was just after the time some talk had started about Jerome's Uncle Glen. Some of the church sisters were worried that Jerome was spending too much time with him. I didn't know Jerome's Uncle Glen that well, but I did remember my Mom telling me once that Glen had so much sugar in his veins his blood had turned to syrup. At the time I didn't know what exactly she meant, but I did think Glen was sweet. He brought Jerome fancy, new clothes from places like New York, Paris and Los Angeles. The way his Uncle Glen would say "Los Angeles" made it sound like it was part of a different country. These gifts were a big deal to a Midwestern kid like me. Uncle Glen's gifts were apparently a big deal to the church sisters, too. I had heard some of them say the clothes Jerome's uncle had bought him were too effeminate and part of a "recruitment scheme." Recruitment for what, I wondered.

Around the same time the talk had intensified about Jerome's dressing habits, I had started keeping a personal journal for the Human Growth and Development class at my junior high. Of the twenty pages of banal entries I had made since the assignment had been given, about eighteen of the pages were either directly or tangentially about Mrs. West, my gym teacher. Everything she said, wore or did was documented, a fact that would come to haunt me a few months later when Mrs. West would pull my mother aside and tell her that she thought that I was gay.

I bring up all of these things, the rumors and the history, because they were all part of the atmosphere, floating in the air that evening Jerome and I ended up alone in his basement. That Sunday, Jerome became one of only two boys I have ever kissed. The kiss itself was nothing serious, just a few seconds of lip-to-lip contact. For a brief moment we had followed the example of the couple on the fan. We were bit actors in the church's Everyman drama for our lives, perfect replicas of what Pastor Locke wanted us to be, albeit prematurely. If our kiss didn't exactly set the world on fire, at least Jerome proved that he was a boy, despite his spit curls and notched eyebrows, and I proved that I was girl who liked boys, at least for that evening.

This became our secret. We never spoke of it again.

Several months later Jerome was shipped off to spend a summer with my Uncle David. I was told the purpose of this trip was to make Jerome more like a man. When Jerome came back the gel had been eradicated from his hair. His eyebrows were going in every direction like weeds, not perfectly coiffed as they had been when I kissed him that Sunday evening. And all of his clothes were toned down to a boring shade of boy. I'm not sure what the long-term effects were of this crash course in black masculinity. To my knowledge Jerome has never had a serious girlfriend. Like my uncle had, I suspect he learned the fine art of camouflage.

My Uncle David was gay. My aunts and my grandmother will

tell you that he repented from that "lifestyle" before he died of "cancer." I have never believed this story, but I include it here because in addition to being gay, my uncle was also a Christian. It wasn't until my twenties that it dawned on me that my uncle's one-time roommate Courtland was not in fact his roommate, but his boyfriend. They had sexiled themselves in the California desert in an attempt to escape our family's whispers. My mother and I visited them one summer, two gay, black brothas out in the middle of the Mojave trying to make it in the world without going crazy.

Uncle David died on my birthday a week before I was to enter university. He left a house full of things, including a collection of dog-eared, marked-up Bibles. I was later told by my cousin that my uncle had been careful to dispose of all of his "embarrassing items" several months earlier when he'd had a minor health scare. That's when I suspect all the *Ass Master* magazines went in the dustbin. In lieu of these magazines and whatever else I might have found had he not been so diligent in the months before his death, I was left with a collection of Bibles, all of which I stuffed in my suitcase. I never had any real intention of reading the Bibles, but they were not something I felt I could just throw away.

I had stopped going to church when I was thirteen, the age of accountability according to our church, and didn't start going again until my sophomore year of college when I became obsessed with my sexuality, obsessed with the question of whether or not it was a sin to be gay. This is when I pulled the Bibles out to see what they might say. I flipped to the key passages, looking for anything my Uncle David had highlighted, jotted down or bookmarked. There was nothing of importance or at least nothing that was relevant to my quest for answers. All of the Bibles were curiously silent in the key passages, except for the one in Romans where Uncle David had scrawled in the margins, "ABOMINATION."

Of course, this came as no surprise to me since this had been his public stance on homosexuality since I was kid, even during the times when he was finding love in another man's arms. What was troubling about the proclamation was that the only place he had bothered to write it was in the Hippie Bible. He had two King James, one Catholic, one New Revised Standard Version, and then this Hippie Bible. What separated it from all the others was the absence of thee's and thou's. The Hippie Bible was written in 1970s slang and sported a green cover with a mostly white cast of twenty-somethings with headbands, peace necklaces, beads and guitars, seated around a campfire, presumably riffing on what a groovy dude Jesus was.

This discovery just set off a whole new wave of anxiety for me. No matter how hard I tried to shake the feeling, going to the mostly white University Chapel had this Jim Jones type of vibe, like I was drinking the communion Kool-Aid. Perhaps their God was one of unending love and unconditional acceptance, but the one I grew up with whooped asses. The fact that my uncle had only taken the time to scrawl "ABOMINATION" in this particular Bible made me feel like he was saying, "I'll be damned if I join these white kids and their pot-smoking Jesus in the Lake of Fire."

At that point in my life, I desperately needed some black clergy to tell me that God loved me as much as the white clergy said He did. The only problem was that I was too ashamed to admit to the one black clergy member on staff that I was gay. After all, gayness was a *white person's disease.*

Then one Sunday Dean Roberts, the black minister I was afraid to talk to, abruptly changed his sermon halfway through to discuss the story of the eunuch that came to worship at the temple and those who wanted to turn him away. "We don't know if the eunuch is a eunuch by birth or by choice," Dean Roberts said, "but either way there is God's work for him to do."

His words reminded me of something Mother Locke had once said to me. Mother Locke, Pastor Locke's wife, had been born with a caul over her head, which people said gave her the power of vision. I was nine when she told me, "God's going to use you. He's gonna really do something special with you."

What would God choose me to do? Maybe God would have me speak, to tell the truth and shame the devil.

All of my concerns about my soul back then were on some level hypothetical. I had never even kissed a woman, let alone slept with one in college. I wasn't technically a *ho-mo-sex-u-al*. I just had *ho-mo-sex-u-al* thoughts. After an exhaustive two-year exercise of reading literally hundreds of books and articles regarding homosexuality and the Bible, the Qur'an and the Talmud, my amateur theological studies ended mostly in a draw. I found as many religious scholars that pronounced gayness a sin as I did scholars who dismissed it.

It became abundantly clear to me that there was no clear-cut answer to the question of my soul. Loving women would require an act of faith on my part, based on my somewhat shaky belief in God's all-inclusive love. I remembered thinking of Dean Roberts' sermon about the eunuch and saying to God, "You'll just have to work with what you got."

While I may have been unsure of many of my values back then, I was sure of at least one. I knew that I valued love, or at least its possibility, more than anything else in the world. I had witnessed for myself how love's absence had the ability to ruin lives. I saw the depression it caused in my mother and the perpetually single women that attended my childhood church. These were women who wanted to know the warmth of a lover's touch as much as they wanted to hold the hand of God. Although I had considered many times just being celibate as a way to avoid the question of my sexuality, I often wondered what religious ecstasy could be without the possibility of real ecstasy.

I was always amazed at the number of religious scholars I ran across who were willing to advise gays and lesbians to just give their sexual desire up to God, to be less than human. This was simply unacceptable to me. How could it be possible to believe in a God of Love when commanded to deny love here on earth?

Embracing my sexual identity needed to be a part of my testimony, a part of my becoming a witness.

Shortly after I made this peace with myself, I moved to Texas for my first job after college. One night at a friend's dinner party I met a young woman named Cynthia who was a graduate student at UT. We hit it off immediately, discussing her research on Caribbean cultures and enjoying bowl after bowl of seafood gumbo. When our host ran out of wine, Cynthia and I volunteered to make a run to the liquor store. Although it was an errand that required only one person, both of us went. I suspect we both saw it as an opportunity to be alone together. By the end of our little liquor run I found out that Cynthia was attracted to women, in particular me! We started dating shortly after that night.

I still remember the first time I kissed her. While my kiss with Jerome had felt slightly dirty, her kiss made me feel redeemed. It was as if all of my desires had been answered and my questions resolved in one single act. I remember chanting, "Thank You! Thank You! Thank You!" to the God of my mind. They were the same words that poured out of the women who caught the Spirit at my church years earlier, said with the same intensity as just before the ushers with the white sheets came to surround them. It was the ultimate expression of gratitude because, for the first time in my life, I really believed that I could be loved.

Yes, it's true that Jesus had always loved me, *but Cynthia let me know.*

I made the choice of "coming in," a process of learning to understand and become comfortable with myself without the need for acceptance from others.

Shamanism: My Path of Self-Discovery

By Anthony Farmer

Sunday morning rolled around once again, as it always did in Memphis. My Sunday morning ritual consisted of getting up, then walking and feeding the dogs. I then went across the street to purchase a paper. I read the sports section, the funny pages, the sale flyers and the classified ads, in that order. After breakfast, I got ready for church.

At that time in my life, I considered myself a black, gay man. The more comfortable I became with my sexuality and myself, the less tolerant I was of attending a black Baptist church to hear the "Adam and Eve, not Adam and Steve" or the "you are an abomination and a sinner in the eyes of the Lord" sermon. My patience for the "you are going to hell, but you could ask Jesus to forgive you and repent your sins, and don't forget to pay your tithes" rhetoric had flown out the window. I attended a non-denominational church that had a predominantly white, gay, lesbian and bisexual congregation. My partner wanted to attend a place of worship that was affirming of us, and our relationship. After we split up, I maintained my membership and attended frequently. The message at this church was "God loves you." This was a message I could embrace.

Sunday morning worship service at this church consisted of a reading from the Old and New Testaments, and prayer, followed by a musical selection. This led into the reverend's sermon of the day. His sermons were generally good. However, as time went on, I found myself feeling not as spiritually fed as before. I remember driving home, thinking, "What is it lacking? What am I missing?" At first I thought I was missing the toe-tapping, hand-waving, amen-shouting, spirit-moving experience of the black Baptist church choir. As time moved on, my feelings intensified, and the "what is it" became "WHAT IS IT?"

One particular Sunday, the reverend spoke from a passage of one of the gospels. He said he preferred this particular gospel to the others. I thought to myself, "Don't they say the same thing: the teachings of Jesus Christ? And if so, then why is one better than another?" I realized I was overreacting to his statement, but his statement only added to my confusion and frustration. My quest for "what is it?" continued.

Then the bomb dropped. During another sermon, the reverend told of his missionary work in central Africa. He shared his experiences of converting the people from being of Catholic faith to being Methodist. He said, jokingly, how they preferred being Methodist to Catholic because the rules are more relaxed. My response to myself, but reflected on my face, was "You are assuming that the spiritual practices and religious beliefs of these indigenous people were wrong, or not worthy, or were somehow inferior to Christianity, and that unless they became Christians, worshipped Jesus Christ and adopted the crucifix as a symbol, their salvation was out of reach."

Granted, I had read a lot into what he'd said. Basically my question was "What gives you the right to go into someone's home and tell them that what you believe is what they should believe? Would we God-fearing, church-going, Christian-Americans welcome into our homes with open hand and heart someone from another land who came with the sole purpose of converting us to their way of religiously believing, living and thinking?" I began to wonder if my "What is it?" was now "Is this it?"

I listened to the reverend's sermons with a more discerning and critical ear. Sometimes I agreed with what he said; however, most times I did not. On a rare occasion or two, I remember visibly disagreeing with him by shaking my head. I realized then that my issues with the "straight" church were more connected to a disagreement with the doctrine and my understanding of Christianity than the Church's stance on homosexuality and fire and brimstone sermons. Within the context of Christianity, I did not hear "the word of God" or feel "the love of God." What I heard and felt was someone else's interpretation of the word of God. What I heard was that "the road to heaven passes only through Jesus Christ and that prayers will go unanswered unless tithes are paid." There was very little talk about loving your fellow human or cultivating and nurturing a sense of community, or about how being of service helps everyone including oneself. I heard none of that.

I started to feel the same way I'd felt at the black Baptist churches. I remember going to a church in the inner city across the street from a housing development. The pastor talked about the congregation being half the size it once was; however, I heard nothing about reaching out to the people living two blocks away. It was these old thoughts and feelings that I was experiencing again. I now understood the "it" of my "What is it?": It was my disenchantment with the Church and Christianity.

One Sunday my morning ritual changed ever so slightly. The new ritual consisted of getting up, then walking and feeding the dogs. I went across the street to purchase a paper. I read the sports section, the funny pages, the sale flyers and the classified ads, in that order. After breakfast I asked myself, "Are you going to listen to the sermon or are you going to argue?" Without uttering a sound or having any further discussion, I got dressed and went to the park.

There, sitting under a tree, I read a book, felt the wind, did a crossword puzzle, watched the squirrels, wrote in my journal and listened to the birds. I began to notice how peaceful I felt. I began to wonder if the blowing of the wind was more than just air moving. I began to speculate about whether the chatter of the squirrels was more than just noise. I began to question if the warmth of the sun, the songs of the birds and the busyness of the bees were more than just that. In her poem "Nothing Is Just," Nikki Giovanni wrote, "Nothing is just, a movie, a book, a song, a piece of cake."[1] I add that nothing is just the warmth of the sun, the song of a bird, the busyness of the bees. I continued to wonder...

The Dream

Sometime later I went to dinner and a movie with a co-worker. Afterward, we walked the dogs, and talked about the movie, life, work and our past relationships. It was a nice evening spent with a good friend. That night I had this dream: I was riding in a car driven by my co-worker's former partner. We stopped in front of a two-story white house. We went in the front door. Suddenly I was on the second floor, not the first, and I was seemingly alone. I looked around and saw sheep, cows and goats, as if I were in a barn. I walked around the room naked. I then heard a deep masculine voice behind me saying, "I want you to bear my seed." Whatever or whoever it was that said this then became intimate with me. Out of the corner of my eye, I saw what appeared to be a horn. The dream ended.

I called a friend the next day to share my dream. My first thought was that since I left the church I was being recruited by team evil. However, something inside kept me from totally believing that. My friend said, "Tony, you were chosen. There are cultures that speak of people being called or chosen through similar spiritual experiences." I asked, "Chosen for what?"

After that dream, the dream floodgates opened. I had dreams of visiting other places and other worlds. I dreamed of cliff-side dwellings similar to those of the Native Americans living in southern Colorado or of the Dogon people of Africa. Most other dreams involved animals in combat.

There was one particular dream in which I stood in a pen that had very tall walls and several raised platforms, each one being a step higher. The way out was to climb the platforms. All of a sudden, a door opened and several lions came out and headed toward me. I fought the lions so I could climb up out of the pen. My goal was to get out alive. I made it. As I walked away, I made eye contact with several antelope and deer left in the enclosure. I felt they were trying to communicate with me.

Then the dream changed. I walked around the side of a two-story wood house. I came to a wooden staircase in the back and started to climb. At the top, I saw my mother. I thought she was wearing a bleached blonde, bob-styled wig. As I looked closer, there was a bright, white light surrounding her head like a halo. She then became pure white light. As if I understood what I needed to do, I turned around and headed back toward the animals left in the pen. The dream ended.

I was dreaming all the time, which was nothing unusual for me. What was unusual was the number of dreams I had and remembered each night. I would go to sleep, wake up and write them down. I would go back to sleep, and wake up in the morning and record more dreams. I called my faithful friend to share my dream experiences, and he responded, "Oh lord, Tony, not again. You and your dreams!"

I was concerned about the quality and quantity of sleep I was getting, and about being so wired about the dream experiences. To help me relax, I started meditating. It was slow going at first and I would lose concentration rather easily. Once, while sitting in a chair with my eyes closed, breathing slowly and deeply, I imagined that I became an eagle and flew out of the room. I flew over the land toward the sea. I flew along the coast for a while and then returned to the room. I opened my eyes and wondered what I had just experienced. My spiritual awakening had begun.

As I experienced my new spiritual awakening, I began to have sexual and physical feelings for women. Up until that time, I had all but accepted my sexuality. I participated in and enjoyed intimate sexual and physical relationships with men. Some of my family and many of my friends knew the truth about my sexuality. However, I found myself watching women walk down the street, taking notice of their figures and flow. After a few moments, I would ask myself, "What is going on here?" I wondered if God had a sense of humor and if I was the victim of some heavenly prank.

In an attempt to get some understanding of what was going on, I read many books on life transformation, letting go of fear and choosing the untraveled road. I searched for answers to the many questions about my dreams and my changing, or expanding, sexuality. The books were helpful, but only to a point. When I finally read a book on "spiritual emergency," a light bulb went on. I realized that my emerging feelings were part of my spiritual awakening, rather than a mental breakdown.

I had spent countless therapy sessions coming to terms with and accepting my sexuality. However, my spiritual awakening brought with it a much broader question of "Who am I?" I had acknowledged being "gay" and come out of the closet; however, I did not feel totally connected to the gay community or the black, gay community or even the black community in general. I felt like I was on the periphery of each of them. I needed more than each of these communities offered. These communities did not provide me much support in understanding who or what I was. I made the choice of "coming in," a process of learning to understand and become comfortable with myself without the need for acceptance from others. The underlying question of "Who am I?" was the focus of my "coming in."

The terms gay, homosexual and bisexual did not come close to describing how I was feeling. I found them limiting, clinical and relating more to sex than anything else. I felt my life was comprised of more than just physical attraction to other men and—by this time—women as well. My path of self-discovery and my journey to me were driven by the desire to better understand myself, not just sexually or spiritually, but completely and wholly.

Memphis, Tenn. to Washington, D.C.

Several years ago, my life journey led me to Washington, D.C. to take a new job and to move closer to my family in Virginia. I continued dreaming about nature and animals and other spiritual symbolism. Once, I dreamed that I was a tiger communicating in English with other animals. We were auditioning for a movie. I woke from that dream lying in bed in the same position as I had been in the dream. My intimate, romantic and sexual thoughts and desires for men and women continued.

One day I found a local, quarterly publication that provided information on mind, body and spirit resources in the Washington, D.C. area. Flipping through the pages, I noticed an advertisement for an organization that had an interesting logo that was vaguely familiar. I realized the logo resembled something I had doodled many, many times. At first I thought it was a mere coincidence; however, I kept coming back to that advertisement. The organization was the Foundation for Shamanic Studies. Shamanism. I knew very little, if anything, about it; however, I heard a small bell ringing inside.

Shamanism

Shamanism is the world's oldest known spiritual practice, the earth's root spiritual and religious belief system. People living in all parts of the world used various techniques to help with physical and spiritual health, personal and cultural growth, and individual and community well-being. People and cultures separated by land and sea were using very similar rituals and ceremonies to stay connected and balanced with the Universe, the Great Mystery, Mother/Father God and the Creator.

"Shaman" is a catchall word, thought to originate from the Tungus people of Siberia, used to describe people who are sometimes called medicine men and women, witch doctors, sorcerers, seers, visionaries, mystics, teachers, spiritual leaders, guides and healers. Shamans understand and believe that everything is of Spirit and is connected, that humans must live in harmony and balance with nature, and that there is a world filled with spirits that exists alongside our physical world.

Michael Harner, founder of the Foundation for Shamanic Studies and author of the book, *The Way of the Shaman*, states that a shaman is a person "who enters an altered state of consciousness—at will—to contact and utilize an ordinarily hidden reality in order to acquire knowledge, power and to help other persons."[2] A shaman is a person of wisdom who uses his or her unique awareness to guide and serve others. Joan Halifax, Ph.D., in her book *Shamanic Voices: A Survey of Visionary Narratives*, states, "above all, however, shamans are technicians of the sacred and masters of ecstasy."[3]

In January 1999, I began my formal study of shamanism. I decided to attend an Introduction to Shamanism workshop. That month, I began walking the spiritual path of a shamanic healer. My perspective on religion and spirituality, the physical and the spiritual worlds, and sexuality and spirituality continued to change. Throughout my training, I experienced a rapidly expanding consciousness and a deeper self-awareness. My path became unconventional and unpredictable.

The Initial Workshop

The first workshop was a two-day weekend adventure. Shamanism is the practice in which the individual's soul, through a trance-like state of consciousness, leaves the body and travels to a world of spirits, or non-ordinary reality. This is known as a shamanic journey. Non-ordinary reality is a hidden part of the universe similar to places experienced in dreams and written about in myths. Once there, the shaman can assist in his own healing, personal growth and power and balance restoration. He, or she, also can support others in their healing. Spiritual help and guidance are present in the form of power animals, spiritual teachers and other spirit allies. During this initial workshop, I learned to journey, and met my spiritual teachers and power animals. Though this was all very new to me, there was something familiar about it.

One of my spiritual teachers appeared in the form of Odin, the supreme god of Norse mythology. After the workshop, I began reading about Norse mythology, and in particular about Odin. I found the information very intriguing. Odin was considered many things to many people. He was on a never-ending quest for knowledge. It was written that he was a master of death and rebirth, a leader of warriors, and one who sought female wisdom to complement and balance his maleness. According to myth, Odin participated in women's sacred rituals and even dressed as a woman, which is very similar to spiritual practices of gods of some indigenous cultures. Odin was also a poet, a healer and a shaman.

During another journey to meet Odin, I was given a sacred symbol, the rune Dagaz. The spiritual symbolism of Dagaz is the balance or the synthesized mystical union of two extremes, darkness and light, pleasure and pain, life and death, matter and energy, spiritual and physical, and masculine and feminine. This is the paradox of Odin: to achieve balance between extremes. Dagaz also is the rune of enlightenment. This was my sacred symbol.

The intention of one of the journeys was to meet our power animal. A power animal provides one with strengths and imparts wisdoms that can be used in everyday life. During the journey, I connected with two power animals. I discovered that the spirit of one of my power animals was male and the other female. I thought, "This is balance, with me in the middle. Female on one side and male on the other." Did this mean that my two power animals represented two aspects of myself—opposite ends of a spectrum? Was this an example of the paradox of Odin? Did this represent who I was becoming: a mystical union of two extremes, a balance of masculine and feminine, of both male and female?

In retrospect, that workshop was another initiation, a ceremonial crossing of a threshold that came with no return trip ticket or instructions on how to get back. Each workshop and training was a crossing of another threshold, a continuous expansion of consciousness. That dream I had in Memphis was the first initiation.

The "horned god" that I encountered in that dream, I discovered later, was another spiritual teacher. In other cultures, the "horned god" is known as Osiris, Cernunnos, Lord of Animals, Lord of the Forest, or Earth God. The horned god is associated with spiritual and religious beliefs older than most modern-day organized religions. Pictures of a horned god show a part human/part animal entity, which represented the balance of man living with nature. This is a belief held by many shamans and indigenous people.

I further discovered that many of my previous experiences (dreams, visions and meditations) were shamanic in nature. Those dreams with and about animals and the meditative experience of flying like an eagle are all shamanic experiences.

Like Odin, I, too, am on a constant search for knowledge and wisdom. After my initial workshop, I looked for all I could about shamanism and shamanic practices. As I searched for answers and understanding, again I felt I was expanding spiritually as well as sexually. However, I did not have the words to accurately explain or describe this expansion. I began to think that maybe there was a deeper connection between my spirituality and my sexuality.

Gays, Gatekeepers and Nádleehí

Malidoma Somé, of the Dagara people of Burkina Faso, Africa, has written several books on his life experiences as a healer, a medicine man, a teacher and shaman. His book, *Of Water and the Spirit*, spoke of his journey as a boy who was abducted from his village and forced to learn European ways of worship and thought. He escaped, returned home and was initiated into his life purpose. He wrote about many of the spiritual beliefs and practices of his people.

In his book *The Healing Wisdom of Africa*, Somé states, "the gateway is a door to the Spirit realm that is connected to a particular place in the physical world. Healers who bring energy from the Spirit World through the gateways are known as gatekeepers."[4] In an interview with M.E.N. Magazine, Somé talked about these "guardians of the gates" and their connection to our Western notion of gay people.[5]

The Dagara people do not view the gender of a person anatomically, but energetically. Somé states, "A male who was physically male could vibrate female energy, and vice versa."[6] They are seen as people, are not labeled gay or bisexual, and are identified as gatekeepers. He further states that gatekeepers vibrate at a higher frequency than other people, and have knowledge of indigenous medicine and ritual, much like shamans and healers of other cultures. In the Dagara culture, male gatekeepers, even with their sexual attraction for other men, married and fathered children.

Even after accepting my physical and emotional attraction to men, the concept of being gay or using that term to describe myself always felt "limiting." I agree with Somé's belief that limiting "gay people to simple sexual orientation is really the worst harm that can be done to a person. That all he or she is is a sexual person."[7] I held this same understanding of myself. I decided to no longer accept terminology that spoke only of my sexual orientation and not of all of me.

In Somé's interview, he made reference to the Dogon people of Africa. They are noted for many things, including their complex spiritual and religious beliefs. Throughout their mythology and cosmology, there is balance between the masculine and feminine, earth and sky, and physical and spiritual. The Dogon are known for their extensive knowledge of astrology. Somé states, "It is a tribe that knows astrology like no other tribe I have encountered. And the great astrologers of the Dogon are gay."[8]

My continued quest for information about shamanism led me to the concept of "two-spirit." This term refers to gay and lesbian people native to what is now called North America. It replaced the anthropological word "berdache." The two-spirit, or person of multiple genders, bridges the masculine and feminine worlds. Many Native American cultures had a name for gay and lesbian people. In an excerpt from his book *Changing Ones*, Will Roscoe wrote, "Each tribe, of course, had its own terms for these roles, such as *boté* in Crow, *nádleehí* in Navajo, *winkte* in Lakota, and *alyha* and *hwame* in Mohave."[9] Donald Denetdeal, in an interview for the Salt Lake Tribune, stated that "In the Dine tongue of the

Navajo, Two-Spirits are known as 'na'dleh' – literally, 'one that changes."'[10]

The Ute referred to gay men as *"tozusuhzooch"* which means "a male who is not quite a male."[11] These men lived as women and dressed as women. They were in many cases the best in the tribe at doing work that was typically women's work. The two-spirits in many cultures had spiritual roles and responsibilities. In some cultures, they were also viewed as healers. Will Roscoe writes, "Berdache identity is widely believed to be the result of supernatural intervention in the form of visions or dreams, and/or it is sanctioned by tribal mythology. Berdaches most often form sexual and emotional relationships with non-berdache members of their own sex."[12]

I found this information comforting and affirming. I gained valuable insights and deep self-awareness from my shamanic and meditation experiences, my relationships with my spiritual guides, and the information I found in the various books and essays I read. Many of my questions were answered. I felt closer to understanding the answer to the one big question: "Who am I?"

The Journey Continues

During shamanic journeys, a person can engage playfully, intimately, and sometimes sexually with their spiritual teachers and power animals. This is a way of exchanging spiritual energy and strengthening bonds between the spiritual allies and person. From this engagement, the person brings "healing energy" back through the gateway, across the threshold, from the spiritual world back to the physical world. The person incorporates this energy into his being. I had many of these experiences.

After encountering a bear during a journey, I have found that my powers of introspection became enhanced and intensified over time. I developed a deeper focus during my meditations. Bears, in a spiritual sense, bring the gift of intuition and the ability to awaken the powers of the unconscious, meditation and introspection.

From these experiences, I raised this question: If, in the

spiritual world, an intimate or sexual encounter is a means of bonding with a spirit entity or a means of exchanging energy, could a similar experience in the physical world have the same meaning? Does this mean that my desire to be with a man may be a way of exchanging energy, physically, with someone of predominately masculine energy? Can this masculine energy come from either a man or a woman, someone who vibrates with sexual energy that complements my own? Are my sexual desires to be with a woman my way of physically expressing an exchange of energy with someone with feminine energy, which can come from either a man or woman?

I am exploring, through studying shamanism, my own spirituality and sexuality beyond the physical. The paradox of Odin is the mystical moment when two opposites come together in limitless union. Does this fusion of male and female into an androgynous state exceed the conceptual limitations of either extreme? Does this unification of masculine and feminine energies create a togetherness that defies conventional labeling? Is what I experience when I have sex with someone the actualization of Odin's paradox? Could this mean that sex is more than just the physical act? Am I getting closer to understanding the connection between my spirituality and sexuality? Am I getting even closer to answering the question of who I am?

Loving Myself

I understand that my journey is a journey to learn who I am, how to be me, how to love myself and share this love with others. To love myself is to learn to understand me from the inside out and not from the words and beliefs of others. To love myself is to detach from the labels, categories and limited understandings of society, and to redefine myself as I live, think and feel. To love myself is to have the courage to be who I am even when that goes against my cultural norms and I am standing alone. To love myself is to follow my heart's desire to become aware of my life path and then have the faith, strength and perseverance to walk my path—the untraveled road. To love myself is to give myself permission to be what and who I am.

I never felt that Christianity had given me the opportunity to explore who I was beyond the person others said I should be. Organized religion seems to tell people who they should be, what they should do, and how they should do it. Organized religion meant having someone else tell me what Spirit was and dictate my experience with God. Seeking my own spiritual path, life purpose and identity gave me an opportunity to listen and be guided by Spirit.

I continue to study shamanism and walk my shamanic path from the place of heart. This means listening to my internal guidance. My spiritual journey along this shamanic path led me back to the Bible, in particular to the four Gospels. I hold the teachings of Jesus the Christ as a rich source of divine wisdoms that, when interpreted from the heart, give guidance, inspiration and support without condemnation. As I walk my journey, I integrate and incorporate teachings and wisdoms from other Ascended Masters and Spiritual Leaders.

My spirituality is coming alive as I walk, talk and become my path. This is the result of my "coming in" process, my going inside to understand and be with the question "Who am I?" The answer must come from within. Who I am is about discovering, accepting and appreciating all of me, my spirituality as well as my sexuality. The two go hand-in-hand. As my spirituality deepens and broadens, so does my sexuality.

Shamanism is a tool I use to reconnect to peace, purpose, and love—all of which are great companions to have on this journey called "life." To love myself is to know myself. The more I learn about me, the more I learn how to be me. I learn of myself, and how to fulfill my role in community. We are all connected to each other, to nature, to love, to God. In order to find that connection again, each of us has to walk the path of self-discovery. It is not necessarily the path of the Christian or the Muslim, the healer or the teacher, or the path of the gay or straight. However, it is the path with your name on it. It is the path that is all of you. It is a road through the heart, a road through love.

My journey is my journey. It is not for anyone else. At times, I feel that walking and being my path is the hardest thing in the world to do. Often, I question the choices I have made and where my path will lead. Nonetheless, at the beginning and end of each day I stand in front of the mirror and ask myself, "Given the journey thus far, would you again take the road less traveled?" and the answer continues to be yes. Sometimes what seems like a walk away from something is really a walk toward something else. As I walked away from the Christian church, I began to walk my path. My path of self-discovery has led to me.

Endnotes:

[1] Giovanni, Nikki. *Blues for All the Changes: New Poems* (New York: Morrow, 1999), 8.

[2] Harner, Michael. *The Way of the Shaman* (San Francisco: HarperCollins Publishers, 1980), 20.

[3] Halifax, Joan. *Shamanic Voices: A Survey of Visionary Narratives* (New York: Arkana, 1979), 4.

[4] Somé, Malidoma Patrice. *The Healing Wisdom of Africa* (New York: Jeremy P. Tarcher/Putnam, 1998), 75.

[5] Hoff, Bert H. "Gays: Guardians of the Gates." M.E.N. Magazine, September 1993. MenWeb. http://www.vix.com/menmag/somegay.htm.

[6] Ibid.

[7] Ibid.

[8] Ibid.

[9] Roscoe, Will. "What Are Two-Spirits/Berdaches?" 1998. *Changing Ones*. http://www.geocities.com/westhollywood/stonewall/3044/ index.html.

[10] Mims, Bob. "Two Spirits Respected in Indian Tradition: Indians Have Tradition of Respect for Gays." *The Salt Lake Tribune,* December 31, 2000, http://web.lexis.nexis.com/universe.

[11] Ibid.

[12] Roscoe.

I was still conscious, but I knew something was happening that my experience with the Holy Ghost in the black Christian church, and nights at the Sound Factory Bar with DJ Frankie Knuckles spinning House, had prepared me for: I had been possessed.

The Voodoo That We Do: Discovering My Sexual/Political/Spiritual Self

By Kenyon Farrow

Sex, politics and the occult have been three very consistent subjects I have been fascinated with my entire life. The fact that I am a lifelong Prince fan should probably explain those three particular obsessions if you know anything about His Royal Badness. But I feel the need to further explain. As a child, my favorite shows were not *Sesame Street* and *Electric Company*. I watched *All My Children* and *One Life to Live* for the sex. My jones for politics was filled by talk shows like *20/20* and *Phil Donahue*. In addition to reading the Bible, these shows also satisfied my fetish for the occult because of the hysteria around "devil worship" and "heavy metal music" in the early/mid 1980s. For most of my life I have been fumbling for a way to make sense of the need I have to balance my voracious sexual appetite, my commitment to exposing and (hopefully) undoing oppression, and finding a spiritual path that honors all of who I am.

My moment of truth—the place where my spirituality, politics and my sexuality all came colliding together—happened in New Orleans, also known as "The Big Easy." At the gay bar where I had just finished stuffing the last of my singles and fives down a number of boy strippers' G-strings (one of which I was fucking on a regular basis), I found a stack of hot-pink flyers advertising a voodoo ritual. I don't know what it was about that year in New Orleans, but the boy dancers *loved* me, yes indeed! Maybe it was because I was never that queen that thinks that I am the one he's gonna take home, fall in love with, leave the business and run off with me to get married in Massachusetts. No, I know *they are there to get paid*. I am the best kind of customer: I will chat them up, cop my feel, tip them and then send them on their way. I don't try to hog them from the other clients, either. There's more money out in the crowd, and again, they are there to get paid. Maybe it was my reserve, but all I know is, I would tip them, say hello, and they would respond, "I get off at 2 a.m. What 'chu doin' then?"

In any case, I had just had a typical Friday night, about 60 bucks poorer (which is a lot to blow in New Orleans, 'cause drinks are very cheap) and a little bit tipsy. But as I exited the bar, the flyers that read "Chez Vodun's 'Authentic Voodoo Ritual': Every Saturday 9 p.m." greeted me on my way out.

"Hmmm," I thought. I had recently met Sharon Caulder—the owner and proprietor of Chez Vodun, a café/bar, temple and museum in New Orleans. Two weeks prior at a party held at Chez Vodun, I had taken a tour of the Voodoo Museum in the upstairs of her establishment. Sharon has a Ph.D. in depth psychology and was initiated in Benin as a Vodun chief by Supreme Chief Daagbo Hounon Houna. I knew when I met her that she was no fake "voodoo priestess"—one who specialized less in a religion and more in titillating and scaring white tourists for money. As we perused photos from her trips to Benin and shrines to various deities, I knew she knew much more than someone who was out to make a quick buck. She also showed no interest in "entertainment." This religion was her life and work. I had a good hunch that if I went to her event, I would definitely witness an authentic voodoo ritual. So, I took a flyer, did the "Miss Clairol" run through oncoming traffic across North Rampart Street, dipped in my new Ford ZX2 and bounced.

Before meeting Sharon, I knew very little about Vodun, or

voodoo as we call it here in the Americas. I had always been fascinated by religions, and after deciding at fifteen that I wasn't a Christian, I set out on a journey to find a spiritual path that was right for me. At first I started with Rastafarianism, but it felt too much like Christianity by a different name for my tastes. After reading a bit about Haile Selassie I's reign in Ethiopia, I realized he was no God I wanted to follow.

Next I tried Buddhism. I attended classes at Cleveland (Ohio, where I'm from) Buddhist Temple, and went on to study Tibetan Buddhism for five years. This was time very well spent, because the practice of meditation allowed me to become more self-reflective, and to learn to live in the moment. But I got tired of white hippies, and wanted something that spoke to my experience as a black person, and decided to turn to traditional West African religions.

Like most black folks learning about West African religions, Ifa was where I began my search. I have since learned that even though most enslaved Africans came through the ports in Dahomey (currently the Republic of Benin), the reason Ifa (and its western manifestations—Santeria, Lucumi and Candomble) are so prominent in the Americas is because the Yoruba people of Nigeria (where Ifa originates) were one of the last West African people to be sold into slavery.

I read several books on Ifa, studying the orishas and the philosophy of the religion. I met a few people along the way who were practitioners, priests or priestesses, but I knew to be very careful about whom I might choose to study with, or whom I might choose to be initiated under. There can be a lot of unhealthy power dynamics (including sexism and homophobia), people being taken for huge sums of money, and even initiates being physically or sexually abused, which happens in most any religion. So I kept my study of Ifa mostly to books until I moved to New Orleans. Though I had not considered any other West African practice besides Ifa, in New Orleans I learned firsthand the power of Vodun.

The night of the ritual, I arrived at Chez Vodun a little early.

I wanted to have a drink and some food before the ritual began. I was also dressed to party, complete with cute low-rise briefs, 'cause I figured I would hit the bars (and maybe the strippers!) while I was out.

While I was sitting there, eating and drinking, I knew in my heart that I had come to this place on this night for a reason beyond wanting to simply witness an "Authentic Voodoo Ritual." I was at a point in my life where I was stuck—stuck in a lot of old patterns that weren't serving me anymore. I had fled New York because the very things that make the city unique can also be the very things that cause your demise. For each of us (especially those of us who are transplants), the booby traps are different. For me, those traps were the multi-culti art/political milieus and access to sex, because New York has to be the easiest city in the United States to get laid in.

I had been functioning in New York City's Queer People of Color (Q-POC) radical left scene for some time. When I found that community, I thought I had found "it" and did make a few close friends through that world. But after a few years, I began to notice some things that made me less and less content with identifying as a "person of color." It has almost become sacrilege to say "I'm black," or to be interested specifically in working with black people, or on issues that primarily affect black folks. I know that in the South, there is no getting around blackness. New Orleans is unlike any other place in the world, and the racial politics are not exactly the same as the rest of the "Black Belt" states. By accepting a regional job doing anti-prison organizing, I would have the opportunity to work with black folks in various parts of the south—Mississippi, Georgia, Louisiana and Florida, mostly. By moving south, I would be forced to confront blackness and black people in a way that I felt was obscured by the "POC-ites" of the East and West coasts.

Also, I was growing bored with the rituals of fucking/dating in New York City. Everyone in the communities I was part of talked about being "sex positive," which was not so much about reclaiming a healthy sexuality and sexual relations, but a way to excuse fucking anyone you chose while being totally unaccountable to that person, your/their partner(s), and the community at-large. I remember being at a benefit for an organization where a queer Hawaiian woman activist was the keynote speaker. She talked about how it was an acceptable practice in her culture to have multiple partners, and that if one were married, as long as your ass was home before daybreak, whatever you did was all good. After she told that story, the audience erupted in thunderous applause and rose to its feet.

Now, I am not invested in monogamy as the only or "natural" pathway to loving, committed, romantic relationships. But let's be for real. What we do most often is not what this woman was talking about. We live under capitalism. *Everything* is a commodity. Even in this auditorium of NYC's finest Q-POC lefties, we had treated each other's bodies like sexual commodities. I had been sexualized in ways that had everything to do with me being black by non-black people in that room, and I had done the same with other non-black men of color. We were really no better than the larger society we critiqued; we only managed to obscure the specific dynamics of power by functioning under the "we're all people of color" umbrella. As a "radical," how do you *not* look at sexual promiscuity (which is not the same as non-monogamy) as a (potential) manifestation of a culture of hyper-consumption and addiction?

Besides, we also come from histories of racism, sexism, homophobia and transphobia that inform how we even view and treat our own bodies and respond to others' sexually. For me, growing up black means you always have to challenge the notion that your body isn't some freak of nature. We are all taught by racist white culture that our black bodies—muscled, big-assed hot pussies and big black dick—hold a lot of power, but are fundamentally "abnormal." Unlike what black boys/men are supposed to be, I was a skinny black effeminate boy. "Pitiful" was a word often used to describe my chest, thin arms and legs. That is how I began to feel about my *entire* self, that is until I was about sixteen or so, when black men much older than me began to follow me around, try to pick me up in their cars, or make sexual advances. I felt then that my body held an enormous amount of power, since it was now beginning to bring me such attention, but the attention was mostly negative—I was not a "person" to these men, but hot "boy pussy" to be fucked. So I, too, felt the "power" of my body, but that was coupled with a healthy dose of disgust for it, as I was also still grappling with my sexuality. Even though I had been taught to respect and love my body by my mother, I had the entire planet to contend with, which held a different fate for me.

By the time I came out and began to have sex with men, sex became an outlet for me to exercise power—even at the same time I felt a level of disgust with my body. I had grown into a skinny man who doesn't easily fit into a "butch" or "femme" category, at a time when the "thug" represented what was (and still is) sexually attractive for black gay twenty/thirty-somethings. My pattern of sexual promiscuity was about using my body to gain access to power, as a means of escapism, and of following the American trend of hyper-consumption.

I was at a point in my life when I needed healing on many different levels. When the drumming began that night at Chez Vodun, I knew it was time. In fact, I said aloud, "Tonight is the night." I downed my drink and headed upstairs when we were summoned.

This was the first night that Chief (the name I call Sharon, though most of her followers in New Orleans refer to her as "Doc") had offered this showcase, so there weren't very many of us present as spectators. I only remember a young white male/female couple there on a date, and (I believe) one other person. We were seated on red footstools placed in a semi-circle. I was seated in the center seat, just in front of the drummers.

While the ritual was happening, Chief came up to me after saying a prayer and making an offering at the shrine to Mami Wata. She asked me why was I in pain? The answers were too numerous to count, and she began working to expel whatever pain I was holding onto.

My recollection of what happened next is a little foggy. The first thing I noticed was the change in my breathing pattern. It changed to a deep, slow breath—almost like snoring. Next, the muscles in my hands, arms and face contracted in such a fashion that the way I normally held my body and face changed. I had no control, but somebody or something else did. I was still conscious, but I knew something was happening that my experience with the Holy Ghost in the black Christian church, and nights at the Sound Factory Bar with DJ Frankie Knuckles spinning House, had prepared me for: I had been possessed. Chief grabbed me by the chin, and looked into my eyes. "This isn't you," she said. She then began to tell me to fight to stay with her as she worked to exorcise this spirit that had leapt into my body.

Her assistants supported her efforts. As the drums danced, Sister Margaret, another voodoo practitioner and reader, began shaking a percussion instrument up the back of my spine, which arched up and down with every shake of the instrument. I was about 25 percent conscious, but not at all in control of my body. I wasn't afraid; I knew I was in good hands. I recall looking at the faces of the white couple—who clearly had come to see a "performance" and not a ritual—and thinking, "Wow. They are not ready for all this."

This went on for another twenty minutes or more. As the spirit began to loosen its grip on my body, Chief stood me up and walked me over to the Mami Wata shrine, doused water from its pool on my face, and walked me out of the ritual space.

"Why did you come tonight?" Chief asked.

Thoughtfully, I responded, "Because I had to."

"You have a strong spirit, very pure. You're open, but you let too many beings in. You need to learn how to control what gets in. Come and see me on Monday at 3 p.m. and I'll help you."

I was escorted downstairs by a woman I later learned was a local psychic who was present for the ritual. I felt as though I had just run a marathon. I still didn't have full control over my body, and I felt like both my feet had fallen asleep. As I tried to regain full control of my legs and feet, I got in my car, still dazed and confused, and after waiting for some time to regain my faculties made my way home.

As dramatic as that ritual was, it was really only the beginning. I began to work with Chief Sharon three days a week. It's hard for me to describe exactly what she was doing, because all of my experience in West African religion was from books. I had never seen anything like it. Some of it was the spiritual work to help me heal from physical, emotional, psychological and spiritual wounds, but some of it was just our time together and the infinite amounts of wisdom I learned from her. Though she was my teacher/mentor/healer, we became friends. We were both newbies to New Orleans and had a difficult time adjusting to New Orleans culture. New Orleans exists on New Orleans terms, and you have to adjust to it; it won't adjust to you.

We talked a lot about sex and sexuality, as she had identified that as a place where I needed particular healing. Chief made me aware of a few key concepts in Vodun and Ifa (which Chief also knows a great deal about) that helped to shape for me a more balanced view of sex and sexuality.

Each of us has a male or female spirit. This does not have anything to do with our sexual preference per se, as a woman with a male spirit is not necessarily a lesbian, and the same is true for men. It is part of our job here on earth to learn how to achieve balance, which includes balancing our masculine and feminine energies. So much of what Vodun and Ifa have to teach is about learning balance—male and female energies, the spiritual and physical, the temporal and the sacred. Many of the deities, *loa* in Vodun or *orishas* in Ifa, have masculine and feminine aspects. The Vodun deity *Hevioso*, the uber-masculine warrior god of thunder and justice (whose similar Ifa counterpart is called *Sango*), is sometimes depicted with breasts. *Oya*, Ifa female goddess of the wind and change of fortune, is known to have a male aspect and is often portrayed as a very masculine woman, sometimes having a beard.

The most profound thing that I ever learned from Chief

came very near the end of our work together, just before I was planning my return to NYC. I had come in for our regularly scheduled meeting on a Friday. We went upstairs to the room where Chief does her work. As was typical, she took off her glasses and looked at me.

"Where are you going?" she asked.

"Austin," I replied, wondering how she knew I was going anywhere that weekend.

"Why?"

"Going to a conference."

"What conference?"

Now I was nervous. There was something in her tone that suggested she didn't believe me, or was picking up on something that I knew was present but didn't want to reveal. I was going to a conference for work, but I was also very much looking forward to exploring what the men of Austin could show an out-of-towner for the 48 hours or so I was in town. I was looking forward to some serious fucking, and I knew she knew it.

I told her the conference I was going to. Though she didn't seem satisfied, she let go of the subject for the time being. She got up, stood right behind me, closed her eyes and went to work.

After we completed our session for the day, we chatted while heading for the stairwell and then she stopped dead in her tracks.

Oh, God! I knew that meant something. The last time she'd stopped at the top of that stairwell with me, she'd said, "Look. The problem is you're depressed. You've been depressed for so long you don't even know what it's like to *not* be depressed."

Her words had hit me like a ton of bricks. But she was right, and I had, for the first time, admitted to myself that I was suffering from a chronic depression that had been with me since I was a child. As an adult I'd learned (mostly) how to cope with it, and while studying Tibetan Buddhism for five years, I'd learned lots of meditative techniques that helped tremendously. I had seen a therapist for about six months, but I was highly functioning, so the depression never was exposed in my counseling sessions.

It's much easier to be in denial about depression if you still can get out of bed and go about the world every day. My depression has never impaired my ability to work, or to function in general. But it's always present. It's as if I'm on the brink of tears all the time. Chief's confirmation of something that I knew was a problem deep down helped to ultimately set it free. I am now much more able to recognize what triggers depression for me and how to take care of myself until it passes.

So after recalling the last time she'd stood at the stair and nonchalantly delivered a life-altering message for me, I was more than a little anxious this go 'round, waiting for her to speak.

"Be careful who you have sex with," Chief blurted out.

I gazed at her, making no attempt to mask my hurt and disappointment. *This is on some homophobic shit,* I thought to myself. *People are cool with gay men as long as they don't have to confront the fact that you fuck. As long as you're not fucking, you're OK. You can do their hair, cook their food, sing in their choir, play their piano/organ and all that, but the minute they have to think about you as a sexual being, it's a problem. No, it's* your *problem.* I was beginning to get pissed.

"You know I don't care who you fuck," she snorted back. "I mean, when you have sex with somebody, there's an energy exchange, and that person's energy is with you the rest of your life. You don't want to be carrying around someone else's bad energy and giving them your good energy. There are a lot of people out there who are energy drains."

I nodded my head in agreement, and then we proceeded down the stairs. I held on tightly to the handrail, for I was weak in the knees. It seemed like a simple enough statement/observation, but every nut I've ever bust came gushing back to haunt me, and I wasn't even waiting for HIV results. It really forced me to question all of my ideas about being sex positive—ideas that allowed me to use and be used by people in search of something that had absolutely nothing to do with the act of sex. It was about wanting to connect, to be engaged, to be present in my body. Sometimes it was about escape and depression. But I was now forced to consider my sexual politics in a way that I had not done before—how my sexual and political politics were completely disjointed from their practice, as they are for many activists. Even my love of the boy strippers was yet another manifestation of capitalist consumption of bodies. Mind you, the stripper desires aren't a love that I have given up *entirely*, but at least I am clear on what is really happening and can make choices in a more thoughtful way on how and when I engage it.

I left Chez Vodun that day, got in my car and drove to Austin. It took me months to fully think through Chief's statement to me and what it meant in my life. Her comment raises very difficult questions for black folks involved in radical sexual politics: How do we practice sex positivity, non-monogamy, and/or polyamory, in ways that do not perpetuate capitalist consumer culture? How do we as queer black folks incorporate spirituality and/or religious practices in our lives and work in ways that enhance us as human beings and give us tools to fight oppression? How do we change the way we think about our bodies and sexual selves as a way to battle oppression, and the depression that comes with internalized anti-black racism and queerphobia?

I left New Orleans shortly thereafter, returning to New York to begin a relationship with the man I had met the summer before I left New York. My work with Chief has helped me to create a more grounded spiritual context for my life and how I cope with the political/sexual politics of New York City. I am not practicing Vodun nor Ifa, but am still learning about both, debating which path to take and looking to find the right community here before going through an initiation. Not all, but many houses in New York are pretty homophobic or adhere to some unspoken version of the "don't ask/don't tell" policy, which is so dominant in the black community.

One year since my return to New York, I am still learning valuable lessons from that experience and my continued relationship with Chief. The more I fight to understand myself as a sexual/political/spiritual being, the more I know that I am on the road to self-recovery.

For me, that was NOT an option. I told them that for the first time in my life, I had a peace within me that I never thought could exist. And I know it was the peace of God that was telling me that I was becoming who God intended me to be, a black Christian lesbian.

Fearfully and Wonderfully Made

By Rev. Wanda Y. Floyd

At the age of twelve, I found myself walking down the aisle of Shiloh Baptist Church of Henderson, N.C. This was no ordinary journey. I was on my way to becoming a full-fledged member of this church—the place I had called home all my life. The place, on this day, I had decided to give my life to Christ. As I stepped out of my pew in response to the preacher "opening the doors of the church," it was almost like a dream. Here I was dressed in my favorite pink dress, my hair in ponytails, wearing my black shoes, walking in a kind of trance toward the minister. Little did I know how that walk would be the beginning of my spiritual life with God.

On the first Sunday of the following month, I was baptized, my mother and my aunt watching very proudly from the front pew of the church. As we slowly walked up the steps to the baptism font, many of the other children were frightened. I was not one of them. I walked up ready to be baptized. Ready to become a new creature in Christ. Ready to be given the "right hand of fellowship" as we say in the Baptist tradition. It is amazing the things that one recalls from their youth. Obviously, this was the beginning of my spiritual life within the church.

I soon became involved in the Baptist Training Union, youth

missionaries, usher board, youth choir and 4-H, and was secretary for Vacation Bible School. I did the traditional plays and speeches at Easter and Christmas and can still recite most of the Christmas story from the Gospel of Luke.

I was very fortunate to have grown up in a very affirming Southern Baptist Church. I never heard the minister preach negatively about anyone or any set of people. Perhaps it did happen and I just do not recall hearing it. However, the one message I heard over and over again was this: "God is love." I consider myself very blessed to have received such an affirming spiritual beginning. It obviously has helped me become who I am today.

In school I often would hug on girls. Just run up to them and hold on. This continued until my third grade teacher told me, "Hugging on girls is inappropriate for other girls." Again, it is amazing the things you remember from your childhood. I remember how confused I felt and how her tone suggested something was not quite right. Years later, upon reflection on that incident, I realized that part of me shut down and laid dormant until my college years. I continued to go to church and be as involved as ever and pretended that all was well.

Throughout my youth, I continued to do the church thing and fell into society's "appropriate" behavior for girls. I had a boyfriend every year while in school except for my senior year. For my senior prom, I took the last boyfriend I had. The one my mother felt that I would marry. The one that felt that women should not make more money than men and felt that, even in high school, he could tell me what to do. Needless to say, we did not continue in our relationship.

Once college began, I stopped going to church. Not really sure why. I believe I was afraid that any church I attended, especially a black church, would be a place of negativity for me. I wasn't really "out" as of yet, but something inside of me kept me from pursuing locating a church home in my early years of college. I have no doubt that, once again, it was God shielding me from things that I did not need to hear. Things that would have hindered me on my journey to where God wanted me to be.

I became involved with my first girlfriend in school after breaking up with my boyfriend of two years. He and I met the first week of school and were together until I was finally able to acknowledge that I was a lesbian. I did not share this revelation with him at the time.

Once I came out, actually me and my girlfriend came out together, we attended a Church of Christ together until we spoke to a female mentor of hers. On the phone, the mentor began spurting all the scripture that has come to be known in connection to gay and lesbian people. I have to admit, she seemed very well versed in them. She then told the elders of the church who immediately began preparation to have us live separately with families within the congregation. For me, that was NOT an option. I told them that for the first time in my life, I had a peace within me that I never thought could exist. And I know it was the peace of God that was telling me that I was becoming who God intended me to be, a black Christian lesbian. I was even further along on my spiritual journey.

Later, once I stopped attending the church, I contacted the local gay group on the university campus that I was attending. The facilitator wrote back and told me about a church in Raleigh that had a wonderful pastor, and it was a Christian church with an outreach to the gay and lesbian community. I held on to that letter for two years before finally attending in 1987, the year of my first gay pride march. Once I entered the doors of St. John's MCC, I, again, felt the presence of God in and around me and I knew that God had called me home. The Universal Fellowship of Metropolitan Community Churches (UFMCC) was founded to preach God's all-inclusive love for everyone, including the gay and lesbian community. The pastor, an older, straight, white woman, embraced me as her own and for the first time since leaving my home church, I knew I had found the pastor of my adulthood. She was an amazing woman. Sunday after Sunday she preached about the Good News of Jesus Christ for all of us. That God does not discriminate based on our sexuality. That Jesus died for everyone. John 3:16 came alive for me!

I began to really put together all of the things that I had heard of God's love for everyone from my Southern Baptist Church. How God had kept me from finding another church to attend while in college. And now, here I was listening to a woman, a straight woman at that, affirming me as a Christian lesbian in God's house. I was truly HOME!

My journey began to take on another direction. I began to sense more and more God's presence in my life. I got even more involved in the MCC church and that is where I met the girl that I thought God had for me. She was in the military and loved God as much as I did. We would spend time together on the weekends and attend church together. Since we were not at the "Don't Ask, Don't Tell" stage, whenever I visited the base where she was stationed, I had to "de-gay" my car. I would pull over to the gas station outside the base and take off all my stickers. I was not ashamed of who I was and my car reflected that image. However, I was aware that the military could be very hard on gays, even lesbians, and so I would go through the changes necessary to have a pleasant visit on base.

We were together for three years until she was killed in a fatal bicycle accident not too far from where we were living. I survived with a fractured back and many battle scars that are with me to this day. During my time of recovery from the accident, God and I had some very long and hard conversations. Actually, it was more like me yelling at God for what had happened as opposed to me listening to God. Oddly enough, I still had my faith and I began to wonder what plans God had for me. Of course, hindsight is 20/20, and I saw later on that God's hand was present, even in her death and my survival.

I remember lying in the hospital bed at night, trying to figure out what was going on with all of this. Why would God bring someone in my life, and within three months after her discharge from the military she was dead? We had spent three years traveling the road waiting for her to get out of the military and now she was gone. Life seemed quite unfair at the time. I was lying in bed one night in the hospital and I heard God clearly say to me in my spirit, "It's time." Given where I was in my life, I did not want to deal with what God had planned for me even though I had an idea.

I continued to hold on to the affirming love of God once I was out; it helped me through this dark time in my life. My faith was strong; however, I made the decision to leave the church. For three months, I did not attend church or really talk to "church folk." It was a reminder that my girlfriend was gone and I could not understand what God was up to. The one thing that did not change, however, was God's presence around me.

It was almost like God was okay with my being angry and yelling and even not attending church. I believe God was patient with me because God knew that I would turn right back around and come back home. God was not worried, but I was and so were my friends. They called all the time. Visited me with food and tried to get me to go to the movies. During that time away, I did a lot of writing. Poetry was especially significant to me. One poem that I wrote signified the pain I was in:

Awareness
At
night
when I dream—
I see your face
I feel your body
I kiss your lips.

My arms
outstretched
enclose your body
and pull you close,
closer
until I
awaken and
all I have

is
the
pillow

and
my pain.

5/25/91© Wanda Floyd

The more I wrote, the more I felt myself coming out of the fog and getting back, closer to God. Finally, in December of that year, I returned to church a much better person and even more filled with the love of God for others.

I would talk to others about the Good News of God. I would tell them that even when we are angry with God, God continues to love us and bless us and support us. I have come to realize that when God can bless us in the midst of all that we try to do to deny the presence of God, that it is God's way of saying, "It is okay. I understand what you are going through. Don't worry, I will be here when you come back." And as always, God was right there ready to embrace me again.

As my life continued, there were several times in which my faith was tried and I had to hold on for dear life. Within two years after the death of my girlfriend, I was sexually assaulted for three hours in my apartment, in my own bed. The strange thing is, I knew it was going to happen. God had given me a vision a few months earlier and I recall discussing it with my therapist. I remember telling her that I sensed that something tragic was going to happen to me. I did not know what, but that I would survive. To this day, I can go back to my journal and find the entry that I wrote in connection to this. Once again, God was showing me that my being a lesbian was not a hindrance to the goodness of God. When the assault happened, it was as if I disassociated from my physical body and watched what was going on.

Later that same year, I was hit by a tractor-trailer while driving a car that I had just purchased in the previous ten hours.

I had prayed and visualized about this car for a long time and here I was being pushed down the highway in 10 a.m. traffic like lint that flies across the floor. Again, I questioned what God's plan was for me. Even in the midst of the accident, God kept me well protected and away from harm. Even when my car had crossed the median and was facing oncoming traffic, no car hit me and I was able to bring it to rest safely in the grass.

It seemed almost too much for one person to bear. And at times, it almost was. It was not always easy. There were times that I questioned why I was still here because of doing things that were life-threatening—such as having a one-night stand with a crackhead that eventually led me to free-base cocaine for a weekend, or driving while impaired. Through it all, amazingly, I remained true to my foundation of the love of God for me. That one thought pulled me through so many situations in my adult life and kept me centered and focused. Again, I can see it was all a part of God's plan to get me to where I am today.

I can see how the life experiences that I had have enabled me to minister to those that God has brought into the congregation that I am honored to serve. There were times that I can now see I needed to go through in order to help someone else, no matter how painful it was for me. For example, a week after my sexual assault, my best friend, a black gay male, was sexually assaulted at gunpoint (mine was at knifepoint) by another man who infected him with the AIDS virus. If I had not gone through what I had a week earlier, I know I would not have understood his fear of reporting it to the police. I did encourage him to report it as a hate crime, which he did while I held his hand. I often think about God's timing in our lives and how things fall into place just as God wants them.

My spiritual walk with God through all of the events, both good and bad, prepared me for ministry within UFMCC. Once I came to the realization of ministry, an even greater peace fell upon me. In my coming to grips with God's will in my life as a black Christian lesbian, my life began to be much easier. I still had challenges—don't get me wrong—but I had a different perspective now. I began to look at things through the eyes of God even more so than I had done before this time of acceptance. I became more content with who I was and God began to move me further along my journey.

I truly began to see my sexuality as a gift from God, and to deny that gift was to deny God. Through embracing it fully and wholly, I have been able to minister to others that otherwise would not hear the Good News of Jesus Christ for themselves. I have heard the stories of churches and pastors that gay bash or decide to preach on homosexuality on the day that someone gay happens to be in the congregation visiting. I have heard the pain in the voices of my brothers and sisters that have been thrown out of their churches and their families and it challenges me in my love for my fellow pastors.

I mean, we are all children of God, and yet people feel they have the right to condemn and judge others based on their own personal biases. I believe that God has entrusted me with an awesome responsibility to show and give a different perspective to God's all-inclusive love for everyone. I believe that one of my purposes in life is to speak God's truth, by any means necessary, to those that have heard lies all their lives. I have gone to the bar and talked to folks about church and God. I have been a member of a gay bowling league in order to show others that "church folk" can have fun, too.

God has called me to minister in a church that is predominately black, Christian and gay and it is one of the joys of my life. To know that God has used me to change the lives of my brothers and sisters through the church makes me feel blessed everyday that I wake up. It has not always been easy, but the blessings have far outweighed the challenges.

Since founding the ministry back in 1997, I have seen people be healed enough to come out to their parents and friends, to march proudly in gay pride parades, to be willing to have their names printed in the local newspapers. Many have developed a deeper sense of self-worth and self-esteem about who they are as a black Christian gay person for God. I am always amazed at what happens to people once they fully embrace themselves as who God created them to be. It is like they finally can hear that God loves them because finally, they have embraced themselves as the child that God called them to be.

Psalm 139:14 reads, "I praise you, for I am fearfully and wonderfully made." I thank God every day for who God created me to be. It has been a very interesting journey and thankfully, God is not through with me yet.

And as I glanced at the pulpit I saw a man who I knew loved men's flesh, and one day last summer tried to love mine. Battle time had come.

A Nation Divided

By Clarence J. Fluker

For centuries this earthly world has been the battleground for a spiritual war. In this fight both sides have held strong to their contention that one is right and the other is dead wrong; both of these opponents claiming to have God on their side. And with God on your side, how could you be wrong and how could you lose? The war itself, along with the fundamental battle cries heard from both sides, have been passed down from generation to generation and I see no signs of this war being over—although I wish it would come to a swift and painless end. Already it has caused much pain, suffering and turmoil. This war has led men and women to fall, left families in disarray and caused nations to divide.

In the heart of the nation's capitol, the District of Columbia, a chocolate city and mecca for black lesbians and gays, on a main thoroughfare under a bridge sits a Nation: one of the city's largest black churches, known throughout the land for its large number of distinguished members, pageantry, engrossing music and exhilarating orators that bless the pulpit each week. It is often referred to as "a Nation of its own." Though there does not exist a particularly large number of peculiar customs in this Nation, it is customary to overlook a portion of its population for what is seen as their fundamental flaw—that flaw being their sexuality. Some may argue that the Nation and the United States military share the same policy of "don't ask, don't tell" when it comes to same-sex love.

I found myself in the Nation one humid summer Sunday morning, unaware I'd be witness to a battle. I didn't know that Sunday morning I'd see a Nation divide. I didn't know that Sunday morning I'd see souls ambushed with no warning of attack. The choir had completed their fourth selection of the service and it was announced that it was preaching time. With ease and confidence, a woman approached the microphone and placed her Bible and notes on the podium before her. Beautiful make-up, a beautiful dress and a distinguished voice that was a cross between college professor and girl-next-door made her most interesting and easy to listen to. She greeted the congregation with a few words, innocent eyes, and a smile, but within moments opened her mouth and yelled, "Attack!" This Sunday there would be no prosperity preaching; it'd be a "get right" service: She wanted the homosexuals to get right—right then and right there.

"Someone needs to tell the truth," she exclaimed, and the sanctuary grew hotter. The climate was appropriate for battle. During the week she had seen three news programs, all with an overlapping theme. The first program focused on New York City's decision to open its first high school for lesbians and gays. The second chronicled the development of a new television show where men would find their perfect man. Finally, she saw a program that announced the Episcopal Church's decision to vote on whether they would allow a gay man to become a bishop. This trinity was the catalyst for her to begin battle on this Sunday.

Her truth, according to her word and His, was that fleshly desires had begun to take over the world and lead humanity astray, down a path away from common sense. "I am not a homophobic person," she said. "I am not a lesbian and gay basher." But then she went on to say that she was against the lifestyle of lesbians and gays. She was against the lifestyle of any man or woman that interferes and interrupts the word of God.

Next to me was my friend who I knew, like me, was a man who loved other men. In the pew below me was a man I knew loved men. On the aisle to my right was a man ushering who I knew loved other men. In the choir I saw men who I knew loved men. And as I glanced at the pulpit I saw a man who I knew loved men's flesh, and one day last summer tried to love mine. Battle time had come.

"What do you believe?" she asked the congregation before her. She righteously announced her belief that no man should ever love a man the way he was intended to love a woman. Amid the cheers of some of the saints co-signing her every word, I could also hear silent souls crying out. Silent souls lined the pews, pulpit and choir stand. Those souls were crying out for her to stop, crying out for redemption; others were crying because they were just in pain. Sitting in the house of their Father they were being lambasted and told to repent, for the final days were upon us. It was time for them to get right and homosexuality was wrong. "The wages of sin is death." Battle was in progress.

"Someone needs to tell the truth," she said.

Throughout the Nation that Sunday, spiritual warfare caused many to re-examine their life with their God. Countless times throughout their lives these men and women had been told their sexuality was wrong and they wouldn't see the gates of heaven; her sermon was designed to reinforce their interpersonal struggle. Just as the Nation was divided that Sunday by those who believed the preacher and those who didn't, so were many of the conflicted silent souls. Silent souls were the men, women and children like me, same-gender-loving people who had been shamed or shunned into spiritual silence. Often seen but not heard. Our psyches, souls and our hearts had been divided and we were perched to fall out of our faith. I must admit, even as a soldier who has fought this battle of reconciling my spiritual beliefs with my sexuality, I almost found myself a victim rather than just a witness to the battle before me that Sunday. Although I years ago had liberated myself and won the war that had waged within me, I could see her weapons—her words—that Sunday knocking out many.

"No weapon formed against me shall prosper."

Her words that were meant to destroy that Sunday were picking up momentum and would only make me more steadfast in my beliefs. "You have to experience the power [of God] for yourself," she told her captive audience. "Yes, indeed," I thought to myself. I looked back on my life and my personal spiritual walk. I'd learned that my relationship with the Creator was unique to me. I couldn't base my perception of who God is simply on what others had told me, especially when there are those who told me he didn't love me. I had to find out differently on my own.

"True Christians at some point will have to deal with pain and struggle in order to see the tremendous power of God."

Not too far off in the past, I had dealt with a spiritual struggle. I had asked myself many prayerful nights and many mornings, "Am I worthy of God's love?" "Am I living the life he meant for me to live?" There were voices in my head: voices like the preacher that Sunday, citing biblical verses; and taunts of those in the neighborhood who said that sexually transmitted diseases were gay people's curses. But there were also voices whispering my destiny: that I, too, would put on the crown that had already been bought for me, that I would sit my natural self beside my Father one day, in His house. This had been the struggle that divided me. Those voices argued in my head so much that sometimes it would hurt. I would feel a pain in my head that would cascade to my heart and cover it. But it was there in that struggle and in those moments of pain that I began to know God. In my mind, there was no one else to turn to, so I turned to Him. My faith grew stronger in the belief that He did exist and was for the natural me, the black gay me. His power showed in how He began to lift me up, in how He ceased the warring voices in my head, in how He removed the pain from my heart that I thought would never go away. I'd gone from feeling downtrodden to feeling uplifted. Little did the preacher know she was reaffirming that I was a Christian.

I had known pain. I had known struggle. I also knew my Lord.

"Resistance gives you the victory."

She was so right about that. When I battled with the demon of spiritual doubt I resisted listening to those who said I'd not be able to grow in the Holy Spirit. I resisted giving in to the voices I heard that said I would not know His graces and mercy. I resisted the urge to walk away from my quest to build a relationship with my Creator. I resisted listening to the voices that said I'd never walk through the gates and enter the Kingdom of God. Because of my resistance I was able to declare victory. I was able to win the war that waged within me, yet the war in the religious sector and world around me continues to wage on.

That Sunday I thought that I'd only play the role of onlooker to the spiritual war, but eventually I decided to take arms and get involved. While she preached, I prayed. When she concluded her sermon and started praying, my prayer intensified. She prayed for the Nation, she prayed for the world, she prayed that those who were living their lives wrong would give their lives to Christ and begin to live right. I prayed that the Nation would not divide its congregation and that the word of God be used to unite; I prayed that the silent souls would one day come out of their silence and share their walk with Christ, free and unashamed. I prayed that no one who had heard her sermon that day was pushed or scared further away from their desire to walk with Christ. I knew there were people in the building praying for *us*, and I was praying for them.

The attack was over, signified by the preacher closing her sermon and prayer and taking her seat. She sat in an elevated chair in the pulpit, able to view the charred battleground. The sanctuary was still.

"If you're looking for the Lord, that's where He is—in the Holy place."

The choir began to sing those words, the congregation stood and all over there seemed to be a tension lifting as we all found ourselves swaying to the music and finding personal joy and comfort in what the lyrics meant to us individually.

"I want to walk in the Holiest of Holies—where He is, just to see Him face to face—where He is, to lay prostrate in His presence—where He is—and to hear Him speak to me—where He is."

I learned during my war that the walk with Him is a walk for only the two of us. I learned during my war that any answers I'd be required to give for the life that I lived, any answers would be for Him and Him only. I learned during my war it is in His presence that I am able to lay down my body and my load. I learned during my war that indeed when I am praying, He is listening and that He speaks to my soul.

I just prayed that others were listening to the lyrics that Sunday. I wanted everyone in the church to listen carefully, not just hearing that beautiful sound of the choir but understanding the beauty of the words being sung. I know some of the saints were listening to the sounds. Others, I knew—like me—felt the words. In the Holy place, the Holiest place, inside of all of us, we can hear the voice of God. Surely, if you are looking for the Lord, that's where He is—and only there can this war end.

And if you're looking for the Lord
He's in the Holy place
Inside you.

I call myself a heathen because I have grown indifferent to conventional Judeo-Christian ideas of God. The fact is that I do believe there is a power, an entity, that is greater than any and all of us. … We (God and I) do not apologize.

Why I Am a Heathen
By Tracee Ford

When asked, I tell people I am bisexual. Many folks don't like that at all. "Be straight or gay," they say, "preferably straight, but pick one." Bisexuality seems to be some in between thing. A non-decision.

When asked about my spirituality, I tell people I am a heathen. Again, folks take that as a non-decision. Be an atheist or be a believer. Many people regard heathens as defiant believers, but I guess the best dictionary definition of my kind of heathen would be "one who is regarded as irreligious, uncivilized, or unenlightened." My understanding comes not from Webster's, though, but from the sitcom *Sanford and Son.* I would watch Fred Sanford plod through life, love and family the best way he knew how. Then his sanctified sister-in-law, Esther, would scrunch up her face and say, "You old heathen." I could see that Fred was no saint, but I thought calling him a "heathen" seemed a bit heavy-handed. If Esther had called Fred a sinner, I would have bought that because he obviously didn't adhere to any strict moral code. Esther, however, reached past the words "sinner," "unrepentant" or even "heretic" and went straight to heathen. In addition to just seeming funny, it seemed to say that Fred was unredeemable. He was going to keep on doing and saying things just as he pleased and no amount of Bible-bashing would change him. I think I'm like that, too. I'm an Esther heathen, not a Webster's heathen. Maybe heathenism is my way of sticking my tongue out at people afraid of the rich shades of gray that exist in and around the more comfortable black and white.

Identifying as bisexual, however, is not an act of defiance, but of growth and of validating my own existence. For me, being bisexual means that I am able to create a loving, fulfilling relationship with a person or persons regardless of biological sex. This could include a relationship or relationships with intersex, female- or male-born people. While same sex loving people have made some strides in the social and legislative arenas toward safeguarding our rights, we need not pretend that same sex loving is a generally accepted practice. We don't even talk about intersex people and their partners. They're just too marginalized for folks to dialogue around. Sexual minorities (lesbian, gay, bisexual, transgender, intersex and questioning people) regularly find themselves in the position of having to defend their loves and lives. "If it ain't heterosexual and monogamous, it ain't right." Not only does bisexual not fit into that neat formula, but people have told me that they actually don't "believe in it." I tell them that I and other bisexual folks are not Tinkerbell. Some of us may be fairies, but we do not need others to believe in us in order for us to exist. We love, therefore we are.

My ears are particularly sensitive to the ways bisexual folks are told we ain't right by both gay and straight conservatives. These folks perceive us to be noncommittal and deceptive people. Bisexual women disrupt the lesbian community by prioritizing male lovers and transmitting STDs to lesbian women. Bisexual men disrupt the heterosexual world by lying to their female lovers and transmitting STDs to straight women... at least, that is what conservatives like to say.

That's the kind of talk that has made me the bisexual heathen that I am now. Many of the conservative folks doing the talking identify themselves as believers of some loving god. They claim to follow the examples of some altruistic messenger and/or savior. They profess to study examples as recorded in sacred texts. You can input the appropriate names for yourself: God, Lord, Allah, Jehovah, Jesus, Holy Spirit, Muhammad, I Am, Moses, Abraham, Elijah, Buddha, Qur'an, Bible, Missalet, Daily Word, etc. It is in the name of their faiths that many of these folks alienate sexual minorities in their faith institutions, neighborhoods, schools, jobs and families. That isn't loving. Nor is it godly. Yet, these folks will tell others that they are Christians, Muslims, Buddhists, and Hindus and that's why they talk that talk.

Well, I don't want no parts of that. Being from the South, I know mostly Christians, so that is the experience from which I can best speak. I was raised in the Roman Catholic Church. As an adult, most of the churches I attended were Protestant. I even spent a year at Bishop Eddie Long's Missionary Baptist Church near Atlanta, Ga. These are generally good folks. Not perfect, but trying. I respect that. What I don't respect is the sanctioning of sexual minorities based on misunderstood and misrepresented texts of the Bible. A growing number of sexual minority allies are speaking out publicly. More and more of these allies are challenging homophobia and gender phobia under the banners of a truly loving God, but I need more of them to speak out against anti-LGBT demonstrations, like the march that Bishop Long hosted in December of 2004, before I will feel comfortable denouncing my heathen title.

I call myself a heathen because I have grown indifferent to conventional Judeo-Christian ideas of God. The fact is that I do believe there is a power, an entity, that is greater than any and all of us. That co-creates. That loves. I believe that. In fact, I think that I love that God. I believe that God and I are partners in creating me. We (God and I) created me to be a sexual being. We (God and I) created me bisexual. We (God and I) do not apologize. In fact, we celebrate this creation called me by welcoming Love in all its many forms into my life.

Today, I experience the blessing of lasting friendships, chosen family and a fulfilling partnership in my life. I credit these experiences to my God and I welcome Love into my life. Some good and generous folks regularly grace my life with their friendship. This diverse group of queer, straight, young and old enrich my life in ways that I could never capture with words. I only know that I am happy to call them family. They support my five-year relationship with my transgender partner and they help me grow into a more loving person. They don't seem to mind that I am a heathen. Not that they ask. It's the fact that I'm loving and genuine that concerns them. Our God is Love, and our religion is to be loving.

A few scriptures are given, and entire sets of values are based upon them. We believe these "minister-given" values without question and live our lives accordingly. I was no different.

Regardless of or Despite the Church I Love Myself: One Lesbian's Opinion

By Diane Foster

Who am I? A woman, a Black woman, a Black lesbian woman. I love women, I love womanhood, I love the essence of womanhood; I have a woman, love my woman—but most of all, I love myself.

Coming up as a child in the '50s, I was socialized into strong Baptist doctrine. I came from three generations of ministers, deacons and church mothers—that I am aware of. I was seven when thoughts of female intimacy entered my mind. These feelings were kept to myself when playing with my girlfriend every day; I never told her how much I enjoyed lying beside her in her bed. My taste for females was my secret, and remained so for many years.

My teenage years were not much different. By that I mean I still kept my secret. I was no longer around my childhood playmate. My hidden passion was subdued by Baptist indoctrination, and at fifteen years old I was baptized. That same year I discovered the word lesbian while in the school library looking in the encyclopedia for some word that started with "le." I also learned the prefix "homo," then the word homosexual. What an awakening! I remember looking the word "homosexual" up in my mother's Childhood Development book. (She was a teacher. She also made the church announcements each Sunday. Sometimes I would look at her and admire her beauty. To me she was a diva; dressed to kill with a set of legs that would make anyone take notice.) While reading the definition I became aware of who I was. It described me perfectly. I was a female who felt sexual intimacy for other females. After reading about myself I took the book to Mom asking her about it, thinking it was okay. She immediately hushed me up and told me to put the book away. I realized then this feeling of mine was something I had to continue keeping a secret. It became taboo, and for many years I never mentioned it again. But I still fantasized. Staring at girls and following them to their classes became my passion.

In the South, homosexuality was seldom spoken of in the church during the early '60s; God forbid. When it was spoken of it was with such diabolical verbalism that the congregation couldn't give an "Amen." Instead, they would get quiet, and I would think, how was I going to come to terms with myself? My mother wouldn't allow me to express it; I had no one else with whom to discuss it, so my secret stayed.

In the meantime my indoctrination continued in what the minister said the Bible said about homosexuals. With no outlet I buried my desire and lived a heterosexual life. I did the boyfriend/girlfriend things but the fantasies continued. I couldn't stop them; they remained, and I waited for my opportunity of expression.

I never read the Bible for myself and like so many others neither did I question its doctrine; I believed what I was told. I believed the minister had a direct know-it-all relationship with God and "his" word was His word: the God-given truth. This is a Christian fallacy.

We believe what we are told. As a result we become conditioned to beliefs. These beliefs bring about stereotyping, phobias and even hatred for whatever has been taught to be evil. A few scriptures are given, and entire sets of values are based upon them. We believe these "minister-given" values without question and live our lives accordingly. I was no different. I felt shame because of my taste for women and thought I would go to hell if I acted upon it. I hid my secret passion and my passion became a burden. We were taught by way of scripture to cast our burdens upon the Lord and He will bear them, but how was I to cast a homosexual burden upon a God who taught that same-sex relationships were an abomination? I began to feel condemned as so many others like me feel to this very day.

By my seventeenth year I knew I would live a lesbian lifestyle. I also knew I loved God. I believed I was His child and knew that He loved me. Yet my love of self was a problem. I found myself living in polarity. God hated homosexuals and homosexuality yet I believed John 3:16 which states, "For God so loved the world that He gave His only begotten Son, that whosoever believeth in Him should not perish, but have everlasting life." I believed in God. How was this to be? He loved me and hated me? I loved myself and hated myself.

This issue is prevalent with many Christian homosexuals. They love God but hate themselves. As a result there is misery and self-hatred. High suicide rates are a statistical fact in gay/lesbian communities. Unable to come to terms, we love self and hate self, confusion on all sides—and despair. Some continue to go to church in spite of the phobias because of their love for God, yet they live in the duality of homosexuality and secrets. They hide within hetero-culture and they go, despite the church's teachings. Others stay away for fear or shame or hatred of belief systems. They hate themselves because they love God, yet are unable to worship with Christians who hate the very lifestyle they live. Some are fortunate to live in cities where homosexual churches give an outlet for worship, but what about the masses that have no such outlet?

Though I claimed myself as being a child of God, I buried my Christianity and, when I became of age, I stopped going to church. However, the Bible still interested me so I studied it. I read in Ecclesiastes that nothing is new under the sun. I learned from history that homosexuality had been going on since the beginning of time. I learned from the study of science that same-sex relationships exist in the animal kingdom. How could animals carry taboos? How can God, the creator of all, create such animals? Was this a freak of nature? If so, Him being the creator, does He reject them?

At eighteen I had my first lesbian sexual experience. I heard bells ring—literally. It sounded like wedding bells—I knew I found my true self. I loved the emotional and physical feeling, yet I still had the problem of not loving myself. I chose to enjoy this new freedom. Many years went by and I ignored my personal relationship with God and continued my lifestyle. Yet the issue remained.

During the '70s and '80s more was being said about homosexuality and spirituality. Homosexuals began questioning the doctrines of churches and what "thus saith the Lord." Scripture was re-evaluated and looked at from different viewpoints.

By the late '80s the Internet began to explode. Information was readily available to anyone seeking it. I was one of those people and my first searches dealt with lesbianism. This led me to a lesbian minister: What a revelation! I once again thirsted for biblical knowledge as it pertained to the love of God and she introduced me to a new way of thinking. I began to understand biblical context from a different (Christian) theory. As I studied I learned that "parts" of scripture were being used as bases for entire belief systems. I particularly attached my new way of learning to Leviticus 18:22, "thou shalt not lie with mankind as with womankind." The issue of woman-to-woman sexuality was not mentioned. I read the entire book and realized that God named other abominations including the eating of pork. The Levites were told not to wear clothes of linen and wool blend. Hmmmm. I asked myself, why would God-fearing ministers of today's society, dressed to kill in linen and wool suits, feasting on pork chop dinners, denounce homosexuals? I could hear them saying, "Well, times are different now, the way things are we can't grow our own cotton to make clothes of one blend." Really now?

If thus saith the Lord and you are unable to do these things then where is your salvation? Is it in asking Him to forgive the fact that you have no desire to spend your labor in cotton fields? That life is different now and no one does that any longer?

I asked myself who God was talking to: all of us, or the Levites? What about those churches who live by New Testament doctrine only? Are they choosing to ignore some laws and live "religiously" by others? Have they chosen to segregate via convenience? I will not address in this essay the issue of male dominance in the church—much can be said about that. Rather, I'm focusing on how I came to the place of loving myself as a Christian lesbian.

While reading the scriptures "for myself," I came to II Timothy, which teaches us to study to show ourselves approved unto God, that a workman need not be ashamed, rightly dividing the word of truth. I read that I was conceived in sin and born into iniquity; that sin was in me. We all sin, hetero and homosexuals. I read that God looks upon the hearts of His children and that ANY who have the love of Him in her/his heart was part of His fold. I read that God is love. I realized that if I was in love with a woman then it was of God because Satan is not the author of love; God is. I John 4:8 states that God is love. How could I feel love and not be of God? I also read that God forgives seventy times seven. *If* I want to believe that homosexuality is a sin then I would also believe that I am forgiven. But I do not believe God sees my homosexuality as sin.

Many churches use the story of Sodom and Gomorrah as the basis for God's hatred of homosexuals. The sins of Sodom and Gomorrah were many, brutality, greed, lust and being inhospitable among them.

Upon discovering the lifestyle of the people of Sodom and Gomorrah I learned that God was displeased with them because of their lust and insensitive ways toward humankind. They were a very wealthy nation that hardened their hearts to the conditions of those around them. They lusted after things they had no need of. They should have been content with such as they had. When the men of the city tried to invade the body of God's angels, it was a bit much for Him. It's like He said, "I don't like what you're doing anyway and now you've gone and messed with my sons. That's enough, you've crossed the line this time and I'm going to do something about it."

I continued dividing the word of truth and began feeling better toward myself. The scripture teaches us there are many books of the Bible that deal with the ways of God. Yet, how many of us look for them for ourselves to discover the true nature of God? God said His mysteries are many. If there are so many why do we not try to discover them based on our lives, and lifestyles? It is because, sadly, we believe what we are told.

God looks upon the hearts of (wo)man. If the heart is wicked we are wicked. If there is love in our hearts then we have the compassion of our Father. It took me a while to learn this. I was in my forties before I began to love myself. Having experienced His love, His mercy and His many blessings I knew He worked in my life. I know my heart isn't wicked therefore I must be a good person. I believe in loving my neighbor as myself, which is the greatest of His commandments. I knew I didn't lust after another woman's woman. (Not to the point of acting on it, anyway!) I believe in modesty and all things good. I honor my mother and father and respect my elders, so why would God not love me? Why would I not love myself knowing that I try to live a Christian life?

Of course there is room for improvement. I have my carnal ways. We all do. Scripture says first there is carnal, then spiritual. This means I live in the flesh before I live in the spirit. I've come to terms with the fact that I will never be perfect. I've come to terms that God knows this. Why should I feel that I must be perfect? I can only strive to be a good person. God knows my faults, and I do not believe that my being a lesbian is one of them. Before the foundation of the world He knew me. He knew I would become a lesbian and He blesses me. Why should I not accept His love and love myself? This was my turning point.

At this stage in life I've been able to discuss such issues with my minister, or ministers that I trust. It shames me not to boldly speak my Christian lesbian opinion. I'm relieved to discover that some ministers of God are beginning to see from a new perspective. This pleases me but there are still too many looking through the glass darkly. As a lesbian I'm free to love myself— and my woman. How is it possible to love another before we love ourselves? It isn't.

For those that live in this place I say take these words for your strength. Dwell upon them. Search the scriptures for yourself if you believe that God doesn't love you because you are homosexual. Rid yourself of Gospel Psychological Chains of Homosexual Enslavement. Love yourself that you will be able to love someone else. If you have a partner or mate and can't deal with self-love you are doing the relationship injustice. Use these words to break the chain.

Greater is she who conquers self than she who conquers a nation.

God, as an entity, as an idea, did not work for me. When I got the courage, I let it go.

I Hate God
By Steven G. Fullwood

If you believe that you have a spirit or a soul, then you might also agree that most of your life you do not think about it. It's just there, and when you compare it with the needs and wants of the body, at times the soul seems to be non-existent. I do believe that I have a soul, mainly because I spent a great deal of my life trying to avoid thinking about it. It terrified me to think that inside of me was something that could be granted access to heaven (if I was good, and judged so) or sentenced to hell (if I were bad, and found guilty.) Complicating matters greatly was that I was a man who loved other men, and that everything I ever read or heard about men who loved men was that those who dared walk that path inherited a first-class, non-stop ticket to hell. A good reason if there was one to avoid thinking about souls.

Not that my soul was having it, because it did not. My mind is never still. From a very early age, I knew that I was a special sort of child. Every day, inside, my soul chattered away like a schoolboy, telling me to lift my head up and look at the boy looking at me from across the room, or to beware this particular alley because a rabid dog was waiting for me. I sometimes listened and took the advice, or ignored it and missed an opportunity for fun or suffered a bite. But it wasn't until I went to church that the voice was mute, and something else took over. Something not so good.

But first, a little history. Me and Christianity go way back.

This is the part of the story that I know. My grandfather Steven, on my father's side, was a Baptist minister in rural Arkansas. His son Lucious became a Baptist minister as well, and now lives in Chicago. My own father sang with a short-lived gospel group called the Horns of Zion, and they toured parts of Michigan, Ohio and Indiana. My mother was raised in a Lutheran church in Ohio, and was sometimes taken to a Baptist church by her grandmother, Buela. My mother raised us kids in a Lutheran church (my father refused to go for some reason), and it was there that I formally met the Father, the Son and the Holy Ghost. I would have been better off not making their acquaintance. It was not an amiable relationship.

First, there was the venue: church. How could anybody stay awake in church? The purr of the minister's voice was a guaranteed snoozer. He'd read from his prepared sermon or the Bible in a monotone that alternately made me want to laugh or sleep. Laughing was guaranteed to be rewarded with a slap from my mother; sleeping kept me quiet for fifteen minutes or so before she or my older sister would shake me awake. Outside of the church, I endured constant threats from God filtered through my mother about where bad little kids like me were likely to go. That, coupled with what I thought were far too simplistic stories in Bible class about sin, crowded my thoughts daily. These and other fucked up thoughts told me all I needed to know about God—He was judgmental, and didn't like little boys like me much.

And I didn't like Him. In fact I hated Him. What did he ever do for my family except provide a temporary reprieve from our miserable lives on Sunday mornings? My mother worked like a dog throughout my youth. My father had no less than two jobs his entire adult life, and still with their combined incomes struggled to raise five children. Understandably, my parents fought constantly about who was responsible for this or that. Did He step in and break it up? Or come with food when the refrigerator was empty? No.

God, as an entity, as an idea, did not work for me. When I got the courage, I let it go. The day it happened was like any other day for me. I was a rambunctious child with an opinion that I was willing to share with anyone in earshot. After becoming particularly sassy with my mother, she banished me from the kitchen and into my room. I only made it as far as the top of the stairs so that I could plan retaliation. Carefully, I sat there thinking of a way to get both her back and God back for punishing me. I patiently waited until my little brother Darryl came close enough to hear me before I uttered the words that would have a profound effect on my life forever.

"I hate God."

He didn't hear me at first, and asked me what I said. Once again, with perfect diction, I slowly walked the words out: "I-hate-GOD."

The plan worked beautifully. Darryl tore through the living room like an ambulance screaming "Awww!" and ran into the kitchen. I readied myself for the confrontation that never came. In her usual flippant fashion, my mother told my little brother, "Let him hate God, I don't care. Hate God all he wants. He's still on a punishment. Tell him that."

Next stop: Hell.

After I made that little declaration, my list of complaints against God mounted by the day. Picked on at school, at the park, at a friend's house. Not enough food, heat, or time to get up in the morning to go to school. My brother took my stuff, my older sisters were bossy and hogged the phone, and the younger one got any and everything she wanted just by crying for it. My clothing was old, raggedy and out of style. Mom and daddy gave everybody but me everything. And what did God do? Not a thing. This God was sadistic. Praying seemed fairly useless, and so did acting like I believed that it worked. So I stopped.

That's when the spirits started visiting me. The first time it happened I thought it was a dream. The second time I wasn't so sure. The third time I was convinced that I was nuts. The encounter would normally start out with me in a semi-conscious state while lying on my bed or the couch. If I were on my bed, I would be facing the wall; if on the couch, I'd face the back of it.

The only way to describe what was happening to me is to liken the experience to listening to the noise that results from fumbling with the knobs on a transistor radio while trying to find a clear station. My whole body would be frozen while spirits roamed through my body, some talking, some crying or screaming. I never knew how long it would last, but while it was happening I would try to move my petrified limbs. First a finger, then a leg. Gradually, my life force would again inhabit my limbs and allow me to move again. Scared, and terrified that it would happen to me again, I would sit up, dizzy with fear, and try to comprehend what had happened to me. I felt like a way station for wayward souls.

I remember telling myself that what was happening was ridiculous. I didn't believe in God. Did that automatically mean I was going to hell? And if so, were demons periodically hanging out in my body? And I was already poor, so, like, could God or Satan go pick on someone who was better off? I offered up this prayer to whatever entity was listening: "Leave me alone, at least until I get myself together."

The incidents/visits stopped, and so did my anger toward God. Surely, it had to be God with whom I had brokered the deal. Still, a nagging sense inside told me that I just faked myself out to get a little breathing room. That a raging puberty and insurgent sexuality almost immediately filled the little opening that either God or I made for myself. Overwhelmed and incessantly horny, I decided to try to be a good Christian and go to church.

Once again in church, I sat alone, without my mother or siblings. The pews were brown, cool and slick under my pants, and I carried a Bible that I got from a thrift store. The pastor I knew as a child, a white man, had retired, and now another younger white minister stood in the pulpit. Everything was basically the same: the monotone lecture, the red hymnal books secure on the shelf in front of me, the alert faces of the adults, the anxious or sleeping faces of the children or elders. This time, however, I listened with a matured ear. I was twenty, had my own apartment, and was in complete denial of my sexuality. The thought that someone might discover that I was homosexual terrified me so, hence my trying to wash it away with a weekly trip to the church.

But it didn't work. The ascent of my consciously acting on my desires for other men was directly proportionate to my waning interest in attending church. Though I stopped, I was still interested in God, or better put, matters of the spirits. As I made my way through college, I wrote poetry that started to question more than the existence of God; the poems became a way to dialogue about the ways in which spirituality manifested itself. Godstuff was my preoccupation for a number of years, until one day I had a dream that not only confirmed for me the existence of God, but also clarified that what I had been doing all along was looking for a dragon.

Next: The Resurrection

I was in the backyard of my parents' home. It was dawn, and spring was busily breaking up the ice. Mud and water commingled at my feet. I looked up in the sky. Frozen in a block of ice was a dragon upside down, floating in the air high above me. The ice was rapidly melting, and I feared that the dragon would fall on my head. The block actually floated a few feet away from me, where the dragon dropped out from the now completely melted block of ice and into a neighbor's backyard. It came toward me. Suddenly, I was looking out of my bedroom window watching the dragon follow me around the house while my father followed the dragon. I didn't feel like I was being chased, nor did I feel that my father was chasing or hunting the dragon.

Freaked but not scared, I related this dream to a co-worker the next day. She was shocked. Rolita, a budding spiritualist and all-around good woman, and I talked about the significance of the dragon in Chinese cultures, and how the dragon represents feminine energy. She gave me a copy of the book *Jambalaya* by Luisah Teish. It changed my life.

Jambalaya chronicles Teish's development as a Yoruba priestess in the Oshun tradition. The book provided a brief history of Ifa, and how it consecrated with Christianity and formed, among other things, voodoo and hoodoo, and a whole mess of things. Teish's personal narrative helped me to get closer to the idea of Ifa, and I read everything I could about it, voodoo and hoodoo. Orishas (representatives of energy in the Yoruba pantheon of spirituality) by the hundreds. I felt close to these ideas of the spirit. Teish recounted stories similar to my own. She laughed and told great stories about healing and growing and finding her spirit. Who knew that religion could be so much fun?

For once, spirituality began to make some sense to me, particularly the Orisha named Elegua. After Olodumare (God), the next most powerful being is Elegua, the divine messenger. Elegua is the deity who removes obstacles and opens the paths, doors and roads of opportunity and success for humans. He also takes the prayers of humans to the Orishas, and acts as a conduit for their energies. Without him, no ceremony can be done nor can spiritual work be fully realized. Hmmm. What I found most intriguing about Elegua is his energy, which is seen as mischievous and playful. Throughout my life I have enjoyed joking or pulling the rug out from under people, literally and figuratively.

So bring on de fun!

Ultimately, I didn't (and won't) join any group or any religion (who needs an intermediary? I can talk to God myself!), but if I had to choose one it would be Ifa. My exploration in this religion led me down a much more familiar spiritual road, one where I didn't have to stop being me—the rambunctious me, the one I like being—to be right with God. Ifa was a good introduction to the different ways that one could experience the spirit with many names and various manifestations. This was a relief to me. I even stopped hating God. It could all work, you know?

See, before there was Eshu, there was Jesus, and before there was Jesus, there was God, and He said unto me: Boy, you better get right with God. And I did. By getting right with me.

We had to deal with more church sissies, church queens, than anything. Because the older ones were so brainwashed that they didn't feel worthy; they wanted the younger ones to sit down, be quiet. The silence of the South.

Southern Sanctified Sissy: An Interview with First Lady/Regional Mother Anthony R.G. Hardaway

By Lisa C. Moore and Anthony R.G. Hardaway

I first met Anthony Hardaway through my co-editor, G. Winston James, when James was touring with his volume of poetry, *Lyric*, in 1999. Hardaway was adamant that black gay authors include Southern cities such as Memphis, Tenn., and Jackson, Miss., on their book tours; "our people are hungry for your work" was his common refrain. Referred to as "The First Lady" in parts of the black gay South, Hardaway is known for being surrounded by "the children," younger black gays that he introduces to art, history and culture. He has a passion for educating Southern black gays and lesbians about black LGBT history, and documenting Southern black LGBT culture. Even more, Hardaway has a talent for pushing black gays and lesbians toward all things positive. As co-editor G. Winston James says, "People see God in Anthony. He touches them."

Lisa C. Moore: Give me a little background about your history with the church.
Anthony Hardaway: My city, Memphis, Tenn., has at least eight community choirs (besides a person's own home church choir) for the chil-ren to sing in. In every one of those community choirs you have what you call the "sissies" or "punks." (The ladies

in the church called them "sissies," and the straight men called them "punks.") Now, mind you, no one could out-sing ANY of them. They were known as those "punks who could really sing you up under a pew."

I am one of those sissies that can sing you up under a pew. I've sung in at least five of those community choirs, plus my home church choir.

I have attended Mount Pisgah Missionary Baptist Church all my life. I was reared there, every Sunday and throughout the week, from Sunday school up to 7 p.m. church services and gospel concerts. It's a Southern thing—to still be affiliated as an adult with the church you grew up in.

I started singing when I first started talking; I imitated how people sang. I must have started singing in the choir when I was seven or eight years old. I sang there until I went to college, and when I'd come back from college on weekends and holidays, I'd come back to my home church choir and sing. I'm still a member of my church, though I don't actively sing in the choir because I'm busy with HIV/AIDS work and theater work.

When I sing, I close my eyes and sing from my heart. I sing out of my pain; I transform and go into a whole other world. I'm not a person standing up there; I'm a spiritual being. And I'm healing myself. I help move the people toward connecting to the Spirit, getting happy and shouting through song. Some people [who sing] stand up and sing, then go sit down. [But] I sing from the microphone to my seat. That's a Southern thing, too.

LCM: Has gay sexuality ever been an issue in the church, in your experience?

AH: Oh God, yes! Nobody wanted to be gay. My parents didn't want a gay child. I wrestled with it tremendously all the way up to college. You were lower than the devil if you were gay in the church. You could be the biggest ho in the church and get respect. [But not] being gay. And when you came out to people…

I came out to my family through events. I invited people to events, black gay events. Once [my family] realized what it was, they could leave or they could stay. Once they realized their [gay] nephew was there, the [gay] lady that lived up the street was there... It was our way of telling the village, "We're OK." Once the straight people were there, and they realized that we were all gay, they didn't want to have to think about who else might be gay.

My sexuality was not questioned when I was in church. I was a very effeminate male, and I think people recognized that. It was never said or spoken. But I heard what other church people said: "It's a shame all them sissies in the church," but it wasn't directed toward me. I never heard the word "gay" in church, or "homosexual"; it was always "sissy." In the South, [a sissy] could direct the choir, or play the piano... They didn't expect you to lead in certain ways, [but] they expected you to lead the choir.

We had to deal with more church sissies, church queens, than anything. Because the older ones were so brainwashed that they didn't feel worthy; they wanted the younger ones to sit down, be quiet. The silence of the South. Look how many of us didn't know about James Cleveland until after he died. *After* he *died!* We weren't raising a ruckus; we were just coming together. [But] there's still that silence; dare not speak it.

That's one of the reasons why I don't want a funeral; I want to be taken straight to my grave. I can't stand the lies. If you really want to honor what I've done, teach someone who's black and gay. Teach them about their history. That's how you eulogize me.

LCM: How did you come to be called "First Lady"?
AH: "First Lady" comes from the southern church. It came from when I was in Jackson, Mississippi, in college in 1990. I imitated a lot of the women in my church. I didn't imitate the men; I imitated the women—they were dressier. There was something about them. These women wore the biggest hats. They were the nurturers of the church. There was *something about them.* Us gay boys, we immediately imitated them. Down South, for gay men, [the gay church community is] like a silent club, a silent group. Gayness is not spoken about, but you know each other. I wore the big hats, the furs. It really had nothing to do with the spirituality

part; it was something we played. My gay friends locally and nationally named me because of the way I dressed and conducted myself. They said I carried the church with me… and the name stuck.

LCM: Do you have particular beliefs about spirituality and sexuality?

AH: I think, sexuality-wise, if someone asks if it's a sin for a man to be with another man: To me it is a sin if anyone, any two individuals, are with each other and the connection is not on a spiritual level. That's not good to me. That's something I had to teach myself; I had to learn for myself. If there's no connection, I'm not equally yoked.

I think we have been brainwashed in things spiritually. In my heart, I really don't believe I'm an abomination. Why? If He's all-powerful, then just a thought from the Divine can take these feelings away from me. Who's to say that my being same-gender loving and being spiritually connected to the Divine will not help someone else get spiritually connected?

From the moment we realize we like the same sex is when we start trying to hide things from our family. I think you can be connected spiritually and sexually to the same sex, but we've tainted that so much; we're defining ourselves by what other people have said and thought about us.

I don't think there's any orgasm that two people can have that the Holy Spirit can't be a part of. It's divine order. I think it is a sin for a man to lie down with a woman when he knows he is not spiritually, mentally or nowhere near emotionally attached to that woman. To me that's the biggest sin; that's why we have rules to go by. A lie is just a lie.

LCM: How did you reconcile your sexuality with the teachings of the church?

AH: I reconciled [my sexuality] by seeking out the truth. When I prayed, I felt that He was telling me that I was not anything that was not clean; you are of Me. Then I sought out the artists and the writers. The core of them was that they were pure, and beautiful. That's when I came into [believing] I'm not a bad person; my gay friends are not bad. We were such a rarity, so powerful and magnificent, the common people don't know how to take it. Anything that is so beautiful, too beautiful to be touched or expressed, we tend to destroy. Look at our great leaders. They were too beautiful, too exotic. To me, spiritually, some people recognize it, but fleshly they have to destroy it.

Reconciliation… It's like taking a mirror and thanking the Divine for making you who you are. It's like making love to yourself. To wash another man is so spiritual to me. I started seeking my inner truth, and I found beauty.

My church is the doctrine that disconnects me from my ability to have a healthy relationship with God. I walk with this assurance: that God wants me to break through the barriers that come between us and God. I walk with the confidence that the teachings of my church are my barrier and I must let them go.

Same Spirit
By Dorothy Harris

Laying Aside the Weight

Wherefore seeing we also are compassed about with so great a cloud of witnesses, let us lay aside every weight, and the sin which doth so easily beset us, and let us run with patience the race that is set before us. (Hebrew 12:1)

I am. I am an African-American lesbian. I am an African-American lesbian mother. I am a saved African-American lesbian mother. I am a saved African-American Pentecostal lesbian mother butch daddy. I am a saved African-American Pentecostal lesbian mother butch daddy who knows that my spiritual calling is sure, who knows that God's love is bigger than any of my insecurities, bigger than any doctrine. I know God's love and God's love for me is perfect. I am. I am loved. I am loved by God. I am loved by God for being this African-American Pentecostal lesbian mother butch daddy.

I am. I am weighted. I am weighted by the doctrines and teachings of the Church of God in Christ. I am burdened by the teachings of my people who taught me that God is love while simultaneously teaching me that God doesn't love homosexuals, and therefore does not love me. I am burdened and weighted by the doctrines and teachings of the church in which I learned to seek the kingdom of God while also learning that homosexuals have no place in the kingdom of God. I am burdened by the church that tells me that we all have a right to the tree of life, and on the other hand that homosexuals have no place and no opportunity for a place in the sight of God. I am weighted by the rejection of the church that taught me that God has no respect of persons while teaching me that God does, indeed, have persons whom he does not respect. I am. Weighted. Rejected. Cast aside. Forgotten by those who taught me that God throws our sins, not us, in the sea of forgetfulness. I wonder where this God is. I am weighted and I am thrown into this sea of eternal forgetfulness, the Bible tied around my ankles to assure my drowning as I am reminded that God will never forgive my sin. God, who loves everyone, abhors me.

My Bible tells me to lay aside the weight and the doctrine that so easily besets me. My church is the weight and it teaches the doctrine that besets me. My church is the weight that obstructs my view to and my relationship with God. My church is the doctrine that disconnects me from my ability to have a healthy relationship with God. I walk with this assurance: that God wants me to break through the barriers that come between us and God. I walk with the confidence that the teachings of my church are my barrier and I must let them go. I must lay aside this weight if I am to be free from oppression, if I am to be free to live the will of God. I cannot continue to support the contradictions that are inherent in the doctrines of the church. I cannot sit comfortably in a congregation that teaches homophobia to thousands of people who in turn reach thousands of people. I cannot support a congregation that teaches people to hate me, that teaches me to hate myself. I cannot participate in my own slaying, in my own drowning, in adding to the weight that burdens and easily besets me. My first step toward spiritual healing, therefore, was to leave the place that offered no redemption. My first step in my spiritual healing, then, was to leave the church.

My Religious and Spiritual Development

Train up a child in the way (s)he should go: and when (s)he is old, (s)he will not depart from it. (Proverbs 22:6)

I came to consciousness in the church. Like many other people who were raised in the church, I learned the sixty-six books of the Bible from front to back. I can quote scripture, book, chapter and verse for most topics. I can talk about the God of wrath and the God of love. I can tell you about the triune god, the basic doctrines of the Church of God in Christ, and the ways and reasons to be saved. I was raised in Sunday school, vacation Bible school, YPWW (Young People's Willing Workers), Prayer and Bible Band and weekly choir rehearsals. I was in church several days a week and in three services on Sundays. I am a product of the church.

As an adolescent, I taught Sunday school, directed the choir and was involved in all youth activities. I embraced much of the culture of the church. I was active in my local, district and state programs. I also became skilled in both reading and interpreting the scriptures before I finished high school, even though I did not profess to be saved.

In our congregation, being saved was a serious commitment, and you could not say that you were saved until you were ready to leave all that is worldly to live for God. We were pretty strict about the "all the way or no way at all" policy that was preached. Either we were saved or we were not. There were no gray areas. Although my background in scriptures and in church was a major part of my youth, I was eighteen and in college before I decided to accept Christ as my personal savior. When I did accept Christ, however, I accepted him in the only way I knew... I went all the way.

I became deeply involved in my spiritual journey. I sought God both day and night, believing that if I were to acknowledge God in all of my ways, as I had been taught, that my paths would be directed. I learned experientially about the power of prayer. I learned firsthand about the reality of God's love. I learned for myself to commit myself wholly to God who would, in turn, take care of all of my needs. I learned that God is greater than all of my problems. I learned to trust that God would make a way out of no way. I learned that if God was for me, God was more than the world against me. I learned to pray without ceasing, to fast evermore, and to always know on whom I could rely.

Not long after I became saved, my diligence became evident. I became president of our junior missionary board. I continued to direct our youth choir. I became respected in my church, in my school, and in my college and local communities for being a sincere Christian. Everyone knew that I was saved, that I believed in God and that I took this relationship very seriously.

By the time I came out, at thirty, I was deeply involved in the church. Of course my struggles with the church's teachings did not begin with my coming out as a lesbian. My concerns began with the development of a feminist consciousness while participating in a sexist faith. I was already feeling conflicted about having to fight each week against the sexist practices that were exercised and preached in the church. I also knew that my ministry would never be realized in a church that did not support women's ministries. Discovering that I was a lesbian, therefore, just compounded the concerns I had with my personal philosophy and the church's doctrines. Somehow I wanted to make it all work. I wanted to stay in the church, especially because I earnestly believed that I needed to fellowship in the way in which I was accustomed, but I also wanted to maintain all of my identities.

My Spirituality and Sexuality

Wherefore let him that thinketh he standeth take heed lest he fall. There hath no temptation taken you but such as is common to man: but God is faithful, who will not suffer you to be tempted above that ye are able; but will with the temptation also make a way to escape, that ye may be able to bear it. (1 Corinthians 10:12-13)

During the first few years after I came out to myself, I really believed that I had fallen to the place of no return. I was in major spiritual crisis and did not know how to get out of it. Not long after I came out to myself, I married the man I had been seeing for six years, even though we never really got along. I hid in my marriage and in the church because I was afraid that this new reality, my acceptance of my sexuality, would surely lead to condemnation. Even though my marriage publicly verified my heterosexuality and ensured validation from the church, I was extremely unhappy. My spirit was not at peace; my consciousness was in turmoil.

I tried to remain active in the church; I tried to be a model mother, but I did not rid myself of the pain with which I walked daily. I felt that I was unforgivable, that I had fallen to a place from which there was no redemption. How did this happen? I wondered. How could someone who was so in love with God, so in love with the church, someone who lived so dedicatedly to the Spirit fall so hard and so far? I beat myself up with the scripture that precedes this section, "let him that thinketh he standeth take heed lest he fall." I was certain that this warning applied to me. I thought I was strong, I thought I stood upright, and I didn't think that I'd fall, but I did. Hard. I could not get the next verse; I could not see the reference to God's faithfulness and to God's ability to make my burdens bearable. I was not happy in the church and I was not happy outside of the church. My marriage was bad, I was living a lie, and my spirit was not in tune with the Divine Spirit.

When I came out to my husband, he decided on aggressive action. He outed me to my church, to my job, in the community, to my family and to my colleagues. Because of this experience, I was forced to deal with all of these communities from who I'd hidden my sexuality. In many ways, he actually forced me to deal with my own sexuality.

My friends and the church community justified my fears. They reinforced those doctrines that were so much a part of my conscience. In their visits and in their phone conversations with me, they supported my husband, exacerbating the shame and anxieties I harbored. In fact, upon hearing of my suicide attempt, one of my friends reminded me that the demon of homosexuality is a five-star general in the devil's army, that this demon is so evil that he will, in fact, make you want to kill yourself. In the same conversation she also made it clear that she didn't want this spirit, or me, in her house.

At this point I was certain that I had fallen from grace. I felt that I had sinned against God, against my family, against my community and against my church. I was certain that God had turned a deaf ear to me, and that there was no redemption without repentance, nor any opportunity for repentance. I had the scripture to support this; I held the tools for my own destruction.

My difficult divorce, complicated by child custody and support battles, my loss of friends, church, and community support made it difficult to be connected to any of the support systems, including the church, on which I had relied. . Eventually I did leave the physical church because the fear, the shame, the guilt made it difficult for me to fellowship comfortably with those with whom I'd been fellowshipping. I left the church because I no longer belonged; I was no longer welcome. I left the church because I no longer had a place in the house of worship.

Nevertheless, more than any time before this experience, I needed a church. I needed a relationship with God. I needed a place for spiritual fellowship. I needed a place in which I could walk in the only way I knew to walk. I needed to try, even if I didn't feel it, to make things right with God. I could never quite leave the spiritual church, but the guilt, the shame, the fear mounted each time I sat in the pews in silence

Saved and Gay

There is therefore now no condemnation to them which are in Christ Jesus… The Spirit itself beareth witness with our spirit, that we are the children of God. (Romans 8:1, 6)

A ministerial friend told me that she had been teaching tolerance to women in her new women's ministry classes. Although I had been outed, I wasn't really out, and did not realize that she had already heard (as had many of my friends) that I was a lesbian. While she was not necessarily surprised, she figured that being outed in this way was difficult for me and decided to approach the topic with me gingerly. Creating a safe environment for me to come out to her was a major goal of hers; sharing some ideas that she had about her new ministry seemed to provide this environment. Implicit in her ideas for the women's ministry was the conscientious effort to teach straight women in her congregation to be open to the gay and lesbian members of her congregation. Imagine my surprise that this friend of mine, who had recently bailed out of the church to which I belonged, was being so progressive. She had left to become part of a ministry that supported women in the pulpit, and her work with the women's ministry of her church was one of the first assignments she was given. The discussion of the work she was doing in her church and with the women of her church opened the door for a conversation that would have an impact on the way I identify myself as a spiritual lesbian.

I was saved. She knew this. That's how all of my friends knew me. And I was gay. She had heard this. She also knew, more than those who were less familiar with me, that I'd have great conflict about this. In that regard, she knew me exceptionally well. I was, indeed, in major conflict about the contradictions that had become my life. That afternoon she allowed me to share my anxieties, my fears, my concerns and my disappointment with myself. I told her that I was afraid to even say that I was saved anymore. I lost the confidence I had about my salvation, fearing that I was not acceptable in God's sight, that my life no longer reflected the image of Christ, and that I was afraid that I'd become a reprobate. Even so, I wanted to make it clear that I had not stopped loving God. I had not stopped praying. I had not stopped believing that God is, God exists and that God is a rewarder of those who diligently seek Her. I certainly had not stopped seeking God, nor had I lost the desire to walk in the Spirit. I wanted to know that the years I dedicated to serving God would not be negated just because I realized that I was attracted to women.

As we talked, she refused to accept the self-sabotaging, doctrine-embedded language I used. She also affirmed any assertions I made about still being saved, still loving God, and reminded me that I did not have to give up on God to be a lesbian. I don't remember every word we shared on that afternoon, but I still remember her firm, calming voice as she said, "You're no reprobate." "Dorothy, I believe that you are still saved." "I believe that you are gay." "I believe you still have a commitment to God." "God still respects your commitment." I also remember the moment in which I visibly and audibly trembled as I said aloud, "I have decided that I am saved and I am gay. That's it... I'm saved and gay."

While this was a significant moment for me, it was only the beginning of what would be a consistent struggle. I could not quite stay in the church, but I could not stay away from the church. Whether I wanted to admit it or not, I was quite the church girl. One could tell by the way I walked, by the way I talked, and even by the way I dressed. I was marked, as my mother used to say. I was the daughter of a missionary and a preacher. Everyone could see that I didn't belong in the secular world. By the time I became an adult and by the time I discovered that I was a lesbian, it was clear in my community, on my job and in my church that I was really one of them—one of those church ladies. Yes, I was truly marked.

We were taught in our COGIC training lessons, that we should let our lives be a mirror that reflected the image of Christ. Others should see us and know that we are of Christ. This also meant that when others saw that our behavior did not mirror the image of Christ, we should be concerned. Of course this meant that when I had moments of diversion I walked in guilt and shame. My diversions would cast negative reflections on me, on my family, on my church and on the body of Christ. And, like young folks in the church, I had several periods of diversion. Accepting my sexuality, however, became one major diversion.

Coming out was not just about facing my family, friends, colleagues and my church community. This was hard enough, but the hardest part about coming out was facing my own self. I was in major conflict with the discovery of my sexuality. Honestly, I shocked my own self! I belonged to the grand old Church of God in Christ, one of the strongest, proudly open adversaries to homosexuals. We believed that homosexuality is wrong, that it is a sin, that it is an abomination against God and the church. We taught that homosexuals are lost souls, reprobates, who are unable to ascertain right from wrong. Our preachers added to the sincerity by which we taught against homosexuality by saving their strongest negative comments and their most vivid aspersions from the pulpit for those lessons against homosexuality. Our leaders often reminded us that homosexuality is the one thing about which God was consistent from the Old Testament to the New Testament. Often supported by the audience's overwhelmingly unanimous confirmation and snickering at tasteless homophobic jokes, very few members contested the ministers' condemnation of homosexuality. While I cringed at this language and behavior even before realizing I was a lesbian, and while I spent many Sunday afternoons in conversations with our church's Bishop about my concerns with his use of pejorative language and images to describe homosexuals, I remained a part of this congregation much longer than I should have. Thus, being a lesbian was contrary, not only to what our church taught, but to the doctrines that my early development, adult membership and participation clearly supported. If I were going to be a lesbian, my entire way of being and living would have to be transformed.

Obviously being saved and gay was not a popular declaration in my church. It wasn't even a popular declaration in the region in which I lived. My Bishop suggested that I stay in the church and remain quiet about my sexual orientation. I had the option to be closeted, and to deny the rumors about my sexuality so that I could remain active in the congregation. I did not want to give up on God. I didn't even want to give up on the church. And, once I stopped suppressing the questions I'd been asking about my sexuality for years, and once I started finding answers to those questions, I did not want to give up my new sexual identity. What made sense for me as I worked through the early stages of my relationship with my own sexuality was that I'd claim both my sexuality and my spirituality. I decided to accept that I am not less of a lesbian because I am spiritual, and I am not less spiritual because I am a lesbian. This was the beginning of my journey.

Same Spirit

Jesus Christ, the same yesterday, and today and forever. (Hebrews 13:8)

The most important realization in my development has been the realization that I am, in many ways, the same person I was twenty-seven years ago. I am the same person I was fifteen years ago. I have the same yearnings for the Spirit. And I know that God's Spirit is the same. This is the same Spirit that saved me, the same Spirit I sought when I prayed and fasted. It's the same Spirit that taught me to trust, to love, to believe. Being a lesbian does not obliterate all of this. Being a lesbian does not mean that I have forgotten my experience with God. Even when I want to think otherwise, even when I was not part of a church, even when I did not fellowship with others, even when I did not worship in a physical structure called a church, being a lesbian does not stop me from loving and serving God. Being spiritual, being Christian, being committed to God is still a major part of who I am.

It actually took years for me to regain comfort with my spirituality. As a child, I learned of the love of God, of the forgiveness of Christ, and of the promises of the Holy Spirit. As an adult, I learned that my spirit would continue to seek its connection and its fulfillment in the Holy Spirit as long as I love, regardless of my experiences.

My desire to live for God, to love God, to be close to God has not changed with the gender of my partner. It has not changed with the recognition of my sexuality. I learned to embrace the assertion I made years ago that I don't have to choose to either serve God or be a lesbian. I can, indeed, do both. I have faith that I can surrender, totally surrender, to God and still be a lesbian.

I've accepted that being a lesbian does not mean that I have forgotten my love for God. Being a lesbian does not mean that I have lost my desire to live and walk by and in the Spirit. I have such a strong foundation that I can never walk away from my own faith. I have faith that God will show me directions for my future. I have faith that God will lead me to my ministry.

I have decided that since Jesus Christ is the same yesterday, and today, and forever, and since God's Spirit is the same as it was when I first claimed salvation, then my commitment to God does not have to change or be altered because my sexual orientation has changed. I believe that God requires the same dedication I had before I realized that I am a lesbian. I also have a desire to offer the same level of dedication. I still believe that God is love, and she who dwells in love, dwells in God and God in her. I still believe that there is therefore now no condemnation to those who are in Christ Jesus, gay, lesbian, trans or bisexual, who walk not after the flesh but after the spirit.

Singing a New Song

Praise ye the Lord. Sing unto the Lord a new song, and his praise in the congregation of the saints. (Psalms 149:1)

In the lesbian/gay/bisexual/transgender community, there is a need, a serious need, for spiritual healing. There is a serious need for love, true love, to permeate our hearts and minds. There is a need for renewal, for forgiveness, for reconnections with God. This love and peace of God that surpasses all understanding needs to be taught, lived, walked and it needs to emanate from our very beings.

I have moved to several towns over the past ten years and have visited many churches. In my fellowship with gay and lesbian congregations, or open and affirming congregations, I recognize the same rhetoric that I heard in our straight churches. I am concerned that when we move from traditional congregations, we take some of those same oppressive behaviors with us. We bring the same messages of condemnation and retribution to a community that needs our love and healing. We mimic the behavior that fueled our own painful experiences in the church and in our new community. If we are preaching the love of God and the God of love, then we need to really offer God's love to everyone, regardless of who they are. We need to offer the hand that we wished we'd had.

I meet other people in the lesbian/gay/bisexual/trans-gender community who were raised in the church but who have also been cast out or who decided to leave their churches because of their sexuality. I've talked to many people who are turned off from the church and religion because they feel that they cannot live for God as openly gay people. I recognize the pain in their voices; I relate to the hunger in their spirits; I acknowledge the longing for fellowship that we've been raised to seek.

While some of us do not fellowship anywhere at all, and some stay in the traditional churches, some of us have found solace in open and affirming or predominately lesbian/gay/bisexual/transgender churches. I, too, have found solace in such a congregation. It is wonderful to be part of a congregation that accepts me into its community, regardless of who I am, of who I love, of where I have been. I love having the opportunity to hear affirmations from the pulpit and the pews of the things I used to embrace. There is something comfortably familiar about walking into a community of gays and lesbians who are singing songs from my childhood. However, we need to sing new songs.

I have recently found a church home and a place in which I can move forward in my ministry. As I continue to seek the right direction for myself, and as I have finally reached the place in my life of having integrated my spirituality and my sexuality, I also seek direction for ways to reach out to my community. I seek the opportunity to share with those who are still struggling with ways to acknowledge who they are spiritually and who they are sexually. I can safely say, finally, that I am comfortable with my affirmations. I do believe, from the depths of my soul, that we can be saved and gay. I have learned through a long and painful process that our spirits can be in tune with the Divine Spirit, and that this relationship is not contingent upon our sexuality. I am still learning, as I move to a new land, the land of open and affirming spirituality, that I must learn, sing and teach new songs.

I am ready to sing a new song.

It was a woman's voice, depth and nectar and melody. Instantly I recognized it as a voice I had always longed to hear. She spoke to me with such enveloping love, and such authority, that I was calmed as soon as I heard her words: Stop fighting the water. If you relax and stop resisting, the waves will carry you back to shore.

Testify: A Spiritual Trek to Irawo Omi
By Michaela Harrison

What y'all want me to say?

I am crouching before my ancestors, leaning into the altar to conjure the words for this essay. I have to bring it to them, ask for direction on how to verbalize the essence of this journey that has been my life as a lover of women who is saturated with Spirit. There is something translatable in this, I know, something that is accessible and useful through the writing—empowering, even, if I can communicate it properly. And because I really want to share the bountiful blessings with which I have been continuously gifted, spread them among my people like dandelions in a field, like a contagion of a different kind, I am putting my hands into this work, calling on the angels who guide and assist me without judgment to help me testify. They are telling me to speak directly to you, my sisters and brothers, and brothers-turned-sisters, and sisters-turned-brothers, who have managed to squeeze out from beneath the constrictions of compulsory heterosexuality and hold onto (at least the search for) your relationship with the Divine. To share a piece of my story, and hopefully a portion of my inspiration, with you.

More than any other setting, Nature has always been the environment that has given me the sense of being most peaceful and most spiritually uplifted, even as a small child. I could talk to animals and they would respond to me in ways I seemed to understand automatically; I could see the auras of the spirits that enlivened the trees and plants during my hours-long adventures in the woods. If there was water nearby, that was best of all: I would get so clear and so high that sometimes I would just slip into another zone, a space I can now identify as somewhere between meditation and trance. Oh, and the Moon and the stars! They have always been some of my very best friends. They would sing me through lonely, only-child nights while I gazed out my window, waiting for dreams and visions that would tell me of past or future events to which my parents, grandparents and other adults around me would listen with utter solemnity, heeding warnings and gleaning messages (and sometimes lottery numbers) from epiphanies that even I, very often, did not understand.

Truthfully, I can say that as far back as I can recollect, I have had both a firmly established relationship with the force I call Creator and a variety of nonphysical beings as well as an understanding that my affections for and connections to other females went beyond what was considered acceptable and "normal" by the larger society. On some level the two facts have always been linked in my mind, because even as a child I had an awareness of being attuned to higher energies, and that awareness prevented me from accepting the notion that I was bad or wrong for having the feelings that I did.

Three events during my early years stand out in my mind as having contributed directly to the path my spirituality and the development of my sexuality would take. Of course there were many, many, but for some reason these three incidents, which all took place before I was seven, left indelible impressions and had reverberating effects that I can trace through my journey into adulthood.

The first happened when I was four. I had accompanied my mother to a doctor's appointment and was entertained and kept company by one of the nurses in the office while my mother was with the doctor. It was already evening and no one else was in the waiting room, so I had the nurse's undivided attention, and I was soaking it up. By the time my mother's appointment was over, I had fallen in love, and she walked out of the examining room just in time to see me gaze adoringly at my new friend and tell her how beautiful she was. (And she really was fine, y'all; I remember.) My mother scolded me afterward, telling me that I wasn't supposed to say such things to women or girls. I was upset because I felt attacked, but I didn't believe her. I had an unshakable sense that what I felt was something good and sweet, even though I held onto what she told me, learning to be more clandestine about my attractions for the sake of self-protection. I could sense the relationship between those attractions and what I felt when I was outside climbing trees or feeding squirrels or smelling roses, certain that I was touching God, or when I was in church singing with the gospel choir, and the soul in the music spiraled to a peak that set the whole congregation to jumpin' up and shoutin' out, folks gettin' happy left and right. Somehow I knew that all those joyful feelings came from the same space inside of me. Still, I engraved what my mother told me onto my young mind. It was unbelievable to me, but also unforgettable.

The next event happened a year or two after the "nurse incident"; I was about five or six. I had the privilege and the blessing to spend every weekday with my grandmother until I was old enough to go to school, at which point I spent afternoons and evenings with her and my grandfather until my mother finished work at 11 p.m. One day we were sitting on her bed, and I pulled out some of the magazines that were tucked into an area in the headboard. They were some of those sexy magazines that used to abound in the '70s—*Pillow Talk* (anybody remember that?) was one of them, I believe. They had erotic stories in them and pictures of scantily clad women that I loved to look at. Well, up until that particular day, I had sneaked peeks at the pictures when my grandmother wasn't around, and read some of the stories, too. I'm not sure why I was feeling so bold just then, but when I started to pull the books out, she asked me in a sharp voice, "What do you want with those?" All of a sudden I remembered my mother's admonishment, and for a second I was afraid I would get in trouble for wanting to look at the pictures of women's bodies. But then I remembered that it was my grandmother I was talking to, my Bertie, with whom I had spent more time in my short life than anyone else. "I want to look at the pictures," I said matter-of-factly. I don't believe I'll ever forget what happened next. She gave me a look that was full of acknowledgment and understanding (even though there was resignation mixed into it), as if she knew exactly what was motivating my desire to look at the pictures and why it was so important that I not be made to feel bad about doing so. We held each other's eyes for long, silent moments, until she finally exhaled deeply and said, simply, "Okay." End of conversation.

We never discussed it, but I understood from that moment on that I had my grandmother's unconditional support, an understanding that became critical during my young adult years, when I was able to bring girlfriends over to introduce to my grandparents without ever having to worry about feeling uncomfortable or awkward. It wasn't until the summer I almost drowned (more on that later) that I came to a better understanding as to why my grandmother seemed so open and familiar with regard to my sexuality. Her sister and only sibling (with whom she had a rocky relationship) was an out lesbian. The troubles between them didn't have anything to do with my great-aunt's lesbianism from what I could discern through bits and pieces of family gossip, and when I connected with this long-lost, Philly-dwelling trailblazer as a late teen, the bond that we developed helped to mend some of the ill-feeling that had stewed between the two sisters for so long. My grandmother, I should add, continues to offer me the same encouragement and support from the other side of the veil of life as she did when she was in flesh-and-blood form.

Incident number three actually happened somewhere in between the first two. I must have been about to turn five, because shortly after I did, my father moved out and never lived with me and my mother again. I came into the living room one afternoon to find him sitting on one of our jumbo floor pillows with his legs crossed, eyes closed, and the tips of his fingers touching each other in the formation of a circle on either hand. I could tell that he was involved in something deep and serious, so I whispered the question, "Daddy, what are you doing?" He opened his eyes ever-so-slowly and replied, "Transcendental meditation." That sounded great to me, and after he gave me a brief synopsis of the calming, clarifying, enlightening effects it was supposed to have, I plopped down on a pillow next to him and started meditating too. It was the beginning of what has become a lifelong relationship with the practice, and even though I only managed to meditate sporadically after my father left, I continued my practice well after his had ended, giving it up sometimes for months before coming back to it, until eventually, in my twenties, I was able to make it a part of my daily ritual. Just in time for it to help me balance and heal from some of the raw and overwhelming emotions that accompanied the process of coming out as a lesbian.

During those early years, I attended church every Sunday with my mother and several members of my family. The official denomination was Southern Baptist, and if you happened to pass by the building while a Sunday service was in session, you could almost see it rocking and bouncing to the gospel sounds. Church was always more about the music and the energy in the air than anything else for me. I often felt offended by the guttural and seemingly angry sermons given by the preacher, and I started reading the Bible when I was seven to find out what it was really all about. I only got through Genesis, some of Psalms and all the Gospels, but I read enough to discover that the words spoke to me in a different way, that I could take some of it (the parts that resonated within me, like loving the Creator with all your heart and mind and your neighbor as yourself, and Jesus laying hands on folks to heal them) and leave some of it (the parts that just didn't jibe, like God being so damn angry and wrathful all the time and Eve coming from Adam's rib cage and causing the whole mess with Eden). When we moved further out from Chocolate City and stopped going to church regularly (I was eleven), all I missed about it, besides gathering with family and friends from the congregation, was singing with the choir.

Adolescence brought all the customary challenges plus the added burden of trying to find a space where I could fit in with my psychic gifts and my crushes on girls and women in tow. It didn't happen. I always felt like a misfit, I never had a boyfriend, and I learned that many people, especially adults, do not appreciate being seen into and through. There were some boys I liked, but they were usually unavailable, and the truth is I never really trusted most of them. I couldn't help getting various types of information about people without having it told to me: I could just feel and see things, the way I always had, and that ability grew more prominent as I got older, though I struggled with the lack of guidance on how to direct it and shape it to serve me in the best possible way. Throughout junior high and high school I read books on all types of New Age spirituality, Eastern religions and Native American spiritual tradition, to which I had always felt drawn because of my Cherokee ancestry. While I managed to have plenty of fun, do well in school, be involved in a range of extracurricular activities, make some wonderful friends who continue to be near and dear to me and win the coveted status of one of the "popular" girls, I was depressed a lot of the time, alienated and unfulfilled. I loved my mother dearly and respected her tremendously, but did not feel that I could talk openly with her about the things that weighed so heavily on my heart. Which is why, that summer I nearly drowned, there was a part of me that believed I wanted to die.

Family reunions in North Carolina had been the height of the past several summers, and by the time I was twenty I had gotten familiar with the country terrain and the coastal environment that made up my maternal grandparents' homeland. We had the usual gathering on the beach that year, and I waded out into the water alone, away from the tables behind the dunes where the loud festivities were going down. There was something about the ocean that I could never describe, something so powerfully moving about being in its presence that made me feel I was born to be near that water, if not in it. And as a quadruple

Pisces, in it is probably the more appropriate term for me to use.

I wasn't a great swimmer but I felt comfortable in the water as long as my feet touched the bottom. Walking further out into that liquid joy, I could feel all my worries being cleansed away, and I was conscious of heading toward what I later realized was a sandbar about twenty feet out from where I had already waded up to my chest. Starting to get that dreamy feeling that always came over me in and near water. Letting myself forget about everything. Dissolving into the water until, from one breath to the next, air was replaced by sea in my nostrils, there was no longer sand under my feet, and what had been a tranquil communion with the ocean had become my closest encounter with death. And I did everything someone who's drowning is not supposed to do: I flailed my arms and struggled against the current, wasting my energy in the face of an indomitable force. There was no one near me; if I'd had the breath to call out for help no one would have heard. Swallowing more salty fluid by the second, seeing less sky, under, under...

Really, I was about to surrender; I was tired. Then it occurred to me that even though I was drowning, it wasn't my time to go yet. Somehow I just knew it, with a certainty that wouldn't budge, despite the situation I was in. Then my life changed, from one instant to the next. Right when I was about to suck in what felt like had to be (but could not be) my last breath, a voice spoke to me. It was physically audible, but not from a source I could pinpoint. It came from inside my head, from inside the sea, from the air that was less and less accessible to me. It was a woman's voice, depth and nectar and melody. Instantly I recognized it as a voice I had always longed to hear. She spoke to me with such enveloping love, and such authority, that I was calmed as soon as I heard her words: *Stop fighting the water. If you relax and stop resisting, the waves will carry you back to shore.* There was no thought involved. The tension immediately drained from my body, and I was drifting, effortlessly, merrily, back toward the sand. What a gentle journey that was, floating in the comforting echo of that voice to safety.

When I made it onto the beach, I knew I was transformed. I couldn't speak about it, and I couldn't identify exactly the ways in which I had been altered, but I knew that I had experienced something that would mark me forever, something that carried a lesson that was much more profound than a formula to keep from drowning. I told a few cousins that I had almost gotten carried under, but I said nothing about the voice to anyone for a long time.

The following year I went on study abroad in East Africa for a semester. While I was there, I experienced manifestations of magic and divine wonder that convinced me that the very ground was enchanted. I came to understand that it was so because most of the people there had maintained their openness to the workings of Spirit in a way that allowed for a much more free-flowing interaction between the Dreamtime and Earth time. I had repeated encounters with traditional healers and medicine people, and the undeniable sensation that I was reconnecting to something so precious and valuable that, once I really understood its relevance and meaning, I would never let go.

My only experience of traditional forms of African spirituality up to that point had been through the wretchedly biased and malignant images pumped out by Hollywood and brief mentions in a few novels I had read. There was a part of me that always knew I was connected to them, and that my grandmother was connected to them, since my father had told me on several occasions how she had gone down to North Carolina to have "roots worked on him" after he and my mother separated (which I never doubted). When that voice that had saved my life at the beach spoke to me again, in a one-room library on a coffee plantation outside Nairobi, though, I was sure that I was being called, and that the supplications for guidance along my spiritual path that I had been pouring out to the heavens were finally being answered.

That book seemed to jump off the shelf at me. It was on African spiritual traditions that had survived in the Americas—a subject about which I knew next to nothing. I sat down with it in the solitude of the dusty library, opening it to a page somewhere in the middle, and my eyes fell onto an image that hypnotized me. It was a photograph of a young woman undergoing initiation for her orisha in Candomble in Bahia, Brazil. That was the gist of the caption. I swore after coming back the States that I remembered the book as Robert Ferris Thompson's *Flash of the Spirit,* but I have re-read it and combed it repeatedly for the photograph I saw that day and have been unable to find it. Maybe it was another book. Brazil was a mysterious land to me; I only knew it had Black people and samba and Carnival. But when I looked at that picture, I was overcome with emotion, filled with a longing like nostalgia that was so deep it ached, and I started to cry, to weep without inhibition. I had no idea why I was crying, until the voice spoke to me (my face covered with a different kind of salt water this time), saying *You have to go there. And do that.* Same soothing timbre, same lovingly authoritative tone. There was no question in my mind that I would have to go, but why? I closed the book again and opened to a different page. This one had a description of the orisha Yemonja, the Yoruba spirit of maternal nurturing and abundance, healing and wisdom. Yeye omo oja—the mother of the children of the fish. Honored widely in Brazil as the Queen of the Sea. I inhaled understanding that spread warmth throughout my body. I had a name for the voice that spoke to me. I had a place in a tradition as old as time. I had to get to Bahia.

My first journey to Brazil didn't happen until two and a half years after I returned from Kenya, but I'd had my sights set on it since that day in the library. I continued to read about Yoruba-based spiritual traditions, and it all made so much sense to me: reverence for ancestors, interaction with the spiritual beings animating the forces of Nature, cleansing and healing with herbs, dancing and singing praises to the rhythm of drums, sanctifying food through sacrifice before consuming it, possession by divine entities. And goddesses! And priestesses! Women who were spiritually empowered and respected as leaders. Yes.

As for how I finally made it to Bahia and found myself fully embraced by one of the largest and oldest Candomble communities in Brazil, I can only say that there were several angels placed in my path who opened the way and made it possible for me to get to that place that immediately felt like home. I actually looked like the people in my spiritual house, most of whom were related to each other in some way. And they recognized me, and received me as a family member from the first day.

Speaking of family... I was amazed to find that there were so many gay men and lesbians, not only in that particular house, but in most of the *terreiros* (spiritual houses) I visited. In my *terreiro,* the numbers included several of the highest-ranking and most respected elders in the community. It was the first time in my life I had been around people who expressed their sexual difference openly and without shame in a spiritual setting. I felt more comfortable and more affirmed than I had ever felt in any religious context, though that is not to say there were no problems. There were occasional snide remarks about various individuals' sexuality. There was homophobia among the usual suspects—those people hovering so close to the verge of jumping into bed with someone of their own gender that it made them vehemently resistant to anything that even suggested such a lifestyle. But there was never a denial of anyone's spiritual worth, or of their contribution to the community as a whole, based on their sexuality, of which I was made aware.

By the time I went through the first phase of initiation (called *assentamento,* or "seating") in Candomble, I was completely comfortable with the idea of putting my life into the hands of my godmother and the women who would take responsibility for every aspect of my existence during the seven days I was *recolhida* ("recoiled," in isolation). My godmother, a dark, graceful Amazon (no, not from the rain forest), performed my initiation and presided over my care with such affectionate concern and gentle consideration that I knew there was some very special purpose attached to my embarkation on this road of ancient mysteries. In the solitude and silence of that period, interrupted only by my godsisters and my godmother two or three times a day, I came into a new relationship with myself as a spiritual being, with the orisha whose voice had carried me over the waters of the Atlantic in more ways than one, with the One I call Creator, with my ancestors and guides, with time, with different levels and dimensions of reality, with patience and with peace.

When I emerged from that room that had become a womb, I was a different woman. Yemonja had transformed me twice, and has continued to do so since then. I have been back to Brazil four times, and am preparing to take another trip, moving ever closer to the day when I will be fully initiated as a child of Yemonja. The journey, so far, has been soaked with as many challenges and trials as it has been packed with miracles and magic. In the years since my *assentamento,* I have developed a much keener control over my psychic abilities; I can dream and get guidance about a topic or a person at will and have a much clearer interpretive grasp of the information that comes to me involuntarily; I can direct and receive telepathic messages with increasing accuracy; I am better able to direct the healing energy through my hands into other people. I honestly believe that every person is gifted with such abilities, and that a sincere and devoted spiritual practice will bring those gifts to the fore in ways that are useful and productive.

Other things happened after my initiation. I began to look upon my love for women not only as something that wasn't sinful, but as something that was blessed. I saw it as an indication of my capacity to experience and express a spectrum of love and affection and intimacy that was vaster than what so many people would ever allow themselves the freedom of knowing. Everyone who completes this initiation receives a new name, a Yoruba name that is chosen by the godmother or godfather to reflect the individual spiritual attributes of the initiate. Even now, years after hearing mine for the first time, I smile when I think of it, because it bears such lovely witness to both the heights and the depths of my passion for creation.

Now, I don't want to make it sound like I have it all worked out. Such a long way I have yet to go on this spiritual trek, but I cherish every footfall. The women still drive me crazy, and I still get weighed down by the woes of the world at times. I envision a day when I will have evolved to the point when even my prayers and offerings and rituals will be unnecessary; I will be such an embodiment of Love and Grace that I will no longer need to do anything but rise up each morning and give thanks for Life and my fantastic voyage through it, trusting that with each breath I am acting in attunement with my divine purpose, manifesting my spiritual and creative potential with every action. Ever the dreamer. In the meantime, though, I do my voodoo, and it works. I can testify.

Oh, what was the name, you wanted to know? Irawo Omi: Star of the Water.

I want to shine like that forever...

I believe that if we listen and are open to hear, there are divine voices urging us to action at every moment of our lives. … To hear the voices (call it God, a guardian angel, the spirits of those passed on) we must believe that they are real to us, and to listen to them we must have faith in the universe's intentions and in our own ability to know the truth in our bones.

The Simple Truth
By G. Winston James

I asked myself how to come to terms with my sexuality and spirituality for years before I realized that the question was moot. I stopped attending Christian services not because of anti-gay rhetoric, but because in general such formal, staid environments did not speak to me. I realized later in life that I had always found God (my higher power) in quiet places in nature and in occult objects such as mirrors and runes—objects that facilitated my own inner looking. What I came to realize was that my desire for men was everywhere in me that I looked. My sexuality was inextricably tied to who I was, yet neither my plants, my pets nor the sky seemed to care. My internal conflict came from wanting to be what other people said I should be, rather than accepting who I was. I finally realized that God had made the terms of my sexuality and spirituality, and that if I could accept the challenges of that simplicity, I might work wonders in the service of truth.

As I sit down to write this essay, I find the years of my life rushing through my mind. I can honestly say that I have never been what most people would consider "normal." As a toddler in Jamaica, my mother tells me that I used to run around with a Bible trying to preach to people. When I was four or five, I had erections that I would, hands free, make bounce up and down.

Thinking I was the only one, I told everyone in my family that I was "magic," though I never told them how I had arrived at that conclusion. During my childhood, I believed I had the power to command the clouds to cover the sun, and to affect other people with the energy of my mind. In my pre-teens, fascinated with demons and black magic, I attempted on several occasions to summon not just any demon, but Satan himself. I wanted to talk with Lucifer about God since my prayers had always seemed to go unanswered.

At the same time, I became captivated by animals, plants, insects and earth. In urban Paterson, N.J., I was the black child who took up bird watching. I am sure that I am one of only a small percentage of Patersonians to have noticed our city's woodpeckers and finches; one of few children to have sat in the midst of husking sparrows, having gained their trust. Even now, I can feel tears rising in my eyes as I remember lying under the picnic table in our back yard during a storm, with a waterlogged sparrow as my company.

I so loved life. I would wake at dawn to watch the bees stir among the flowers. Capture and feed praying mantises and large spiders. As a paperboy, I took cuttings from neighbors' plants in the early morning, rooted them and planted my own gardens. I found stray cats and dogs. Sat with my neighbor's German shepherd Sheba and Afghan hound Brandy on separate occasions as they delivered and licked clean their litters. I would visit their owners' yard when they were not at home and sit with Sarge, their Doberman pinscher. Pet him. I was comfortable with those animals. Unafraid.

If nothing else, though, I was and am honest. I must admit, therefore, to pinning some of those bees to the flowers with dissecting pins. To vivisecting worms from our garden. To pitting mantises against one another and relishing watching one devour the other. I must confess to hurling knives at my brother and to starting numerous fires. I must concede that before I was seven, there was a time when I visited funeral homes regularly to view the dead on display. I must acknowledge my impetuousness and overwhelming curiosity. I must register the fear I have always had about my potential for detachment, cruelty and obsession. I must admit that I rely on the candor of mirrors and friends, and the truthfulness of my poetry to allow me to see the darkness and the light of my soul.

These, though, were the early years of my life. Years when I began to learn how to exist comfortably at various points between the extremes of what our society deems as "right and wrong." I think of these youthful times and remember a common thread running through all of those wondrous moments: I was almost always alone and reliant on voices that did not speak in any conventional sense, but kept me company all the same.

"But what does all this have to do with spirituality?" some might ask. I am comfortable, though, in knowing that some who will read this already know that the times and experiences I have recounted have everything to do with grounding myself in the physical world and struggling to find my place in the Universe. These incidents concern Yin-Yang, good and evil, countless other cosmic dualities and the continua that exist between such poles, and those of birth and death.

For me "spirituality" is the understanding of how I am connected to all things—seen and unseen. It is the acceptance of my own impurity, imperfection: I am neither all good nor totally evil. Spirituality is learning that in fact such words have little to no meaning to "God." Spirituality is the acknowledgment that I am on a journey, along which I will stumble. I am not the master of the path onto which I was born, but I choose the acts and energies that I embrace. For me, spirituality is undergirded by the acceptance of responsibility for my own actions and inaction. The first call of Spirit (as with any seed that is planted) is to grow. The charges that follow are to learn, to accept the things we come to know, to embrace the truth, to love and finally to leave the god in us behind (reverberating endlessly) when we are gone.

I believe that honesty and acceptance of our duality, divinity and connectedness to all things are required for us to be strong and to transcend the noise that is everyday life. As sad as my solitude has made me at times over my thirty-eight years, I recognize that my isolation brought me more closely in touch with my own inner workings, the simplicity of the Universe, the six charges that I mention above, and the one "truth" that shields and fortifies my soul today: "In the grand scheme of things, nothing that happens here matters."

While that may sound pessimistic, that is far from my intention. It is to say that my goal, following the charges that I have been given by Spirit, is to "be in the world, but not of the world." To not limit myself to the humanity-imposed demarcations of the world. To not allow the responses that come along with human form—pain, pleasure, anger, sadness, joy, FEAR—to constrain me in the pursuit of my cosmic intentions. To recognize that others—racists, homophobes, community and family members, etc.—may assail me, but "my feet rest in the palms of God," therefore, none of them can truly harm me.

Though I do not consider myself a Christian, I was raised in the Baptist church (including Sunday School) and attended Catholic high school. By and large—and sometimes against my will—my references and spiritual vocabulary stem from my education in these institutions. While I am willing to discard much that I experienced in these establishments, certain things have stuck with me over time. The most important of those is the notion of the "still small voice." I believe that our televisions, radios, bars and streets are too loud, and that many of us have forgotten how to listen to the voices that are speaking to us, guiding us, empowering us, consoling us.

I remember being at a particularly low place in my life just a few years ago. I felt as if I was on the verge of losing "everything." I was crying all of the time, and wanted to give up on life. One day as I exited the train station near my home I passed two elderly women who were speaking to one another. Just as I transited within earshot one said to the other, "No. God never gives you more than you can handle." As a man who had been hit by a car as a child and had gotten up unscathed, I knew instantly that message was for me. To remind me that adversity can destroy us or it can strengthen and educate us. It can teach us how better to walk down and cross the road tomorrow. The choice was mine. As a gospel song that speaks to my heart recounts, I had fallen down, but I chose in that moment, due largely to that still small voice that cares for me (and that oftentimes speaks through others), to get up.

I believe that if we listen and are open to hear, there are divine voices urging us to action at every moment of our lives. Our challenge here relates to the second thing that has stuck with me since Catholic high school: the difference between the words "belief" and "knowledge." Ultimately, one requires faith, where the other does not. I regard the faith and trust that coincide with belief as compulsory to each of our inheritance of our spiritual power. To hear the voices (call it God, a guardian angel, the spirits of those passed on) we must *believe* that they are real to us, and to listen to them we must have faith in the Universe's intentions and in our own ability to know the truth in our bones.

I learned very early to hear the voices. As a writer, I believe I was born susceptible to channeling them. I have not always, however, been willing to listen and to act. I am still growing into that submission.

The third thing that has remained with me is something I learned in high school English class. My teacher was very precise and cared a great deal for the meanings and nuances between "synonymous" words. The difference between "will" and "shall" for instance, is striking, and speaks not only to inevitability, but also to intention. The word on this particular day, though, was "meticulous," whose definition is "extremely careful and precise." Our teacher, however, pointed out that the root of the word is from the Latin "metus," meaning "fear." From that day on, I thought about how fear can drive us (to become too extremely careful—too in need of precision), can cause us to limit ourselves and others.

I thought about how classmates in high school had on numerous occasions told me that I walked as if I were conceited, because my gait was long and slow, and my head held high. I talked as if I were white, they said, because of my diction and grammar. Happily, though, I was already an outsider and was able to resist the fear of being ostracized that could have caused me to hide what light I had under a bushel. I resisted the fear that might have caused me to develop and accomplish far below my potential. I resisted the fear that impelled me to become a dull mirror of God.

I have not, however, been immune to fear. At nearly forty, I am still somewhat afraid to be beautiful, worrying what others might think if I allowed myself to truly shine. I am sometimes paralyzed by fear of making mistakes publicly. I am afraid of speaking my mind for fear of hurting other people's feelings. I am afraid to let the truth live on my skin, bound off my tongue and radiate in my eyes. I am reluctant to be powerful.

Even in this essay, I have been hesitant to admit that I still believe I possess some of the abilities I manifested as a child. I have been reluctant to call myself a healer, shaman, witch, a king. I have been disinclined to say that the gift and promise of sex pulsates in my every fiber like electricity, and that I am coming to own that energy and to say that in itself it is good. I have been averse to saying that I and others I know are absolutely brimming with power, and that I know if we joined hands in sacred spaces, opened ourselves and focused in communion with one another we could change our world.

It is the spectre of fear that makes the truth that *"nothing that happens here matters"* and my belief that *"no one can truly harm me"* so important to me. Those words are mantras that I recite when I risk myself in the service of the Universe. Every day I must remind myself of my charges to grow, learn, accept, embrace, love and give back to humanity. At the same time I continually remind myself that I am not important. That, in fact, I do not know of anyone who is important. At least not by him- or herself. I must recall daily that pain ends. That hurts heal. And that I am made of a higher order, and that doubtless I (the transcendent "I am" energy that is me) will endure. The sun will rise regardless of what my neighbors say. No person's judgment matters but my own and the voice that is in me telling me what is right, what is noble, what is worthy. I know that no man can take from me those things with which the Universe has endowed me. Many people believe they can, but I know from my walks in the park, my times in the garden and sitting at the ocean, that their confidence is illusion. I am learning to live my life believing that no matter what happens, that everything is in divine order.

I believe that no single thing that happens here matters—in much the same way as no single leaf on a tree is pivotal—but that the totality of our lives is a priceless treasure that we collect daily and take with us into the next life—be it earthly or ethereal. Our challenge is to live lives rich in learning, high on daring and low on fear and judgment. I try not to live my life concerned with morality and notions of sin. I measure "good" and "bad" based on an evaluation of the possible consequences of my actions. Rather than good or bad, in fact, the true poles in my determination of right action are "beneficial" and "harmful." My connectedness to nature and the Universe suggests that there are a host of stakeholders to be considered in the instant of my decision-making. My spirituality says that it is acceptable to make bad decisions, but that I must ask forgiveness of those I have wronged, and I must accept responsibility for the repercussions of my actions.

I was indoctrinated in the Christian faith and have been curious about Islam and Buddhism. I have investigated the Yoruba tradition and have dabbled in all manner of the occult. I do not reside today in any religion, but continue to be drawn toward the magical and the arcane. Instead of following the religions I have experienced and studied, I have taken what is useful from them and I carry their knowledge into the natural spaces in which I "worship." When the voices tell me to go the water, I go. When they tell me to kneel down, I kneel. When they tell me to be silent, I am still. My sexuality matters no more to the lake than it does to the birds. When I meditate on it, I feel in my heart that it is good. That I am all right. The many aspects of myself are all true. In this way, I know that my sexuality sits well with my God, a higher order under which the words "mistake" and "abomination" do not apply.

All things are right in creation. My sexuality is right in creation. Everything is always in divine order, whether I, or others, like it or not. It is in learning to feel the bigger picture and our part in it that we celebrate ourselves in communion with this divine order. I have learned to worry very little about what others have to say, and am striving to listen and to grow ever closer to my true self and to God.

The crux of the matter is that we are the invisible soldiers. Drafted souls caught in the crossfire of a select human condition. A tumultuous battle for the merit of our lives, against the dogmatic practice and preaching of those who have damned us, adversaries who would render us silent, forsaken and purposefully displaced. …According to circumstantial evidence, we are the world's delicious nightmare. This *is our dilemma.*

A Place at the Altar

By Lynwoodt Jenkins

"I'm mad at God!" whispered Darryl, my best friend, who is black, gay *and* Christian. Darryl's anger erupted one afternoon upon leaving church after having sat quietly deteriorating in the pew as the minister sermonized his disgust for the (alleged) evilness of homosexuality. Darryl's words, profound and shockingly simple, reverberated to rattle in his throat, and my ears. Jumping to his feet, as if to balance his fury and brave whatever backlash that divine power would inflict, he challenged consequence. He was desperate. He had followed The Word, according to instruction. He made no errors. Calculated, by faith, no possibilities of failure. Then consoled himself into believing that abstinence, fasting and tithing would prove a self-inflicted homo-exorcism. But it didn't work. There was no healing. There was no laying of hands. No miracles were received. Or examples to follow. Nor had there been an angelic visit expressing the significance of his fate. Most of all, there was no peace. Bereft of hope, he sobbed. The encumbering cognition of his fate left him wounded, exhausted, inextricably damaged. He had been baptized in his own tears. He was a fray in the fabric of a racist and homophobic society.

Once home, Darryl argued that he didn't request or choose

his sexuality. He couldn't understand why God had allowed him to be cursed. Empathetic, I was familiar with his particular anguish all too well. He was a kindred spirit who struggled with his sexuality, as opposed to his spirituality. But there was nothing that I could've done. What he required I could not provide. It would've been arrogant to assume that an embrace would protect him. It would've been malicious to suggest that it was all an accident of nature as well as condescending to offer sympathetic words of condolence. The depth of his suffering deserved better accolades for his endurance. He had reached a crossroads of sorts, a reckoning and coming to terms with himself. That crucial and definitive hour in which one either stands valiant in fight or lays waste refusing to take arms. There is no middle ground. Sublime, it is the ultimate accountability in which we, as black gay men, must claim *a place at the altar.*

The crux of the matter is that we are the invisible soldiers. Drafted souls caught in the crossfire of a select human condition. A tumultuous battle for the merit of our lives, against the dogmatic practice and preaching of those who have damned us, adversaries who would render us silent, forsaken and purposefully displaced.

The proverbial "black sheep" of the congregational flock. Demon savants. Tolerated *only* when measured by our octave range, athletic prowess, and/or our general public-pleasing abilities. Men who, in the light of day, are looked upon in disdain, while in the cloaking darkness of night are desired, hunted and insulted by dead presidents in exchange for illicit favors. According to circumstantial evidence, we are the world's delicious nightmare. *This* is our dilemma.

However, we must resolve otherwise. There are no black knights in shining armor preparing for our rescues. Science cannot, and will not, produce a heterosexual antidote for us to swallow. Neither will we rise from prayer miraculously changed. Inevitably, what we must do is accept ourselves, absolute. Deliberately and reverently embracing our individual and collective exclusivity. Fully persuaded that our souls are not to be surrendered. Nor bargained. Proving greater than festering silence. More powerful than caging fear. Renewed as indestructible paragons. Warriors of the new millennium. *This* is our lot. Our duty. And, without regret, our beauty.

Therefore, for those who remain steadfast against us, perhaps a full examination of what the Bible teaches is in order. According to text, it supports the tolerance of slavery. It also supports the second-class citizenship of women. These are references that are overlooked. Or they are made malleable to accommodate a progressive society. Seemingly absurd, but accurate in context, for those who think homosexuality is a sin and that no sin is greater or lesser than the other. With gluttony reigning as one of the seven deadliest sins, why are there no blasting and derogatory sermons for the obese? What purgatory awaits the portly members of the tabernacle? Is there no fire and brimstone for them? These factors, multiplied by the dichotomy of clandestine gay clergy members, need to be considered prior to unequivocally dismissing the children of God.

Instead, understand that whether we are black, white, gay, straight, male, female or otherwise, we are divinely created. Our only task is to find the God within us.

Finally, my brothers, having done this purgative and needful thing, weep no more. Wipe clean the evidence of tears. Surely, given the complexity of life, that "crucial and definitive hour" is but a rite of passage toward manhood. So take heed. Load your mindful weapons, guard your newfound posts, then plant your feet on salvaged ground, and fight!

Editors' note: Lynwoodt Jenkins' "A Place at the Altar" was initially published in Fighting Words: Personal Essays by Black Gay Men *(Charles Michael Smith, ed., 1999). Here is Jenkins' update on that essay.*

A Letter from the Altar

By Lynwoodt Jenkins

I was, at first, impressed with the idea and action of fighting against what I believed to be immutabilities that challenged my sexual and spiritual resolutions. I not only prepared efficiently for that war, but also purposefully and precariously provoked the first strike. I was angry because I was hurt. I was hurt because I was lonely. I was lonely because of occasional, conditioned shame— and because of all of it, I wanted to punish others. The truth, however, was that what I desired, needed most was to have enough courage to love and be loved.

As fear would have it, the idea of simply honoring the love within me seemed like such a trite novelty that my ego immediately rejected the available healing. This is exactly what egos do: separate you from self. So, it was not surprising that I rationalized my need to love and be loved as a weakness that needed to be polarized, and plucked out at the root. Like any artful masochist, I imagined that working every day, maintaining my health and practicing my passions proved that I had self-worth. But I was wrong. In my quest to become immune to the world, I jumped from job to job; my health wavered from mild colds to hypertension; and I hadn't written a poem, completed a play, or finished the novel I'd begun. In no time at all, I found myself repeating the cycle of anger, hurtfulness and loneliness.

After having tried all else to end the cycle, I fell to my knees in prayer. With a wounded heart I prayed until my prayer was no longer distinguishable to human understanding. It became more of a soulful language; a cosmic vibration that emanated from deep within to overcome my circumstances. I wanted answers. I needed healing, and all that I had left was hope.

Fortunately, Love showed me that I didn't have to fight at all. I didn't have to lock, load or wield a weapon. I merely had to surrender. I had to systematically relinquish negative external and internal perceptions, and I forgave myself and others in that process. I gave up the homo-ghost, if you will. Which is to say that, yes, I am a black, same-gender-loving man, but I am not at war with or bound by my sexuality. My innate proclivity for other men is not in conflict with my peace of mind or my life's purpose. There is only love and the lack of it. In loving myself more efficiently, I am more stable financially, writing again, and even find myself approached romantically more often by others. Yes, black men do blush.

In essence, when you accept yourself as a *divine design,* you become more valuable, creative and as authentically beautiful as you ought to be!

Love and Healing,
Lynwoodt

You, Daniel, will have few lovers. You will joke that you are celibate, a traveler in the desert, but there is more to the story… Days without water blend into themselves. Better, you will say, to make a dream of water, than to bear a mouthful of sand.

the book of daniel

By Daniel Alexander Jones

7.
Testimony of a flock of ravens,
fourteen in number:

When you first see Daniel, you notice right away that he has only just put his feet on the Earth. There is still something that wants to lift. A blue tinge at the edge of his laughter. A sudden, crashing wave of thought pulls his gaze inward. The bubbles of music that lace his speech, the faces he sketches in the corners of napkins, the secrets he tells you about yourself, the secrets he remembers from next week.

Art, you see, is Daniel's spiritual practice. Art soothes and saves his soul. Art is his reason for staying; it is his place in the world. Making art is the holiest of all undertakings; Daniel's long fingers and deep breaths engage the same elements and forces that comprise and shape the universe. When he writes, performs, directs, paints or composes he burns hot from the inside out; he participates in creation with a single-minded approach. Nothing seems more important. See him then. He is never more himself than when he is making art. He is completely free of all expectation and judgment. Man? Woman? Black? White? Straight? Gay? Flesh? Spirit? He is more than all of these appellations. He practices freedom every time he makes a new world.

Recollection of the house named
José translated by a black cat:

See here? His love affair with art begins when he is a child. *See here?* In the undressed rooms of the bird mother and the lion father. In this small yellow house on the short street. There he is, silver brown eyes and giggles. The bird mother plays records and dances with the lion father. Miriam Makeba. Odetta. José Feliciano, after whom they christen me (this house) José. Daniel watches the music tie his parents together. Daniel hears this house creak side to side in time. *See here?* Daniel draws lines and circles, records this vision of together in red crayon, on the yawning floor, of the yellow house on the short street. Magic, he will learn early on, is not out of reach. He will dream the most fantastic pictures, dream the most elated melodies, dream the most hilarious stories and then with a brush, a tape recorder or an old shirt he will tease them out from the ether. He will make entire worlds appear. He will rush to share them. He will trip and fall. He will stand up. He will rush again. To share them.

One day, the lion father and the bird mother will snap a photograph of their first son, the dreamer, standing next to a sunflower. When, later, Daniel sees the photograph fall from a brown book, he will hold it in his hands and cry, trying to remember which of the two figures is him. Still later, in reference to the same picture, Daniel's brother, the prophet, will explain a secret about the nature of time and space, showing him that in fact there is no difference between the two figures at all.

skin.
Thoughts extracted from residual electrons clinging to soundwaves, 1993:

DANIEL.

God's Hour. Graduate School. Providence. I am visiting several friends who are staying in a professor's house while he is on leave. One of the other visitors is Elias, a homeless man with stark white dreadlocks, who frequently shares lyrical, off-the-cuff sermons about organic vegetables, astral travel and the value of drinking tea. Coltrane's *Meditations* are soaking the rugs, everyone else has drifted off, one friend sighs in his sleep and Elias's words play off Trane's staccato reachings, weaving a mantra of sorts. Although I am already awake, I suddenly wake up and feel myself heighten. The volume on my senses turns upward from 1 to 10 in seconds. Everything around me begins to tilt and move away: Elias... my friends' sleeping forms... the low cushions and brightly colored fabric on the walls. Swiftly. Smoothly. With the surety of birds in flight. The particles of the air seem to dance and spark off to someplace else. Through a sudden set of refractions, my eyesight instantly becomes fully dimensional. The only way I can describe what I see? It is as though I speed in an instant to the far edge of the universe and look back upon a massive breathing form. Space and stars coalesce to form glistening skin, which stretches and lifts as I hear, feel, smell the body, the universe breathing. Our simultaneous exhale brings me back into the room—quicker than a rubber band snapping back from full extension—to a point before I'd "left." I listen as Elias says what I know he will say, as my friend sighs where I know he will sigh and I smile uncontrollably. I stand up, then sit back down. Whether the journey has been without, within or both, I feel, unquestionably, that a veil has been momentarily lifted. The Universe has winked at me, and I appreciate its sense of humor.

6.

Fragments believed to be part of an unfinished entrance questionnaire. Discovered underneath Daniel's pillow. Three questions were found in one small pile. Three answers in another:

Q: Can you remember the sensation of birth?

Q: Define the following words: shame, resistance, tree, October, joy.

Q: What is an appropriate color to wear to weddings?

A: A working example of freedom is perhaps the ultimate gift, of the many spiritual blessings my immediate family has given me. My parents married in the fall of 1968, shortly after the freedom movement suffered two horrifying body blows in the form of the assassinations of Martin Luther King, Jr. and Bobby Kennedy. My parents were not naive. You couldn't have been in the fall of 1968, with forces of rage, war and quantum change spiraling through their world. They demonstrated their personal courage by walking down the aisle together, a white woman and a black man, met by friends and family with a mixture of love, fear, doubt and disdain in a so-called liberal Western Massachusetts city.

A: My parents' love was partly rooted in their commitment to true brotherhood. They met while working with community youth organizations. They wanted a better society, country, world. But the gradual loss of momentum which the movement suffered, in combination with the tangible repression of progressive individuals and the steely restoration of power hierarchies throughout the 1980s, all led to an increasing sense of isolation for many.

A: I was born in 1970 and my brother was born in 1977; together with my parents and a small extended family, we made a tight unit. We had our own language. Our own rituals. We gave ourselves a context. I often say that my brother and I are children made for a world which never came. We are part of a whole generation of children who were raised by people who envisioned a transcendent society. We have unprecedented tools and privilege. We must now make the world which is our birthright.

5.
Residual light from a past incarnation:

That Daniel last walked the Earth as a woman will come as no surprise. In fact, upon reaching adolescence, he will feel tremendously ill at ease in his body for this very reason. It is new, it will take getting used to. It will embarrass him. His spirit will try to force its way out through his skin. He will swell and bend. His bones will grow and everyone will think him pretty, not handsome. The dogs at the side of the road will ask his bird mother, "Is that your daughter?" She will laugh it off. He will not. He will spend the first three cycles of seven remembering and releasing his old self, and its expectations. But he is to be a man this time. He will learn his own grace.

3.
A secret map marked
-desert:oasis-
sketched in thin blue lines on
the inside of Daniel's thigh:

EAST—You, Daniel, will have few lovers. You will joke that you are celibate, a traveler in the desert, but there is more to the story. Your desire cuts through the glare with river twist. You will hear it before you see it. You will see it before you feel the change in the air pressure. You will dip your fingers into the water before wetting your lips. And still you will hesitate before drinking. A mirage can lead to madness. Days without water blend into themselves. Better, you will say, to make a dream of water, than to bear a mouthful of sand.

NORTH—You will imagine the kisses of many. At four years old you will imagine holding the hand of X., the littlest girl, with the afro and the A-line dress. At seven you will silently pledge your devotion to S., the girl with the flowered pants, and picture running through a sunlit field to meet her, dancing around and around. At night you will dream yourself into your future. *Always,* there is a lush, romantic score. *Always,* your heart aches with uncut passion. *Always,* the lips you kiss, the necks you nuzzle, the backs you caress belong to people in your waking life, who, you are certain, barely know you exist. At fourteen you memorize the contours of J.'s body in the locker room, you study his every gesture, name the colors in his coppery skin, practice the words you will say when he invites you to come home with him to an empty house. You make a long list of desired lovers and desired acts. You mix things into paint—your spit, an accidental drop of blood, a stolen dash of cologne or a down-deep wish (written on thin paper, torn into bits). Then you paint these lovers into existence, and stare for hours-on-end into their eyes. Years will pass. They remain as you brushed them—perfect, unspoiled, abstract.

WEST—You will come upon one of the few lovers. You will have known each other before, in some simple way. As the night blooms, you will speak to one another. You will feel the awkward beauty of arousal. You will not be sure. Then the words will stop. The silence will embrace you both. You will kiss. Again. Longer and again longer. You will hear everything. His mouth will be sweet like melon. The night will caress all of you that his hands cannot cover. You will pull off his clothes and stare with joyful amazement at the possibilities. He will pull you down onto the bed and you will drink more deeply than you ever thought possible. He will remark that your eyes seem to glow, silver brown. You bask in his glory. You will rock together, stretching, sliding through each other. You will both feel the same joy. Here you will lose all sense of direction. You will only feel the spin. You will only hear the spark of stars.

ABOVE—When you wake, you are once again alone. You blush at the thought of his tongue, his hands, the ticklish spot below your navel. You welcome the sun as it spills upward. The light seems different from the heat; today, it nourishes you, it does not sap your energy. You move to run your hands through your hair and your fingers catch in the green and gold. Seeds fall from your eyes and you feel cool fingers of water weave their way through the core of you. You have flowered. At your feet, seven signs of gratitude from a weary traveler, who happened upon you, who drank fully, who basked in your glory. The caw of black birds above. The rustle of leaves in the sweeping wind. The sands gleam at the distant edges. You find that you have become the oasis for which you had searched.

1.
A Whisper Recovered from the
northwest corner of the blue room
in the yellow house, leaning:

"Angels exist between us. Between words. Between moments. Between breaths. Between day and night. Between death and life. Together, we are all the living fabric of infinity."

I opened the note to find few words, none helpful to my situation, and a final sentence that read: "I spoke with my minister and he said to come by the church right away to be healed." Healed?

A Connection to the Divine
By Kaija Langley

My mother likes to tell stories. About other people. About herself. But mostly about me. One of her favorite stories is the day I spoke my first words. A grade school teacher by trade, she used the summer months to bond with me, her only child. On a sweltering July afternoon she prepared pork and beans and franks for our lunch. She sliced the wieners into bite-sized pieces that my sixteen-month-old mouth could handle and added pinchfuls of pepper for taste. With the last dash of seasoning a mild breeze whirled through the kitchen, sending the curtains into a flutter and causing the pepper to scatter. She sneezed.

"God bless you," you said and kept right on playing with your Tonka truck. I pretended to sneeze again. "God bless you," you said again. I pretended to sneeze all afternoon, even after we'd eaten lunch and up until the time I tucked you in the bed that night.

That my first words were not "Mama" or "Dada" was not terribly surprising. My mother made a habit of saying "God bless you" to anyone who sneezed, stranger or friend. And I had deep Baptist roots. Gospel played on the record player, words from my children's Bible were enunciated and shared with dramatic detail, and my immediate family believed that Sundays were sacred.

We didn't even wash dishes on the Sabbath. If you wanted to eat on Sunday, you'd better cook on Saturday because Mama wasn't having it. All day Saturday we worked the fields and cleaned the house and on the seventh day, the Holy day, we rested. That's what the Bible said.

Growing up my weekdays were filled with Catholic school masses, weekends brimming with visits to predominantly Black churches throughout the city (until Mom found one she felt was just "right" for us). At night my mother knelt beside me while I prayed: Now I lay me down to sleep, I pray the Lord my soul to keep. If I should die before I wake, I pray the Lord my soul to take. My soul to keep. My soul to take. Especially after my mother's brush with death.

I've seen the other side. You weren't but about eight then and I asked your Daddy not to bring you to the hospital. I felt myself slipping away. I was surrounded by a tunnel of darkness and at the end there was light. I walked into the light, baby, and I spoke to God. I asked Him to spare my life in order to raise you up and see you to be a woman.

The doctors said she flat-lined for at least thirty seconds before she came to without resuscitation. Though I was not in the room with her that year, there have been several times since when I have witnessed her frail body in the ICU, cloaked in tubes and washed in an eerie fluorescent light. Too many times my mother has been at death's door, knocking with one hand as if to say "let me in" and with the other dangling by the thread of her strong will, a whisper of Psalm 23 on her lips. She lives. We are survivors.

I was eight when I first understood that women were something special. With my mother so sickly, I was shuttled between family, friends and neighbors. Those women took care of me as if I were their own: combing my hair for school; providing enough food for a restful night's sleep; holding my hand throughout phone calls to my mother in the hospital. There was a tremendous amount of love in those moments, a love that said I did not have you but you are a child of mine.

But it was Mikki and her pregnant, chain-smoking self that unearthed my first crush. Many months along in her pregnancy, ripe and big with life; the smell of her pregnant self as she fed me lunch; the shape and curves of her body defying space as she moved through the small apartment; the form of a hand pushing on the walls of her belly, changed me forever. It was then that I knew, instinctively, that I would always cherish a woman more than a man, always somehow bury my existence and my love in their great power to concede life and prowess to nurture it.

In the coming years there were more girls and woman than I can now correctly remember. Nicole and Djuana and Sonja. Kim, the neighborhood bully and my hero, whom I had risked life and limb (and a very embarrassing beating) to get to her house and play with in the attic. And Ms. Hall, my sixth grade teacher, whom I listened to records with before class began and walked home with after school.

In high school I fell crazy in love with a basketball player. Athletic and smart and wild, Anitra had an energy that attracted boys and girls, men and women, teachers and coaches and I'd never met another girl or woman like her. I had crushes on the other girls but they were passing fantasies that I dismissed as part of growing up. My feelings for Anitra, however, were full of sexual energy and longing. I daydreamed of her in class and during practice and entertained thoughts of flowers and picnics and boat rides in the spring. I summoned enough nerve to confess my attraction to my teammate Zoe (because my intuition told me we had something in common; years later I found that we did). She shunned me for two months.

Later when Zoe approached me with a note in her hand, her strides fervent and eyes averted, I stood in the hallway shocked. Never mind that the bell rang and I was late for class; I stuffed the note in my pocket and rushed to the nearest girls' bathroom. My hands trembled with expectation. Did Anitra feel the same? Would I soon be holding her in my arms? If not, did Zoe have feelings for me? I opened the note to find few words, none helpful to my situation, and a final sentence that read: "I spoke with my minister and he said to come by the church right away to be healed." Healed? It never occurred to me that my love of women—their scents and shapes and emotional tides—was sick nor required healing.

As my romantic feelings for Anitra intensified, and she continued to resist, I began questioning my nature and what my attraction to women would mean for my life emotionally, physically and spiritually. Mostly spiritually. Neither my Catholic nor Baptist backgrounds offered me anything more than I was an abomination in God's sight. When Anitra graduated and went away for college, I found consolation in an artist named Kevin.

I knew you were seeing that man before you told me. Mothers have intuition. We always know. I wasn't happy about it, not one bit. That man was old enough to be your father. He should've known better. What was he thinking messing with a seventeen-year-old girl? But at least it was a man.

I was baptized my senior year of high school. There in my underwear, in the cold basement of the church, I stood with four others waiting to be cleansed of my sins; I was petrified. The sheer white cotton robes threatened transparency once met with water, but I was more concerned knowing that once the pastor lay hands on me and I was immersed in the Holy water, my impure thoughts about women would vanish and I would be left with the life God wanted for me: man-woman love, servitude and children.

That year:
My soul to keep
My soul to take.
No more.

❦❦❦

I left Kevin behind and escaped to Baltimore for college, away from the hectic northern city living and the over-protection that only a mother with one child can provide. In an attempt to bury the self I knew most true I dated men. Wary, yet prepared, I lay down with those boy-men, held brief conversations with them, locked eyes with them, desperately needing assurance. This is my fate OR this is not my fate. Before I fell victim to disease or abuse or both, I fell in love with a woman who just so happened to love me in return.

I'd stopped reading the Bible I'd gotten as a gift for my baptism, except to glance at the Ten Commandments on occasion, and managed to avoid the subject of attending church whenever I spoke with my mother. One Saturday afternoon while I was with my lover, her head cradled in my arms, her unruly hair tickling my chin, my mother called.

"Don't forget to iron your dress for church in the morning. Are you going to the early service or the late?" she asked.

"I'm not sure."

"You are going, aren't you?"

"I'll see how I feel in the morning." That was my standard response, but on that day there was a long, heavy silence. My mother cleared her throat three times.

"Have you met any nice young men lately?"

"No, but I've met a wonderful woman."

We both cried.

The relationship with that young woman didn't last long. It was a whirlwind introduction to the world I'd fantasized so much about, for so long. And between club-hopping, girl-chasing and, admittedly, male-bashing, who had time for church? Besides, who was I to pray to a God that would only banish me to hell? I remained ignorant of the actual scriptures of the Bible that condemned same-sex love, thinking that if I didn't read them somehow it would save me from my fate as a woman-loving woman.

My mother bought me books rebuking homosexuality, mailed photocopied passages from the Bible, and dug up letters from long-ago boyfriends; I threw them all away. Once while she was visiting Baltimore we were out shopping and she noticed an effeminate male sashaying down the aisle. She nodded in his direction, whispering, "There's one of your people."

My patience was tried the most when I went home for a visit. Before my duffel slipped from my shoulder to the floor she had whipped out the dress, and heels, and makeup I'd be wearing to church on Sunday.

When you were two I dressed you in the cutest pink outfit with frills and bobby socks to match. I even put pink and white barrettes in your hair. My little girl. I wasn't out of the room but a minute and when I came back the ruffles were bunched around your feet because you'd torn them off the dress! I knew then you weren't a frilly child. I knew then that you were different.

It was during those times when I felt most like a fraud: clapping my hands to the songs, paying my ten percent, and squirming through the sermons when the pastor insisted on preaching about every woman finding a man, children who wouldn't obey their parents, and that disease in the homosexual community that was beginning to take the lives of those who lived righteously.

I'd learned growing up that church was a place of deep pain and immense joy, genuine laughter and glorious song, but most of all church was a place of community. Church was where you went when the bills were due and you were low on cash. Help me Father! Church was where you brought your husband if he had gone astray and you needed to release your burden to a higher power. Praise Jesus! Church was where you felt at ease to jump out of your seat and holler when the Spirit hit you, and on the days when you felt truly moved you could run around the church waving your hands in the air bearing witness to the power of the Almighty. Hallelujah!

On my nineteenth birthday when I accepted that who I was was all that I would ever be, I saw the doors of the church as permanently closed to me and my kind.

Standing on the outside looking in I began to see the cracks in the façade of the church. People who clearly judged when the Good Book said not to; people who used hate as a weapon and tool when the Word called for love. I delved deeper to uncover my godself through prayer and meditation, and I began to shed the rigid confines of any one religion. I realized that there was always a godself within that I could commune with and call upon whenever I was in need. No dresses, no stockings, no makeup required.

I became skeptical of anyone wearing a WWJD sweatshirt, leery of drivers with religious bumper stickers, and annoyed with anyone who felt the need to say "I'm a Christian" or "He/She is a Christian" before anything of substance. Though oftentimes my skepticism was for naught, there were too many times when I encountered "religious" people who were the most racist, homophobic, abusive, Bible-toting, verse-quoting, gossip-mongering men and women to walk the face of the earth. It's as if some people believe that if they say they are of God, if they say they do God's work, that their words absolve them of the ill will of their actions.

Two girls from Seton Hall came to see me about your room today. I asked them what their religious beliefs were. That African girl, she said she was a Christian. But that other girl, sweet as she seemed, was from India. You know who they worship, don't you? I was happy she didn't take the room because I don't know what kind of spirits she might have brought in my house.

I believe in God, in a Divine higher power, though I don't honestly think I ever stopped believing. Too many blessings, too many miracles. I know that my upbringing and my sexuality have converged and given me a more balanced view of God in the universe. Where I once was carried in the womb of strict religious convictions, I have since been born to the true spirit of God within myself and others.

Still, in my quest to make peace with what I've been taught to believe versus what I now know, I have had to acknowledge and accept the dichotomy between religion and spirituality. Religion demands conformity; spirituality encourages individuality. Religion divides us by pointing out our differences; spirituality unites us by emphasizing what we have in common. Religion implies that there is one place to feel the Spirit of God; spirituality says God is everywhere. Religion is manmade; spirituality is a direct connection to the Divine.

These days when I go home to visit I pack my clothes for

church. If my mother feels up to it we go to the early service and I sing and clap and listen wholeheartedly. My mother peers over at me from time to time, her facial expression a mix of shock and gratitude, probably wondering how I continue to love God so much and women too. I know better now. My mother has shared many stories with me over the years, but not one yet about how God loves me just the way I am.

I did not know the teachings of the Buddha because, as my sister had asked me once, "What does Buddhism have to do with black people anyway?" Well, it had something to do with me and I was as black as black gets.

Still Waters Run Deep
By Earthlyn Marselean Manuel

The loud voices of anguish among the descendants of African slaves have been heard throughout the centuries. As a child I witnessed the tears of my parents as they struggled in hope, resistance, and faith, engaged in the lifelong pursuit of wellness and the good life in America. They worked harder perhaps than necessary, yet remained close to God. They worked against dehumanization to ensure that their three daughters would not suffer to the extent that they had. In the end though, my sisters and I did not miss out entirely on the suffering our parents had endured.

As I grew into adulthood it occurred to me that we, and other black folks, had simply learned to cope with unfulfilled lives. We had not learned how to alleviate suffering. We did not know how to acknowledge feelings of limitation and lack. Although Christianity offered God as a liberator and the Church as a community to ease the pain of isolation felt by displaced Africans, we had not learned how to eliminate the sense of inferiority that pervaded our bodies. Social movements gave us a political ideology of equality while education taught us how to assimilate. We had not, however, healed the wounds we so often expressed through our music, dance, and written words. When I saw the depth of pain in my parents' eyes, I wondered if we, black people, could ever overcome the suffering we historically and continually endured.

The need to understand and heal such suffering led me through Christianity and Yoruba to Buddhism. The teachings of Shakyamuni Buddha offered a different kind of liberation; one that brought forth an innate wisdom that in the past I had sought from the Christian God and later from the African Orishas of the most ancient spirituality I have known. Although I still carried the basic teachings of Jesus Christ and the messages of the Orishas in my bones, the Buddha way became the path along which I could relieve the sense of being weary, drained, and suicidal, and come away filled with life.

The teachings of the Buddha helped me to release all the perpetrators I held hostage and put my life back into my hands. I opened my heart to let go of the person who burned a cross on our lawn in Los Angeles, to let go of a black man that raped me, to let go of the white two-year-old girl who called me "niggi," the fair-skinned African American boy who spit in my dark face, the young men who verbally attacked me for being lesbian.

Because I let all these people go, it did not mean that they had not done the deeds that had hurt me. Letting go of them meant freeing myself of them so that I had enough life force to live, so that I was no longer separated from the world in which all of us lived. Clearly, it was my responsibility to heal—to not suffer. I did not come to this realization overnight; it took years to pardon all those soul snatchers. It took even longer to acknowledge the hurt I have caused in the world.

I stumbled into Nichiren Buddhism with no altruistic ideas about being a Buddhist. I did not know the teachings of the Buddha because, as my sister had asked me once, "What does Buddhism have to do with black people anyway?" Well, it had something to do with me and I was as black as black gets. I was a Pan-Africanist and a stone advocate for Black Power. No one could have convinced me that Buddhism could blunt any of the sharpness I felt from being born in a dark body, or from the male dominance in religion that deferred my dream of becoming a minister.

Seventeen years ago, I attended my first Nichiren Buddhist meeting. I was hungry. I mean that literally. I wanted to go out to eat at a restaurant with two friends of mine. They both agreed that if I wanted to go out and eat with them, I had to first follow them to a Buddhist meeting that evening. With some anger I gave in and off we went to the meeting. They were chanting *Nam-Myoho-Renge-Kyo,* a translated title of a Buddhist scripture called the Lotus Sutra.[*] I was completely resistant to chanting, yet one month after that night I created my first Buddhist altar on which sat a scroll with Japanese writing. I was chanting. Why? The hunger I had on the evening of my first meeting was a much greater hunger than that of the physical body. It came from deep within my soul, regardless of my devout belief in God and the Orishas. The Buddhist teachers would ask, "What are you chanting for?" I would say, "I don't know," being too ashamed to tell them I felt a deep pain that I could not name.

After about two years of chanting with overwhelming pain, I realized that the suffering I felt was tightly woven into a larger place of suffering in my heart. Eventually, I recognized that I felt separate from the rest of the world, that I did not belong, and that my differences based on race, gender, sexual orientation, and class, were not acceptable in the dominant culture. I was paralyzed with feelings of isolation as a black lesbian. By agreeing with those who misused power and who proclaimed that I was not enough, I had created an internalized treason, making it impossible to trust my innate wisdom. Oppression distorted the nature of my life.

I came to Nichiren Buddhism through the lay organization called the Soka Gakkai International. There I learned about the nature of my suffering through many of Nichiren's writings. In most Buddhist schools, the first Noble Truth of suffering includes several aspects, including the path to end suffering. Nichiren simplified the Buddha's teachings on suffering to what he called the four sufferings: birth, illness, old age, and death. Also, He claimed that these four sufferings are caused by the idea that the self exists independently of nature and the universe. In other words, the four sufferings derived from the idea: "I am the absolute being."

When I understood that the self does not exist independently, I understood how I suffered—how I felt isolated in my dark, feminine-masculine body. I was awakened to my own innate wisdom. What I knew was that I was worthy of a place in the world like any other human being; that I was not separate from all other living beings. But I had lost track of such wisdom because I lived in a world that thrived on individualism, making a social intimacy among us feel impossible. As I chanted, I understood that I was part of the world; that despite oppression I belonged. With that wisdom, I would not be an accomplice to my own disappearance in the world.

Although chanting saved my life, embracing Buddhism felt different from the Christianity of the black church in which I was raised. Christianity for my parents and my contemporaries was a communal effort to change our plight as African Americans. It was how we survived together. At the start, Buddhism seemed to focus on the individual without any mention of discrimination. Therefore, it was difficult to embrace a spiritual awakening within myself and trust that I was doing the job of resolving suffering in the world. Later, I realized that understanding suffering in my life provided the clarity I needed to help others. How could I help relieve suffering in the world without understanding my own? To achieve such understanding it was important to apply Buddhism to my daily life.

I discovered promptly that the teachings of Buddha could not be figured out in my head because it was not a school of thought, an ideology, or a belief system to add to the other beliefs I had gathered along the road of life. The Dharma was not a theory to be absorbed intellectually. It did not matter that the language of most Buddhists schools was foreign to my Black English tongue. Even as I wrote this essay, I was aware that

Buddhism could not be talked about easily because *Buddhism is a lived experience.* I could not know it unless I lived it. I could not even practice Buddhism as if it were something that would eventually become a habit. Otherwise, I would be forever becoming something else and not appreciating daily life as a black lesbian, praising all of who I am.

In understanding *Buddhism as life,* I was able to create a path that acknowledged all that was important to me: the wisdom of the Buddha, the political and historical impact of slavery on my life, and most importantly social justice as spiritual well-being. I did not turn away from my Pan-African lessons for the sake of spiritual growth. I did not ignore either my cultural identity or my queerness for the sake of enlightenment. But rather I found enlightenment in my identity as a black, queer woman and received a glimpse of what life would be like without such labels once humanity freed itself from hatred.

To be awake, to feel in this queer dark body, was the journey of the Buddha way. Before I could have compassion for the man who raped me, I needed to feel the pain and suffering of being raped. I also needed to be aware of what I have done with my life because of that pain and suffering. There was no need to analyze the mentality of cross-burning on our lawn when I was a child living in a suburb of Los Angeles, to understand injustice, but rather remain acquainted with the terror of hatred and still invite intimacy into my life. This was the path toward liberation from suffering in a dark queer body.

I continue to learn about such liberation each day as I transition from chanting into zazen, a Zen Buddhist way of sitting still and being silent. As I return to silence, I am learning to "stay on my *zafu* (meditation pillow)," which means metaphorically to stay in my life and not to focus on others' lives in comparison to mine. I pay attention to where I am. Am I awake to where I am? This awareness is not a selfish agenda for happiness but rather an honest response to the world. However deep the suffering, however deep the waters, I respond awake.

To my sister's "what does Buddhism have to do with black

people anyway?" I say that the teachings of Buddha have everything to do with us and with every other suffering living being. There is suffering and something can be done about it, without imposing religious sanctions or political correctness, but rather by becoming humane enough to feel the pain of the Earth. Then we can understand suffering. We can understand that within the stillness at the bottom of dark waters there is sustenance for our healing, where loud ancestral voices of anguish can scream deep into wellness and awaken us from bold breathless nightmares. Though deep waters run beneath our caves, therein lies a sanctuary for our crying, where the haunted emerges unfolded from desperate fear and the liberated howl of the wolf calls us back to feeling ourselves alive. The still waters that run deep and cold are undisturbed by our dipping into the cool of its darkness. As we bathe our broken hearts, we cleanse away what we have had to suffer and move on toward fulfilling our purpose in life, which for many of us is to help others.

---

* The literal meaning of Nam-Myoho-Renge-Kyo: *Nam* or *Namu* means to have devotion to or to take refuge in the teachings, *Myoho* means the oneness of the law and everyday life, *Renge* means the principle of cause and effect and *Kyo* means sutra or teachings (dharma).

I am as all is, of the spirit, even as the spirit transcends all. Desire knows my flesh because I am born, and I am born of the spirit. My skin is both blanket and conduit.

Spirit Body *
By Bahíyyih Maroon

The first time I met God
she was a three headed serpent
dancing on a wet rock

TRANS   BLACK
          BI   SPIRIT
   SEX
                DUO
                              RE/ALITY

At the loom I recheck my yarns. They have been picked and carded by hand. I take the three sets of colors in my palms, knowing they are too brilliant to be named easily, and begin posting them to the loom. I am here with these strips, dyed in story, memory and wind.

No sermons, no doctrines.

Only quest.
I come from a place over from here now. I live
there as an anthropologist, looking for secrets on the faces
of the living. There is the belief where I live, that truth requires
evidence.

I know this, because all evidence has been destroyed. I know that truth needs no evidence, because what comes of the dust of sacred tablets is only what has ever been in the air.

I have walked for twenty-eight days to enter this cave of my own skin, which is really but a cloth lent to me by ancestors. It is, my skin, steeped in their herbs and the voices of their lives. Inside myself, I reenter them who gave me life in the first.

I tighten the yarns into place and begin weaving. It is high sun out when I start. The heat burns me into water and salt. The sweat stings my eyes.

I remember I didn't walk in on them. It wasn't private; everyone was allowed. The wimmin erupted around me. I was a child. The moaning made it seem like the ground itself would pick up any minute. Their bodies would convulse and shake in a rhythmed seizure sweet as last drops of rain on the hottest day. Making love to the lord was sanctified ritual carried out under the slight itch of the most thoroughly starched collars around.

A womon humming the blues leans over me. She looks at the few bars that have been made in the canvas so far. I wonder if she, like me, has this memorized in a place she hasn't seen in too long to know already what the picture will emerge as. As she smiles at me the orange shadows come gone. There are clouds strattling in with alto grey.

The cloth begins to come up in shapes/ black strokes touching each other as in symbol.

/_/door

There is no way to enter Blackness, for it is that which is never absent—ever present, no? But through channels, the mind can rejoin the texture of its skin's history. A texture of braids, plaited around and about the skull as a nest ready for a basket to be perched. The texture of a womon's head/hair. In this doorway I watch an uncle, a forefather, a cousin without name, walking around on yellow soil, his feet gone mustard brown with the stains. In this door I know his name in translation is diviner/man of spirits. He is the wife of an Orisha. His body bears the traits of a man—his clothes the marks of a woman. His crown in the braids of a sister. His skull is one of a black man. The Head— possessing spirit-is a mommi. He leans toward me from the doorway. A dozen beads on a gourd. His voice shakes until the wind comes quiet to hear what he speaks.

I am your blackness child. I am your father. I am the wife of the spirit. A man of woman. I have always been. And I am now. Forget nothing of me. I am real. He shakes his braids which fall down and look for just a minute as dread knots. He, who is babalawo, smiles at me, says; don't worry 'bout that 'ting eider chile. Dem dread too will remember me/remember where they come of, one day soon enough.

      Trans   @
times I am aware that there is something which misses
the point[lessness] of having a gender. It feels I've been given
the gift of a useless thing. Gender
is a building/a demolishing. Is no difference—where I'm taking
it/ Line diving in public is only me saying

                      there is no gender
between my legs.   there never was—There—androgyny.
     is the middle of a /\
/\ duo
                Couple/let

Once. I saw two wimmin. They were one next to the other. Laying down. The way their pubic bones touched, the waves in one muscle, it was like that. Tight and fluid at the same time. And there were their eyes, just rolling back in

their heads. Finally one yelled Jesus and the other Yemaya
and they just fell on holding each other while they panted
back down. I saw them once
knew I had seen
magic

The yarns are near half come together
It is raining on me. Inside the short clear drops there are
flowing
       Robes of ordination. She stands in them as
           the preacher I always waited for when
              the wimmin were making love to
the lord.
              "My people!!" The rows of church
pews and restored rickety wood go back for miles. All
around there is the flutter of paper fans, stirring the
dust and teasing the heat. "My people look to Egypt.
Yes, my people I say look upon the land from whence
you came. Here is your salvation. You know now, yes
you do, that you are the children of the   P h a r a o h s
and the Pyramids ruled

             [Flashes make a
colored girls chorus]

            By
            The Laws of Creation. That's right,
now. I tell you and you must know that we have come
from the Mighty. And my people I tell you today, we
have always known that we must bury our dead. For it
is in, yes indeed; It is in this burial that we say; Ohh
Lord, Our God this is a child of our tribe. Look unto
him, Look unto her and know they are as much beloved
by us as you. That's right now, that's what we say. And
so I tell you, yes, to look back. Mmhhmm. Look back
and see this grave I have seen. For there is a resting

place in our mother land, where the dead do lie together as they did in life. That's right. Buried with their arms around each other to proclaim, Lord we have loved each other as we have loved you! EGYPT my brothers and sisters, in a tomb older than the memory of dust. And two men, that's right, man to man they were with their arms 'round each other. And I know as you must know today, that someone loved them who loved each other in the face of their God. Yes they did. And I know they were not stoned, were not outcast. No they were not. I'm telling you this my people.

Take it with you. Take it with you how we were when we still knew the beginning the story…"

I re-enter a woven text in synonyms under B: binary: biradial: bifurcated: biology—surrounds—sexuality,
the bed

is merely a   place, not the point. I am speaking of a way of seeing. I begin in energies, coming to force. Them which interconnect act together. I know that this is a rule. I know too that   binary   force   is   not   always   action/reaction, exertion/resistance. I know that what differs in force may flow and emanate around and with each other. What differs does not just have to be walled against sides.
I am more than one body, more than one sex. My sex is made, my body gotten.
I leave my sex and return to my body as a (*)

spiritual.

I am as all is, of the spirit, even as the spirit transcends all. Desire knows my flesh because I am born, and I am born of the spirit. My skin is both blanket and conduit. In flesh I know lover/to be/what is inside. As in is with
—Creation/Life/the force of a being which makes all. In spirit I come as a body fused to Soul. The spaces
of ascension.
touching   **spirit**

I return to the place I live with cloth under my arm. Before it fades, I will have memorized its pattern and tattooed the pictures onto bone. The patterns speak of pasts and visions. They speak a code within code. As with a line like touchstone, poised in the air for thousands to see. For some it will be the symbol of the bed they share. For me it will be like a moment back inside the oldest cave, witness to a fine black mark etched forever into the rock which holds eternity, a black mark shaped as a pubic bone, a triangle, a womon's center, a man's beginning.

I carry back fragments waiting to make exchanges with others who have gone seeking. Waiting to pull all the pieces into one; Something that will end up perhaps as the shape of explosions or springtime. Something that will end up as evidence of what we have all already known by the breath of our own lives.

I was giving love and being loved. I was becoming active—thinking for myself rather than living as a container for others' thoughts. I was experiencing, for the first time, a joy in being alive. If God was goodness, then I felt I had entered God's land.

Taking the Reins
By Jorhán Mbonisi

The time had come for me to act. I had not been to church in a year, not since I left my husband and moved in with Melanie. I was too much like Papa really. He and I did not believe in half-stepping, in straddling the fence. As we saw it, you didn't believe one thing while living another. So I dared not show my face at the church knowing that I lived in contradiction to its tenets.

It was not the most pleasant realization that I was like Papa. He was so rigid. Mama had always been more lax and open. Funny how through my child's eyes it was Mama who had seemed the imperfect one simply because she showed an interest in things outside of the church and Bible and was generally accepting of all people. Papa looked down on members who were not abiding by church rules and treated nonmembers like pariah; yet, he had seemed the perfect one. Papa followed the church laws impeccably and lived a life in full accordance with church doctrines. His strict adherence to church practices translated as exemplary character, and through my child's eyes he was the model of an honorable, sincere life.

I, too, believed that if one belonged to a group, organization or church, then one followed that group's tenets one hundred percent. One ultimately strived to be the best example of what the organization represented. To be a vital member of any group, one first had to accept and agree with the principles and tenets put forth by that group. I no longer believed in the tenets of my father's church.

It had not been entirely easy for me to walk away from the church. Everyone I knew were members—my parents, grandparents, friends. Jacob's House was a powerful, nondenominational, Bible-based organization with a host of original beliefs and practices. They considered themselves the true lineage of Israel, the original Jews to whom the Bible referred, the descendants of Judah, Jacob, Jesus. Rules abounded pertaining to appropriate dress, appropriate speech, appropriate behavior. One belief was that homosexuality was a sin. According to my family, I was now living in sin.

For a year now I had not attended any church and was better off for it. How was I better off? Could it be that I was worse off and didn't know it? What I knew was I felt better, healthier, improved. I was giving love and being loved. I was becoming active—thinking for myself rather than living as a container for others' thoughts. I was experiencing, for the first time, a joy in being alive. If God was goodness, then I felt I had entered God's land.

I had not known goodness during the time I attended church. The environment of judgment and indoctrination had left me dismal, empty. Nor did I know goodness immediately upon walking away from the church. Goodness had come slowly and steadily as I evolved throughout the year. It took examining my beliefs, engaging in new activities, and witnessing change within myself to know it. As I embraced new concepts, beliefs and practices, my enthusiasm for living increased. Some things we simply know in our soul, and I knew I had entered a realm of goodness.

So after months of thought and experience, I concluded that I did not agree with my family and the church at all. Homosexuality could not possibly be wrong.

When I examined their belief from a biblical standpoint, their assertion was weak. Most churchgoers followed the teachings of Jesus Christ. The truth was Jesus never spoke against homosexuality in the scriptures. One cannot find a word uttered by Christ that condemned homosexuality. In fact, when Jesus was asked, "Which is the first commandment of all?" (St. Mark 12:28-31), Jesus answered that he had two commandments, and none were greater than these two: 1) Love God with all thy heart, mind, soul and strength, and 2) Love thy neighbor as thyself.

Jesus was all about love. Nothing more, nothing less. Sins were found in the things that were not based in love—i.e., judging, rejecting, despising, hating, evoking fear, feeling fear, arrogance, hating one's self, hurtful action, and of course the refusal or negligence to value, appreciate and pay homage to God, the life force, the creator. These were the things Jesus spoke against.

I knew that my lesbian relationship embodied love.

So where in the Bible was homosexuality condemned? In the Old Testament in Leviticus, a commandment was said to have been uttered by God to Moses. There is no direct quote. In the New Testament, Paul simply reiterated Moses' words. Sodomy mentioned in Deuteronomy and Sodom and Gomorrah in Genesis was not specifically tied to homosexuality but referred instead to any and all unusual sex for pleasure. In the land of Sodom, Lot did not want to offer his sons-in-law to the hedonistic men, so he offered his virgin daughters instead.

So Moses was responsible for the ruling against homosexuality in the Bible. But Moses issued many rulings in the Old Testament, and if one considered herself or himself a follower of Moses, then one would abide by all of his commandments.

One would make animal offerings to God—kill animals at the altar, sprinkle blood on and around the altar, and burn portions of the animal there. 2) One would not eat pork, shrimp, crabs. 3) Mothers, after giving birth, would not be seen for approximately six weeks, and after their time of seclusion, they would go before the altar with an animal sacrifice. 4) A menstruating woman would be secluded for two weeks, after which she, too, would bring an animal to the altar to be sacrificed. 5) One would not eat any rare meat—all blood was to be poured or drained from the animal before eating it. 7) One would not genetically mingle animals, nor plants. 8) One would not cut his or her body—no piercings— nor paint the body—no makeup. 9) No bald heads. 10) If one hid her eyes from the deeds of evildoers, one would suffer the same consequences as the evildoer. 11) One's first fruit was to be offered to God. 12) One was not to eat until an offering of food was made to God. 13) One was not to oppress another. 14) One was not to curse his father and mother. 15) One would not have sex with a family member, a neighbor's wife, a married person, a member of the same sex, two people in the same family, or with animals. 16) One would not lie or gossip. 17) One would not bear a grudge. 18) One would always leave food for the poor. These were rulings set down by Moses in Leviticus.

I, being one who expected people to abide by their beliefs and principles, had to query anyone who stated that homosexuality was wrong per the Bible:

"Why mention to me what Moses said when you do not follow his beliefs and commandments?"

And if he or she replied, "Some of Moses' beliefs are old and ancient, and times have changed."

Then I'd say, "Homosexuality is one of those old and ancient beliefs. Times have changed. After all, even Jesus Christ did not speak against homosexuality."

In truth, my beliefs no longer required biblical substantiation. As I saw it, the Bible was written by a host of men no different from you and I. In all records of history, and the Bible is one, some viewpoints had been left out, and some erroneous interpretations had been recorded.

I had come to see that my dependency on others' opinions and beliefs was robbing me of my own connection to the life force. When we confer greatness to others, we devalue ourselves. When we find others more worthy of being heard and followed than ourselves, we diminish our personal power and subdue our life force. As I saw it, every one of us needed to write a book of the Bible and express what we had come to know as truth about life and God.

The clock read 7 p.m. I picked up the phone and tapped out the bishop's number. There was something exhilarating about taking the reins of my life, making decisions and being responsible for myself. I knew it was only a matter of time before I received a letter from Jacob's House announcing my excommunication. How audacious of them to presume that it was their decision to make about whether or not I would spend my life with them. I knew their rules. It was up to me to decide where, with whom and how I would spend my life. I was glad I'd made a decision before I received a letter from them.

The phone was ringing. I felt a bit nervous; I was going up against the big boys now. He answered.

"Hello."

"Bishop, this is Jorhán."

He was silent, listening.

"I'm calling to let you know that I don't want to be a member anymore."

"Well—" He seemed at a loss for words.

"I don't believe in it," I said.

"The Bible says—"

"I don't know about the Bible," I interrupted him. "It's open to interpretation."

"It's God's word."

"I don't know that either. I think it's more a history book."

"God's history."

"I don't know—but I'd feel much more certain about things if I wrote my own history with God."

He was silent for a moment. "Well, I'll pray for you," he finally said.

"Bye, Bishop."

There was so much more I could have said. But why insult or dispute his views? He, like my father, was living a life true to his own beliefs. And if nothing else, I certainly admired a sincere life.

There are no specifics to say whom you must love. The scripture does not say to only love the poor, or the rich, or the Christian, or the women or those who are right-handed; God simply says in the scripture to love one another as I have loved you.

Spirituality and Sexuality
By Dyan "Abena" McCray

Growing up, I was taught to be a religious person, not a spiritual person. Being the only female in a family of seven, I spent a lot of time alone. Unlike most children, my parents did not try to make me fit into a gender sexual stereotype; my brothers had trucks, guns, electric trains, ponies and so did I. Being an avid nature lover, I would lay in the grass and stare at the sky, clouds and birds. I remember one day looking across a blacktop road and seeing heat for the first time. It was a very hot day and the sun was beaming down on the road in front of my grandparents' home and I could actually see the energy from the sun hovering over the road. I realized at that moment that there were probably many things present in the universe that we could not see. So I started watching everything very closely—especially myself.

I realized at a very young age about my soul and spirit. I realized that they were entities that belonged to me and with them I could explore my world. I remember daydreaming that turned into fantasizing, and in doing so I would in my mind take journeys all over the world. I would go to deserted islands, beautiful waterfalls, fields of poppies; I would ride on clouds and travel anywhere in the universe I wanted to. I also learned to protect my space and create boundaries. I learned to survive through my instincts and intuition. I knew that at any time and place I could escape any madness and in my mind go to a place of peace. As I grew older I learned to incorporate this into meditations. These meditations were my guide, my compass, my barometer and a way to connect with the Creator. I grew up believing that the only way to connect with God was through prayer; now I knew a new way.

In church, I had always heard that God created each of us in God's own image; therefore I realized I must be a lot like God. I took this information literally. Knowing that God was spirit and did not exist in a physical form made me realize that God was also without gender, so my identity was very significant. I spent a lot of time reading the Bible and learning the laws and principles God had for me to follow. The Bible was my roadmap to life. Although many times I strayed, that spirit within always brought me back to where I needed to be.

In my twenties I realized that I was very attracted to women. Having both a religious and spiritual background, I felt comfortable with these feelings. The scripture "love thy neighbor as thyself" was something I tried hard to live by. The time I spent getting to know and love myself made it much simpler for me to love everyone else. I learned to treat others as I wanted to be treated. When I would say the Lord's Prayer, I was cognizant of the fact that I was asking God to forgive at the same level that I forgave others. So a foundation had been set within me to understand that love did not recognize gender, color, ethnicity or religion. Love simply looked for itself. So when I pursued relationships with women it felt like the most natural thing to do. Who better to please a woman than someone who has all her life been a woman; someone who is very aware of a woman's feelings, tenderness and nurturing instincts—not to mention being very familiar with her anatomy.

Interestingly enough, I came in contact with heterosexual women who thought I should seek counseling around my sexual identity. I took the time to explain to them that my lifestyle was not a choice; I was born the way I am. I always enjoyed the company of females! I always had camaraderie with men, but I was not interested in pursuing intimate, sexual relationships with them. And I always dealt with men on that level.

I have had numerous conversations with lesbians who struggle with putting God and gay or lesbian in the same sentence. I remind them that God only asks that we love one another. There are no specifics to say whom you must love. The scripture does not say to only love the poor, or the rich, or the Christian, or the women or those who are right-handed; God simply says in the scripture to love one another as I have loved you. If we live our lives based on that scripture, we cannot go wrong.

It is Wicca that provides me with a solid foundation for self-loving. Witches rejoice in the power of the feminine and view sexuality as fluid, constrained only by our own fear and narrow interpretations of it. As a lover of women, I need to see myself and all women clearly in the image of the divine spirit.

And Then I Met the Goddess…
By Monique Meadows

Liberating myself from a life of sexual guilt and confusion has required that I use every reference in my library of healing to ready myself for the type of sexual and emotional intimacy that I've longed for throughout my life. I've used therapy, self-help books and endless processing, but I believe that what has ultimately kept me from resigning myself to a sexual expression warped by shame and repression has been my spirituality.

Born Baptist, I now identify myself as a witch and child of the orishas. In times of despair, very little can calm my soul like a good gospel song. I appreciate my Baptist roots and draw from them on occasion, yet nothing compares to the power I discovered when I first encountered the Goddess, the female representation of the divine in the earth-based tradition, Wicca (commonly known as witchcraft). The Goddess is the One who brings me life, peace, passion and abundance. In contrast to the wild misconception of witches as evil or harmful, Wicca teaches me to revere and celebrate the sanctity of nature, the mystery of the Earth and my body, and encourages me to experience divine ecstasy.

In her book *Spiral Dance*, Starhawk shares with us "The Charge of the Goddess":

"I who am the beauty of the green earth and the white moon among the stars and the mysteries of the waters, I call upon your soul to arise and come unto Me. For I am the soul of nature that gives life to the universe. From Me all things proceed and unto Me they must return. Let My worship be in the heart that rejoices, for behold—all acts of love and pleasure are My rituals. Let there be beauty and strength, power and compassion, honor and humility, mirth and reverence within you. And you who seek to know Me, know that your seeking and yearning will avail you not, unless you know the Mystery: for if that you seek, you find not within yourself, you will never find it without. For behold, I have been with you from the beginning, and I am that which is attained at the end of desire."*

My spirituality is flavored by both Wicca and the West African Yoruba tradition, as well as my Baptist upbringing. Wicca, however, was my introduction to earth-based traditions. It is Wicca that provides me with a solid foundation for self-loving. Witches rejoice in the power of the feminine and view sexuality as fluid, constrained only by our own fear and narrow interpretations of it. As a lover of women, I need to see myself and all women clearly in the image of the divine spirit.

My first encounter with Her was at a sacred sexual ritual more than six years ago that was organized by some of my social justice activist peers. I later discovered that these peers were also witches, shamans and energy workers. They recognized my openness to and hunger for exploring my sexuality and invited me to attend the ritual. Amazingly, I felt very little apprehension about participating. I trusted the organizers and, up until then, had been desperately searching for new ways to heal the sexual wounds of my past. I was given very clear instructions about my participation—come sober, play safe and be open. The first two presented no challenge for me. The last request, however, did. Sexual openness was what I craved, but I was still ignorant about how to acquire it. I tried anyway, and found the evening absolutely magical. I went into trance. I danced. I laughed and made love. I witnessed fat, thin, male, female, black, white, and brown bodies in all of their glorious nakedness making love. The Goddess was definitely present and she was smiling.

I have not attended a ritual like that since that evening, but the experience significantly altered me by allowing me to experience the intimate connection between my sexuality and spiritual life. This shift in perception was drastic for me. Previously, I had understood my sexuality—more specifically my lesbianism—as something to struggle with and resist. That night, I felt I had been given divine permission to delight in my sexual nature and body. This was the beginning of a healing journey still in progress.

Soon after this experience, I began reading all that I could about earth-based spiritualities. I discovered a world of rich and ancient traditions and knew that Wicca—this earth-loving, body-honoring path—would be the source of my salvation. I entered into an apprenticeship with a black, bisexual witch whose spiritual power was unmatched by anyone I had previously met. The first part of my training required that I explore my relationship to the energy of the elements that make up the universe—earth, air, fire and water. Each element has a very real manifestation in our lives and represents a necessary aspect for balance and movement. For example, the earth represents our bodies, our homes and relationships to money. Air represents our mental capabilities— our ability to think and see clearly, our desires and fantasies. Fire relates to creativity, passion, anger and the energy that keeps us in motion. Water represents the moon and its cycles, our emotions and ability to intuit and give life. For most of us, some aspects of these elements are blocked or out of balance, thereby resulting in stagnation, depression or alienation. For example, if an individual has primarily airy qualities and very little earth, she could be absolutely brilliant, but have difficulty functioning in the world because she is not grounded.

My teacher challenged me to discover where my blocks or imbalances existed and how they manifested in my life. There were many, but the first area I explored was my sexuality because my deepest wounds lived there. Over the months, as I proceeded with my exploration, my fear manifested itself as I forgot appointments with my teacher, became ill and failed to complete assignments. While I clearly was unhappy with the state of my love affairs, I was terrified of what I would uncover during this intense examination of my emotional and spiritual landscape. My teacher and the Goddess gently persisted, though, and slowly I stopped allowing fear to control me.

One important step for me was to construct altars representing the elements. Having felt creatively blocked for years, building altars was a perfect opportunity to let my creative and spiritual energies merge. Altars are innately sensual, so I enjoyed creating them. I gathered beautiful fabrics, bright candles, sweet-smelling incense, plants and ocean water. Once the altar was built, I was instructed to be mindful of how particular elements showed up in my life. Beginning with earth, I asked myself the following questions:

- Do I feel settled in my home?
- Do I fear money?
- What is my relationship with my family?
- Do I love my body?

These were hard questions for me, but the answers emerged miraculously quickly. For the most part, I felt settled in my home. Yes, I had issues with money, but they didn't feel insurmountable. My relationship with my family was basically okay. I did not love my body—at all.

That I did not love my body was not necessarily new information to me. Throughout my life, I had felt great disdain for it, always wishing for a flatter stomach, rounder butt, or more shapely hips. I assumed that this experience of body dissatisfaction was part of being a woman. All of the girls and women in my life seemed to be in a constant battle with their bodies. I had no way of realizing that there was another experience of my body, and that the effect of my poor self-image on my sexuality was so severe. And it was. I feared being naked with lovers. I was not in touch with what felt pleasurable to my body and certainly did not feel entitled to ask for pleasure. My low self-esteem also led to making poor decisions about the lovers I chose.

Now, I was being offered an opportunity to move beyond that reality toward something filled with love and light. The mandate from my teacher was clear. If I were to love the earth as witches do, I must also love my body since they are one and the same. With much hope for healing, I participated in many earth-centered rituals. Many tears were shed as I wrote letters to myself and past lovers seeking forgiveness and acceptance. I wanted badly for a miracle pill to exist that would cure me instantly of the physical and emotional heaviness that I had carried for years. But just as it had taken years to arrive at this painful place, I realized that it would take some time to rebuild a self-image that was truly authentic and joy-filled. Fortunately, I was patient with this reconstruction and used it as a base to move forward with working with the other elements.

With air, I discovered how my negative thoughts manifested themselves as truth. I also realized that the wind on my naked skin brings me great pleasure. With the wind comes change, so I prayed for clarity, vision and courage. I delved into my own sexual fantasies and fears and began to identify what I truly desired. Being able to speak freely of my desires unshackled and released my sexual demons. For the first time, I sat emotionally naked with beloved ones and shared my sexual stories.

Conjuring up water energy opened a floodgate of emotions. Past experiences of abandonment and abuse had left my heart bruised and closed. I spent time with natural bodies of water whenever possible. I gave offerings to Her through the ocean, and the bond created ignited my intuition in the most powerful way. I began to trust my gut feelings about people and situations that did not feel quite right. I created and led solitary full moon rituals seeking closure and renewal. Over time, my heart began to feel lighter, less cynical about love—and the love that was always present became evident.

Fire was a trickier energy for me. In some regards, I was

intimately familiar with it. Passion belongs to fire and I belonged to passion, but its pursuit kept me on an endless and frustrating search for more. I satiated this lust primarily with food and, less frequently, sex. For the most part, both left me feeling unfulfilled. My ritual work with fire revealed that my definition of "passion" was far too limited. Passion was, of course, about a strong sexual and sensual driving force. What I failed to understand about passion was that it was also the force that fueled creativity. My creative life was completely static. As a child, I had an active imagination and loved to sing and dance. By my early adulthood, I had decided that I had no artistic or creative talent, so whatever creative energy I cultivated early in life got tucked away. That ignored part of me was yearning for attention. My jealousy of artists probably should have indicated that something was amiss.

My search for my inner artist began. I took belly dancing and African dance classes. I bought finger paints and coloring books. I even joined a gay and lesbian community choir. While these activities provided much amusement, I was still feeling essentially fireless. I had not identified my fuel. More excavation ensued. The answer to the question of the source of my passion eluded me for years, but the fire rituals did expose that my definition of "creativity" was also too narrow. Yes, music, dance, poetry and visual art are all discernible measures of creative energy and necessary for life, but ultimately the most essential expression of the creative flow is through sexuality. I had to reconcile my definitions and experiences of "passion," "creativity" and "sex" in order to understand and express myself more fully through my sexuality.

In its most tangible form, heterosexual sexuality creates new life. As a lesbian, however, what does my sexuality create? I now believe that each time my erotic energy is expressed and allowed to flow freely, I create an opening to the divine source of love, the Goddess. I can tap into this source alone or with a partner. Further, I believe that when I choose to share myself sexually with another, our spirits join and are forever marked by that experience. Sex is sacred for me now. My body and my lover's body are sacred to me as well.

With these new beliefs, I am liberating myself from sexual guilt, shame and confusion. Through Wicca, I know now that a fun, healthy, loving sexual life is my birthright and integral to my journey toward spiritual wholeness. I am grateful to the Goddess for this awakening. Moments still exist when the wounds from my past feel fresh. The crucial difference, though, is that those wounds no longer control me. I know that each time I orgasm, the Goddess is present and she is smiling, and that I am growing ever closer to the oneness with Her and the universe that is my destiny as a healthy, self-loving lesbian woman.

*Starhawk, *Spiral Dance* (New York: HarperCollins Publishers, Inc., 1979), pp. 90-91.

As God's Love is perfect and, therefore, without exception or limitation, when I accept the truth of how I love—and I live that truth with love—I move closer to, not farther away from, God.

Without Exception or Limitation
By Kathleen E. Morris

"*I can understand her dilemma. Being a lesbian goes against the teachings of the church,*" he said.

"*But not against the teachings of God.*"

"*Yes, of course it does.*"

"*No, it doesn't. Do you believe that God is Love?*" He nodded in agreement.

"*And God's Love is perfect?*" He agreed again.

"*Then, if it is perfect, it is without exception or limitation.*"

He interrupted, "*Yes, but I'm sure He didn't mean—*"

"*Well, if God's Love is perfect—then it is without exception or limitation and there are no 'buts'—except those created by man. Perfect is perfect. Without flaw. Without exception. Without limitation. Perfect doesn't need to be interpreted—it simply, perfectly IS.*"

"*I have to disagree.*"

I chuckled. "*I'm sure you do, but with what do you disagree? That God's love is perfect?*"

"*No… it is… but—*"

I held up my hand. "*And do we agree that 'perfect' means 'without flaw'?*"

"*Yes, yes. We've agreed on that. But the Church clearly teaches that people of that persuasion or lifestyle … whatever … are abominations in the eyes of God.*"

"*So … the Church doesn't believe in the perfection of God's love?*" I grinned. *"Well, I sure am glad I'm not a Christian—otherwise, I might never know God."*

He had to study on that for a bit.

Before I left, he asked me for my card and permission to call. He wanted to continue the discussion about God.

"God? We've agreed that God's love is perfect; what else is there to discuss?"

I reached into my bag and pulled out a card. As I handed it to him, I added, *"But if you want to talk about the Church, give me a call."*

☙☙☙

a*bom*i*na 'tion utterly loathsome: detestable.
Webster's New Riverside Dictionary

The Church teaches, with great passion and frequency, that loving someone of the same gender is an abomination, and we suffer because we accept this as truth. Our community is rife with souls in pain.

From our earliest years, we are taught that the Church is the only portal through which we might pass on to Glory. Only in following the "right" way (which changes from church to church—even congregation to congregation) can we truly know God's Love. We accept, in the deepest places in our hearts, that those who do not follow the teachings of the Church will be cast out—of the church, of our communities, and later, out of heaven.

Since the Church has assured us that there is no place for queers in God's kingdom, and we believe it, those of us who remain in the Church must suppress or deny our truths from others and—often—from ourselves.

Others of us march defiantly out of the Church and into the darkness of spiritual oblivion. We try to staunch the flow of grief, anger and regret in the arms of lovers who cannot *possibly* survive the unabated transfusions of suffering and conflict, or the stench of contempt and self-loathing that rots our insides. The belief that love of another woman—or another man—has cost us the love of God poisons our hearts. More than the loss of family, violence in the streets, AIDS or failed relationships, the belief that we are unworthy of God's love rips open our souls, leaving wounds that can't heal, that leak blood and poison into every corner of our lives. It tears at the Spirit until the light in us fades in the face of this horrid truth of who we are. This love that "dare not speak its name" has cost us God. This person, in whose arms we hide, is proof of our damnation.

Giving up Glory is a high price to pay for mortal love.

Eventually, a part of us comes to hate our lovers because they are a constant reminder of all we have lost. Finally, when we leave them—or they leave us—the truth—that our love *is* an abomination—is confirmed.

But it's *not* the truth.

"Before I formed thee in the belly I knew thee;
and before thou camest forth out of the womb
I sanctified thee."
—Jeremiah 1:5 (*Holy Bible,* King James version)

The Church tells me there is no place for me in God's Kingdom. It teaches my family and my community that being gay is wrong, that it is a choice—like what outfit I will wear, or what church service I will attend—*if* I choose to get up and go.

I am a lesbian. My most intimate love is for women. My ability to love is *absolutely* a gift from God. When I love, I testify that God's Perfect Love resides in *my* heart and in *my* Spirit. I prove what the Church has taught me—that God lives in me, and in each of us.

Perfect Love does not change from this Sunday to the next. If I wake up on Wednesday and accept that I am a lesbian, *I* have changed. I have not changed "into" a lesbian; I have changed because I have accepted a truth about myself. I have, by accident or with purpose, stripped away a veil of self-illusion and, having done so, I move closer to living more honestly, more truthfully and more perfectly. As God's Love is perfect and, therefore, without exception or limitation, when I accept the truth of how I love—and I live that truth *with* love—I move closer to, not farther away from, God.

To share my life, my love, my joy, my tears, my triumphs, my failures with another woman is *not* an abomination. If I accept God's love as perfect and without limitation, and I have committed my life to living *in* that Perfect Love, to being *of* that Perfect Love, I must follow my heart. I must follow my Spirit—which is God.

This is the truth, no matter what anyone preaches from any pulpit.

I'd read the Bible cover to cover, twice, by the time I was eight. Both my parents worked nights back then. We had a live-in mother's helper who, at sixteen, didn't care what we were doing, so long as we were quiet and didn't bother her. She certainly wasn't interested in discussing the Bible—or anything else with an eight-year-old—but questions inevitably arise when one reads the Bible, and I was a child who needed answers. So I scheduled daily discussion time with God. Every night, before I went to sleep, we'd go over my questions and observations of the day. Those private moments I shared with God as a child were and are forever mine.

The questions asked and answered by and to me are not open to discussion, debate or interpretation by others. There was just God and me in those quiet moments in the dark and I have confidence in those memories, although I have allowed them to slip from my consciousness for much of my life.

I attended church every Sunday until I was eight. I remember looking forward to sitting at the little tables in the rooms upstairs.

Our teacher read Bible stories, after which we were allowed to color pictures with our choice of the crayons laid out in the middle of the table until it was time to go downstairs and join our parents. I would slide across the polished wooden pews and sit beside my mother. While she listened to the minister, I busied myself waving one of the fans supplied by the local funeral homes. Sucking butter rum Lifesavers as I waved the paper fans, I'd scan the congregation in search of the next likely candidate to "get the spirit" once the choir stood to sing.

Even writing about it now, more than thirty years later, I can still feel the cool of those wooden pews on the backs of my thighs. I still remember the red velvet kneeling cushions, worn through to white thread in places. I can feel the fabric of my mother's dress on the inside of my arm, the arm I used to link with hers when I got sleepy, and I remember the face of the ancient woman who sat in the pew opposite us every Sunday, in veiled and feathered hat. She never failed to smile at me, as an usher helped her stand and then escorted her from the church ahead of the crowd, at the end of service.

I remember other women of the church, who brought their own Bibles with them, but never opened them. They stroked the worn black covers with heavy hands as they nodded, or amen'd or grunted assent with our minister's message. They dabbed their breasts with white handkerchiefs and mouthed the scripture passages along with him. I remember the brass plates, etched with the names of long dead church patrons, on the front pews and beneath every stained glass window. I remember the enormous urns of flowers; the pipe organ, with its long, glistening brass tubes rising to the ceiling; the baptismal pool, rimmed in black marble, that stood ready below and to the left of the pulpit—the pool in which my brother and I were baptized on that day before my eighth birthday.

Those people became a part of who I am. They are at the foundation of all I love about black folk. I felt safe there in Grace Baptist Church; that church was an extension of home. That connection, made in the first eight years of my life, before I was even conscious of the world around me, still catches tears in my throat. It remains with me and of me, despite my passage through more than three decades since I'd let it go.

September 27, 1970. The day I was baptized was also my last day as a member of the Church. I'd spent the days before The Event eagerly preparing. I had to be perfect. I knew that we would wear white robes, supplied by the church, but I was to bring my own towel and a bathing cap. Of course, God saw *everything*—not just the white robe—so I selected my favorite panties, which were covered with little pink flowers. The pink was the exact same shade as the pink in my bathing cap—which was adorned with huge, floppy orange rubber flowers. My beach towel and my flip-flops were exactly the same orange as those flowers. Orange and pink were my favorite colors so, of course, I would share my very best. I knew, too, that God would appreciate how well everything was coordinated.

We arrived at the church and my mother was directed to the sanctuary, while I was taken upstairs to change out of my street clothes and into the white robe. The woman who was to escort me downstairs came into the changing room with my robe. She stared, horrified, at my neon-colored cap and shook her head. "No, no. That will *not* do. You can*not* wear… *that* to be baptized."

She took my cap and towel and replaced them with white counterparts. I had to walk downstairs barefooted, since she didn't have extra shoes and, she insisted, I could *not* be baptized in orange flip-flops.

This is the Church's rule, I realized immediately, *not God's.* God would have understood my sincere heart's offering. I was going to be entered into God's book. This was a joyful occasion, a time to celebrate, and celebration meant colors—colors from *God's* rainbow. I knew that God would *never* take away a child's rainbow. I didn't argue, because children did not argue with adults, but I closed my heart to the Church that day. I swore, under pain of torture and death, that I would never return. I already had a personal relationship with God and that was all I needed.

I didn't know then that I had already accepted that Church

was *the* portal to God. Back then, and to some extent, even today, it is difficult to find language that communicates one's personal relationship and celebration of God, or seeks out ways to be in service to God, or acknowledges or reminds others of their divinity, without inferring Christianity and the Church. I was not a churchgoer and had no intentions of ever being one.

Over the years, I got tired and frustrated with trying to find ways to clearly separate my understanding of God from Christianity and the Bible in discussions and even in my private thoughts. I spoke of God less and less. I spoke *with* God less and less. By the time I was a young woman, coming out as a lesbian, defining myself as an activist and feminist, God and religion (still not separated) were relegated to theoretical debates about the use of God and religion as tools of perpetuated control and subjugation.

Still, there are times when one is struck by something—a brilliant sunset, the wonder of some small, personal discovery that comes with new love—that words or reason cannot describe; some moments that give pause. You know that, while you are a part of it, or witness to it, it is not yours to create or control. There are times when something touches a part of your insides that you *know* you cannot access willfully; that, while felt at your very core, is outside of you… magical moments, when you *just know* that you have been touched by… the Divine.

I didn't know what it was back then. I knew only that, in the passing of those moments, a tender place inside of me was reopened, a place that seemed ever filled with sadness and tears.

It wasn't until recently, in the time my partner and I have been together—my partner, who brought with her the conscious and identifiable sorrow of her estrangement from Church and God—and from conversations with black lesbians and gays who had grown up in the Church, that I realized that my place of tears was where I'd once met with my childhood friend, God. The tears were grief. I missed my friend.

"If your leaders say to you,
'Behold, the kingdom is in the sky,'
then the birds in the sky will get there before you.
If they say to you, 'It is in the sea,'
then the fish will get there before you.
Rather, the kingdom is inside you and outside you."
—"The Gospel of Thomas" in
The Secret Teachings of Jesus: Four Gnostic Gospels,
Marvin W. Meyer, trans.
(New York: Random House, 1984)

We are not encouraged to remember that the church is not God, but a place where we might gather to give praise *to* God. When we are compelled to leave the church—or are cast out—most of us also believe that we have lost God.

Before and after church, however, we have a personal relationship with God. In church, when we give praise, it is because we feel our Spirits swell with Joy. The Spirit in each of us lifts up and merges into a single Spirit of unity and fellowship, seeking reconnection with the Light of Perfected Love, the Greater Spirit, God.

In our lives of constant change, God is our rock, for Perfect Love *never* changes.

"Thou shalt love thy neighbour as thyself."
—Galatians 5:14 (*Holy Bible,* King James version)

This is, I believe, the fundamental flaw of the Church. The Church—and we—*do* love our neighbors as we love ourselves: with censure, limitations and conditionally.

We love ourselves when we are winning. We ace a test, win a race, buy a new home, snag a coveted promotion. We loathe ourselves for getting too fat, for losing a job, for failing at love—and *that* is how we love our neighbor.

I love you—members of my country club or church, my race, my culture, my socioeconomic peers.

I despise you for being old, for not returning my affections; because you have more and thus are more than I am; because you have less and therefore are less than I am.

This is Man's love: imperfect, transitory and conditional. It is *not* God's love—which is perfect and without limitation.

Because we do not know how to love perfectly, we cannot presume to know the breadth or depth of God's love. My faith is the belief that it exists and that I am given my portion of that love, whether or not I am thankful for it, or recognize it—or even return it.

Perfect love does not seek a return on its investment.

It is only when I accept that God's Perfect Love *is* without exception or limitation—*even when such love is beyond my present capacity to understand or manifest*—that I can truly begin to dedicate my life to God. I begin to understand that no one and nothing can limit, control or destroy me in the name of God. I retrain myself to remember that the exceptions and limitations are man-made, not God's decree.

"Every word of God is pure:
he is a shield unto them that put their trust in him.
Add thou not unto his words,
lest he reprove thee, and thou be found a liar."
—Proverbs 30: 5, 6 (*Holy Bible,* King James version)

What is the Church but a gathering of man? Arrogant man—who has not yet touched a single star in God's vast firmament, nor touched foot on the floor of God's deepest ocean; who has yet to decipher the alchemy of his *own* life, which code is locked in a single strand of his own DNA; who has not been granted user access to even half of his own brain... but would presume to know God's intention for *my* life.

Hypocritical man, who would raise me to love God and teach me to pray and then exhort me not to listen to the answers given by the Spirit that gives me life; to reject or ignore that relationship, when it threatens the teachings of the Church.

Dangerous man, who would use the power of my faith as a weapon of oppression against me.

We are a people of Spirit. Like the food and water and air our mortal bodies need to survive, our Spirits need to reconnect with the Greater Spirit, which is God. We need to feel God's presence in our lives. We need to celebrate and give praise to the Spirit; the Spirit in us and all around us: the Spirit that is God.

We know our queer selves are not loved in the Church—*but the Church is family.* The Church is at the heart of the African-American community. It is the wellspring of African-American culture. *Our* community. *Our* culture. We *need* family to return to at the end of a hard day. We *need* the love of our people to make it through to the end of a hard life. Because of this need, we find ourselves making compromises. We allow the desecration of our Selves, even in a place where we have gathered to offer our Selves up to God. We continue to return to a home that will not allow us to bring *all* of our Selves, but expects to receive our full measure of God's blessings—and we give it. When the collection plates are passed, we put our personal blessings in. We *pay* to remain silent members of a congregation that despises us and decries how and who we love.

We have ultimate responsibility for the care and survival of our individual measure of Spirit. Because God has bestowed free will to us all, we have the power of choice. As children, our power of choice is held in trust by our caregivers. As adults, we assume the obligations of our inheritance. What we choose, or fail to choose, and when we relegate our power of choice to others, we have, with or without conscious intent, *chosen* to do so. If we choose not to hear the voice of Spirit, even when it speaks directly to us; choosing, instead, to accept and rely upon the interpretations of Divine message and lessons made by *other mortal men;* and if we *choose* to compromise or deny who we are and who and how we love, in order to retain that privilege, then we are guilty of the mutilation of our own Spirits.

If I enter a church or sacred space with the understanding that I cannot bring all that I am; if I fellowship in a place where I can offer up only a part of my Self; if I lift my hand and praise *any* part of a message that also includes instructions that would lead me *away* from God's Perfect Love by encouraging censorship or intolerance, then I must own my part in the destruction of my—and my community's—Spirit and life.

When we condone the hypocrisies of the Church by denying our divinity, or the divinity of others, we choose to enter into that covenant of deceit, and we are responsible for turning away from God's Perfect Love and toward that false idol, Societal Acceptance.

When I accept that I am a child of God, that we are *all* children of God; when I accept that God is Love Perfected, and that God's Perfect Love is *my* Spirit, which is the very breath of my Life, then I can also begin to accept that there is the possibility that we can transcend the bonds of our human flaws and move closer to—even become one with—Spirit. We can learn to understand, accept and share *true* Spiritual Love—with each other, and with ourselves. We can know Perfect Love. Love without limitation. Love without condition. Love without exception. Flawless Love.

In acknowledging the presence of God's Perfect Love in my life, I also begin to understand and accept that *It cannot be taken away from me.* Divine Love is not conferred or denied, nor can it be controlled, defined or interpreted, by any standard or rule created by Man.

Finally, I discover that, in the light of God's Perfect Love, there is hope. Hope for me. Hope for everyone.

Because God *is* Love, and God's Love is Perfect—without exception or limitation.

Blessed be.

Note to Readers: I acknowledge, gratefully, that there are ministers, within all denominations of faith, who, understanding the responsibilities of a calling to service, struggle to put aside personal ego and social vanities and strive to keep themselves, and those who follow them in faith, on a Divine Path. These seekers and champions of Light are excepted from the ranks of those described above.

There were two rays of light that shone through the darkness. One was my mother. I finally came out to her, near tears. And to my surprise and relief, she continued to love me…. The other light shining through the gloom of my loss, fear and guilt was the knowledge that my creating, loving, accepting God would not desert me, either, and I was not going to burn in hell for trying to live in truth.

Eve and Genevieve
By Tonya Parker

"God created Adam and Eve, not Adam and Steve" has reverberated in my ears, in my mind, in my life for many years. There's no one like a fire-and-brimstone black Baptist preacher to invent sound bites when communicating dos and don'ts. Especially the don'ts.

I'm the youngest of six children born to a poor African-American family in the South. In other words, I grew up in the church. It did not matter that my father seemed to stay drunk and rarely ventured to church; he still read the Bible every morning without fail. My maternal grandfather was a preacher, several uncles were deacons and my mother has been a church clerk as long as I've been living. We started every meal off with saying grace, and my mom read a scripture every Sunday morning at breakfast. Every week was filled with our family's religious rituals, as well as Sunday school, church worship, gospel concerts, Bible study, prayer meeting, Junior Usher Board and youth group. It appeared I was destined to become a card-carrying Christian.

My first memories in church are of Bible stories: Adam and Eve in the Garden of Eden, David and Goliath, Lot's wife, Jesus and the twelve disciples. I drank in these stories full of obedience and disobedience, bravery and cowardice, love and lust. I absorbed them in my mind like I did the Greek and Roman mythology I was learning in school. My childhood was spent living through books, and for me—initially, at least—the Bible was just another big storybook.

It took a while for me to realize that the Bible was supposed to be more than a collection of tales. It was sacred. The stories were "God's word." He had even spelled out a set of rules to follow, called the Ten Commandments. At the time I didn't know what "covet" meant, but I knew I was supposed to follow these rules or I would end up burning in hell with the Devil. Therefore, at the tender age of eight, I gave my life to Christ and started to work toward the African-American dream: depend on God to get through this life of oppression on earth and enter the pearly gates to get my just reward. There, in Heaven, I would find the streets paved with milk and honey, and get to see Grandma, too. Cool!

Being an overly compliant child, probably a function of my father's alcoholism, I took to Christianity like a duck to water. It gave me exactly the structure I needed to be the perfect girl I was supposed to be. My mama sure was happy. Three generations of women had become pregnant before marriage—my grandmother, mother and older sister. Not to mention the cousins and other local girls who had babies as babies. Because I was an "A" student, a lot of hopes and dreams were placed on my shoulders. I couldn't afford to go astray. Don't fornicate, just matriculate.

My Miss Goody-Two-Shoes rendition lasted up until my senior year in high school. Fornication now seemed fun, and everybody else sure was doing it. Thus began a conflict between what I learned and what I lived. That conflict continued as I left my small town for what seemed like a booming metropolis but was another Virginia town, albeit larger. College was a tremendous shock on a number of levels. For instance, I was no longer the big cheese; I was one of hundreds of high school valedictorians. Also, I could study or play on Sundays because no one made me go to church. And to make matters more interesting, there were so many people who looked and believed differently from me. A real change from my small town of black and white, Christian and Jew.

I could not believe that all these nice folk I was meeting would not be able to get into Heaven. After all, the Bible teaches that Jesus is the way, the truth and the light. Not Buddha, Mohammed or Confucius. And what was wrong with a person being gay? Why were they always being picked on? Weren't they made in God's image, too? Major internal conflict was happening. Despite my new friends and experiences, my childhood learning was reinforced every time I sang praises to the Lord in area churches as part of my school's gospel choir. By the time my senior year came around, I was a regular churchgoer again.

That year also brought an answer to my prayers. I asked God for a husband, and I got one. At least I began dating a man who, five years later, became my husband. Tall, handsome, educated, a product of a good, middle class black family. I struck pay dirt! Proof that prayer works. As a thank you to God, I became a more devoted Christian. I was in church almost every Sunday. I wasn't just a pew-sitter, either. I worked hard for the church. I sang in the choir, worked with the youth and co-founded the young adult fellowship.

On the surface, I truly was living the American dream. I had married, purchased a nice home, earned two graduate degrees and was well-respected as a counselor. I had achieved so much so quickly. Then why did I feel that something was missing? This feeling was further accentuated when my father died. After taking care of my family during their time of grief, I began to take a look at myself. I felt like I was drifting further from my family. I didn't want to be perfect anymore. My father's death essentially caused the demise of my overachieving, care-giving role in the family. I started feeling the need to re-create myself based on my needs, not the expectations of others. Yet, I still wasn't ready to totally free myself from my past.

Since my mother had grandkids from all her offspring except me, I decided that maybe a baby would bring purpose to my life.

After years of ambivalence about having children, especially after working with those with severe emotional disturbances, I began to envision myself as a mother. That would be a new and challenging role. Hadn't I played the role of mother in high school and college plays? However, my husband, a waffler like myself, didn't want children yet. Damn! We just couldn't get it right. When he was feeling paternal, I ran. Now I thought I was ready for a child, and he was not cooperating. I started to question more and more our relationship goals. I didn't know at the time I would later be thankful for his reticence.

In the meantime, I had gotten fed up with being an a la carte Christian, picking and choosing beliefs that made sense to me. I began to feel that Jesus Christ was a way, not necessarily the way. I felt guilty that I didn't "get happy" in church. I was barely tolerant of the Holy Ghost shuffle. I fell asleep during sermons more than I paid attention. I got tired of looks and comments about my choice of slacks or lack of pantyhose. Additionally, I didn't see eye to eye with my church's new pastor, and I was astounded when I'd see all the head-nodding when he'd say something I felt was ignorant and fundamentalist. A female associate minister shocked me one day when she told women to stay with their husbands no matter what, and to look at their own actions when the husband was cheating and beating. Sexism and patriarchy all wrapped up in a nice religious package, delivered by a woman, no less. My weekly Sunday mantra became *what the hell am I doing here?* I started feeling less and less connected to my old religion, and to my "peeps."

Thus started the church hopping. I thought that perhaps a younger, more educated minister and a contemporary congregation would be the key. I visited other African-American Baptist churches. Nice people, nice ministers, soulful music, more relevant messages, but still not inclusive of all people and other beliefs. Well, then I thought that maybe the white folk might do it differently. I had been to predominantly white Baptist, Methodist, Episcopalian and Catholic churches over the years. Didn't float my boat. The only all-white service I had enjoyed was a Friends meeting a few years previously. I truly enjoyed the simplicity and silence of the Quakers, as well as the inclusive nature. However, I knew I wanted more elements, such as singing and some ritual. I looked in the local paper and chose a nondenominational church that advertised casual services.

I walked into this community church and was very warmly welcomed. Though I was the only raisin in a bowl of rice pudding, I liked the laid-back environment, the optional offering versus the push for tithes, the snacks we could eat during the service, and thought *this is good*. I got my husband to visit once, but though he, too, was disgruntled with our original church, this new church just wasn't his cup of tea.

I simultaneously was experiencing stress in other areas of my life. I was beginning to burn out as a counselor. I was feeling cynical about my ability to help people who were so resistant to change. Health maintenance organizations were changing the face of behavioral health care. Also, as the token black therapist I was being pulled up to the main office more, having to work harder and longer, and I was resentful as hell. My husband was not happy at this time, either. He was more burned out than I was, and he did not have the work support network I had to deal with his stress. He subsequently quit his job and took the summer off trying to recover from depression and figure out what he wanted to do.

Additionally, I had been experiencing an increasing amount of "sinful" thoughts about women. I had first acknowledged these thoughts in my early twenties, but I discounted them and successfully put them away and focused on my pending nuptials. My counseling training taught me to normalize these feelings; however, I had no intention of exploring anything so frowned upon by my church, and that might jeopardize my marriage. After all, every sister knew a good black man was hard to find. However, at this point in my life, I slowly began spending more time with my lesbian friends, and more time away from home.

I inconveniently took this time to fall in love with a woman. An actual, flesh-and-blood person versus a safe character in a book or a Friday night Skinemax movie. I did not recognize for some time that I was in love, but in later months I was honest enough to admit to myself my true feelings. My husband felt very threatened by this woman and her partner, as well as my other lesbian friends. He suddenly seemed to change into his father, a Baptist minister, and his need for control increased twofold. He started forbidding me to see these friends. When I eventually told him I was in love with the woman in question, he really hit the roof. He started picking apart my personality and preferences, and made a laundry list of don'ts, just like at church. Don't go places with these women. Don't coach these women in volleyball. Don't go to the Bahamas with my girlfriends. Don't keep my hair short. Don't wear pants so much. Don't say no when he wants to have sex. Don't, don't, don't, don't, don't! That period in my life sparked a depression that affected me to the core. For the first time since childhood, I actually wanted to die.

I was a mess. I felt I had ruined this precious man's life. I was considering ruining mine. At least my pragmatic nature and need for approval prevented me from considering ending my life. And what would my mama, the Preacher's Kid, say? To make matters worse, I did not feel connected enough to my new spiritual family for them to help. I didn't think they would understand anyway, since hidden amongst the low-key form of worship was still a strong Bible bent. Well, here I was, quite bent myself, and feeling panicked.

Fortunately, there were two rays of light that shone through the darkness. One was my mother. I finally came out to her, near tears. And to my surprise and relief, she continued to love me. As she put it, I was still her "angel." She told me that some people may not understand my choices and me, but as one got older, one started to understand these things more. I felt so lucky, so very blessed. The other light shining through the gloom of my loss, fear and guilt was the knowledge that my creating, loving, accepting God would not desert me, either, and I was not going to burn in hell for trying to live in truth.

With the tremendous support of some selected co-workers

and lesbian friends, I listened to my heat and my soul, and opened myself up to my woman-loving feelings. I set a date to leave my marriage. My husband, in a panic, began getting friends to call me and to visit—some from other states—to set me straight, so to speak. Supposedly it was a therapeutic intervention to help me see what he perceived as my obvious mental breakdown. However, it all backfired. Most of my friends were supportive and affirming, though admittedly very shocked. Everyone began trying to get to face reality.

At this time I did do some things to appease him. I agreed to marital counseling, and I decided to meet with my new minister and his wife. Counseling lasted all of two sessions. Simply put, our goals were very different. I wanted to negotiate an ending to our marriage. He wanted to reconcile. Ironically, our chosen profession failed us both. Therapy was not enough to bridge the gap between two people determined to follow different paths. This was the end of our love affair.

I was about to move out when the first meeting with the minister and his wife occurred, marking the end of another love affair—that of my church and me. The reverend played it cool during the first meeting, but upon our second meeting, at my new apartment, he essentially turned into a Bible beater. Sure, Jesus loved me regardless, but if I had sexual thoughts about women, I was still sinning. Even if I chose to lead a celibate life, I knew my thoughts of women weren't going anywhere. I felt I was damned if I did and damned if I didn't. Adios to that church. It still wasn't inclusive enough for me. Why didn't people "get it"? I saw nothing wrong with what I was feeling toward women.

During the most liberating, yet the most grief-filled period in my life, I was alone, churchless, marriageless, struggling financially, and in love with a woman who was in a strong partnership with a wonderful person. To make matters worse, these friends were about to move away. I was in dire need of spiritual guidance.

I still don't quite remember what led me to my new church. The Unitarian Universalists had been advertising their presence in the community for years. Different people, gay and straight, had recommended it to me, years before I came out. I assumed the services were very white and overly intellectual, and would not provide for my spiritual needs. But one Sunday morning, three weeks after my separation, I hesitantly walked through the doors of this beautifully constructed church. I immediately saw a familiar face—the wife of a colleague in my former counseling practice. A greeter at the church, she opened her arms and her heart, gave me a huge smile and welcomed me. She pointed out her husband to me, and sent me to sit with him. She joined us when the service started.

And what a service it was. There were members of different local Indian tribes, and the service featured their drumming and religious traditions. I saw a former counseling student from my adjunct teaching days. A Native American, this woman and I had connected on so many levels and continuously had been brought together under what appeared to be coincidences. When I saw her in the church I knew it was no coincidence, and I was meant to be exactly where I was.

I felt jubilant. The beating of the drums called out to me and touched my soul. I felt years of pain erasing, defensive walls crumbling, my heart and mind opening and filling with love. I joined the reading of the church covenant, realizing that this was a spiritual promise that I could keep. Finally, a place where I could skip the a la carte and enjoy the entire meal. A place where my God could be Goddess. Where I could discover my own spiritual truths. Where I felt the freedom to express myself as black and as lesbian. A place where Adam could openly love Steve, and Eve could love Genevieve.

I often reflect on that beautiful, blessed November day when, through my tears, I saw so many faces repeating those same words, making that same promise. A small handful looked like me, but most didn't. Many were obviously gay, but most not. "Recovering" or practicing Christians and Jews, Buddhists, pagans, secular humanists. All different, all the same. All accepting, and united in this special faith community. I knew I had come home.

The myth healed, taking me on a ride back to myself—to the realization that I am meant to be a whole healthy human being who is not only defined as homosexual, but who can just as easily be defined as a brother, a father, a son, a lover, a friend to anyone regardless of their sexual preference or mine.

Reflections Upon the Bambara Creation Myth
By Conrad R. Pegues

Creation has occurred. Consciousness has been dramatically severed from itself. Now there are two parts of it. From a secret recess—a self-containing sphere—suddenly god thought. And that "suddenly," said the countess, was the earliest instance of what later became known as Nyale. (Judith Gleason, 25)

The passage quoted above is taken from a creation myth of the Bambara tribe of West Africa. The creation myth begins with a primal, genderless deity existing as a singular entity within a formless and massless *Nothing*. The deity then somehow, without any conscious effort, turned back and spied itself. When the god saw itself for the first time, it was in awe. Out of that reflection came the first thought—I AM—which led to the creation of what we know as the universe. It exploded into being at this primordial moment. That initial thought and the explosion it engendered over time led to the creation of the cosmos, our star system, Earth with its flora and fauna, and humankind.

When I first read the Bambara creation myth years ago, it struck a deep chord within me. I felt as if I had come home to a realization that this was *the* story I had been looking for my whole life to give my experience in the world meaning and order. The Bambara creation myth, of the deity suddenly exploding into being and consciousness by looking upon itself for the first time, made me consider how we as black folks, and as black same gender loving folks, look upon one another when we meet. Is that element of ecstatic surprise there for us as it was for God according to the Bambara? Do we look at one another and ourselves in the mirror with such wonder and delight? And what kind of reality do we create for one another in our interactions? Heavens or Hells?

The Bambara imply that reality is not solely created for us, but is also created by us as individuals and as a collective. Creation being a product of that Creator god who, time out of mind, looked upon itself with wonder, we also gain the capacity to impact one another's reality from the least to the great. What we believe or think we see causes us to act or speak. Those actions or words can be positive or negative in their impact upon others' lives and our own.

In the Christian religion, Jesus taught, "I have said you are gods." But consciousness was not the only thing born of God. After the deity's primal thought, a vibration was initiated across the distance of the two halves of the whole looking at one another. Within this divine sphere of consciousness was born space and time:

> Now came the explanation: to accomplish thought, the perfect sphere had to divide slightly so that one part could reflect upon the other. Seeing himself as double meant that within the narrow separation between the hemispheres of god were simultaneously created light, distance, and time. And god heard upon this instant his own inner voice in the form of a vibration, which will subsequently animate the entirety of what is beginning to be created. (25)

Through the vibration that was God's voice and vision, God became part and parcel of everything created within its matrix. The Word of God became the ubiquitous building block of the universe. Thus, nothing is fragmented or separate from any other part of the initial reality. Creation could not be born out of singularity. It had to be born out of more than a single isolate entity. Two sides were necessary for all things to come into being, maintaining a tension between the two extremes out of which reality and matter could flow. So it is with human beings.

We are just like the Bambara god in that it takes self-reflection and reflection upon a community of others to define who we are individually and collectively at any given moment in time. The Bambara are saying that we are unfinished gods perpetually creating the worlds in which we live and living in the world, which others have created before us! This is not some new age philosophy where we "create our own reality" without respect to personal responsibility, the right to choose, and historical factors. Rather, the Bambara creation myth places responsibility for our quality of life within our hands and those of others with whom we must live and interact. We become our sister's and our brother's keeper. We are god taking a long look at ourselves in others.

To exemplify the point further of creation being a communal effort, not an isolated, individualistic endeavor, the Bambara say that Nyale, the feminine principle of fire and wind, was born soon after the universe exploded into being carrying the primal word of creation throughout an embryonic space: "Alone... Nyale dispersed creation's word throughout space" (25). At least, Nyale thought she was alone. She later realized that, just like the Creator before her, she also had a double in Faro, the androgynous water spirit, the moisture in the primal Word. Nyale mistakenly believed that she was the only entity that God had created and felt that she should be exclusive in the universe so she tried to dry up Faro in a fiery windstorm. Not realizing Faro to be a part of her very essence, the more she tried to dry him up the more moisture he provided. As long as she existed Faro would exist. So much dried up mass accumulated from the interaction of wind/fire and water that, inadvertently, the earth spirit, Ndomadyiri, was born. So the four elements, wind along with fire and water, and later earth, came to be the foundation of a universe alive and expanding due to its own fecundity.

The process of creation is ever fertile and always establishing new ways of being in the cosmos. The Bambara understand that there is no such thing as an absolute truth in the cosmos that applies to all points and times in experience. As the Creator had to double to come into self-consciousness, so too was Nyale a double regardless of her desire for exclusivity in the universe. Nyale's struggle promoted more and more kinds of consciousness until the earth itself was produced and finally the human being.

Judith Gleason, the author of *Oya: In Praise of an African Goddess,* explains that the Bambara creation myth breaks down into the mechanical processes of speech: "As one speaks, from the mouth issues a mist" (25). When speaking, we start to share moisture and we're already sharing the air over which the vibrations of our voices travel to the waiting ear. Because we're mammals, anything issuing from our bodies will be warm including our spoken words. The information relayed from person to person automatically initiates action based upon what we understand from what has been seen and said. Thus, actions are the concrete end result of our perceptions of the world around us. Flesh fueled by consciousness acts! The Bambara creation myth is a sophisticated means of explaining how cognition and reality work to establish a sense of community as well as providing that community with a sense of how all things came into existence from the common source that is the divine:

> Implicit in this initial act are all four elements, she explained. Wind, together with fire, subtly initiates the process. Water reflects and therefore verbalizes Act into Being. Earth provides resistance.... Earth is the halt preventing diffusion of spirit and ensuring that what is said will be heard, will endure. It is the implicit element of earth that engraves water's sinuous memories upon the brains of evolving creatures. (25)

The first act of creation has come down to us through untold millions of years of evolution in the simple process of our daily interactions in speaking our worlds into being. The act of creation is no isolated incident, but a labor of the entire community of living beings from humans to plants to animals and even including the elements as given anthropomorphic traits in the myth itself. The elements are seen as co-factors helping to sustain the very basis of our material existence in this world.

If we are the bearers of the creative principle that helps to sustain reality along with the Creator of the universe then the things we speak, do and say to one another are literally the forces of construction and destruction, positive or negative. Reality is made by self-and-other and that other can be another person, a tree providing oxygen and shade on a summer afternoon, an ant crawling across your bare foot, or the wind blowing against your skin. Reality is about *Us* and not *I* and I alone. So we are all bearers of an ever living and evolving Word constantly creating itself anew in our everyday existence in the world. We are each, literally and figuratively, the Word of God. With this perpetually creative and communal consciousness must come responsibility and accountability. Our labor in this world is to build community and provide a deeper sense of one another's humanity and divinity. This is the necessity, a moral imperative, if humanity and culture are to continue.

The Bambara creation myth stuck with me because it gave form to the various pieces of my own life filled with the need to connect to black men, black folks in general and all of creation beyond the cultural limits of race, gender and sexuality.

My experience with black men up to the point at which I encountered the myth had no story in which it could be properly framed. The vignettes of my life around black men were like a thousand pages of a novel torn out and scattered across the floor. The Bambara creation myth sparked order where there had been none before. The whole idea of Nyale initially thinking her journey throughout the cosmos to be an isolated one spoke to my own journey of isolation from black men to the overwhelming need to connect with them spiritually and emotionally.

My homosexuality over the years made me increasingly aware of my need to connect to other black men in as many ways as I could, including sexual desire (homosexual desire and homo-social space not necessarily being synonymous). The desire for male affection and affirmation are not always the stuff of sex. I needed black men in ways that affirmed my most basic human qualities: the need for a sense of community and love. Nyale's journey throughout the universe was reminiscent of my movement away from masculine isolation to the realization of a communal sense of purpose where every interaction might breed a larger sense of connection, one person to another. For some time, the options for connection seemed few or non-existent due to the limited definition of "manhood." This left me with a psychic deficit, looking for affection and affirmation in wretched places, often leaving me with the most haunting emotional experiences.

The Bambara creation myth initiated me into a journey toward understanding my life, and my black body as something to be loved and shared; it's been a laborious and disturbing process to say the least. As Nyale, along with Faro, touched the four directions of creation into being at the behest of God, bringing the earth spirit, Ndomadyiri into existence, "...preventing diffusion of spirit and ensuring that what is said will be heard, will endure," so I needed other black men to touch me into being and aid me in defining, in a tangible way, who I can become in the continuum of black maleness in this world. The Bambara creation myth also made me realize that the work of my life, in trying to connect on a psycho-spiritual and physical level to other black men, is not only a laborious task, but one in progress for life.

The Bambara creation myth had taken me full circle to understand that what it is that we need most to create a better world is an understanding that we are divine creatures in need of a space in which we can grow into our full potential as human beings here on earth. The myth blessed me to understand that the years of isolation I had imposed upon myself trying hard not to deal with my sexuality could have no positive end. I had been such a loner up until the time that I read about the goddess Nyale. I didn't want to encounter other people at depth because such engagements entailed change and taking a chance on loving people who might fail me one day or reject me if they knew the truth about my love for black men.

Like Nyale, I'd made the mistake of believing that I was alone in this world and would never really need anyone for any reason. For years, I'd hidden behind sadomasochistic frustration and cruelty masked as spirituality, not wanting the pain of life to touch me. The myth went to the heart of my problem long before I became fully conscious of my own proclivity for self-destructive behavior. I was trying to be a human being in part, denying the fact that I needed people for emotional succor to help me define my own humanity and figure out who I needed to be in the world. I was more than just my sexuality. If I wanted to learn to embrace life, I'd have to accept the bitter with the sweet, with the faith that things could work out for the better in the long run. The myth of Nyale realizing that she was not alone in the universe set me on a path of understanding before I really understood my own process of growth in motion. There was something special in the goddess' realization of her double, her other half, which she didn't even realize she had. Although she tried to destroy it, mistaking it for an enemy and not of herself, not god given, her fight with the double was in vain. She only ended up creating a world. Nyale had to learn to embrace her whole self for the sake of her own continued existence.

The myth healed, taking me on a ride back to myself—to the realization that I am meant to be a whole healthy human being who is not only defined as homosexual, but who can just as easily be defined as a brother, a father, a son, a lover, a friend to anyone regardless of their sexual preference or mine. I was creating the ground from which I could seek out a deeper sense of community with others, especially black men from whom I'd felt so estranged. Nyale's journey was not an easy one and neither has mine been, struggling to affirm myself in a space of lovelessness and hatred in a larger community that thrives on the same mistake that Nyale made: God and creation belong to me and me alone!

I've expended great energy over the years trying hard and failing to fit my sexuality into the mold of Christian and heterosexual paradigms. Like Nyale trying to rid herself of her natural double/self Faro, I've often found myself trying to see where I can fit myself amongst the hate filled sermons, be honest in the face of bible studies where my life is not fully recognized because of my difference, tried to evade the issue at times to keep from cussing out preachers and lay people alike. In essence I've been fighting myself. The resultant world created from that battle has been one of pain and denial, looking for love in the streets from people who can't love me back, in the arms of men who couldn't possibly grasp who I am, and settling for less than I deserve.

I am learning that I cannot fit within the Christian and heterosexual paradigm, but I don't have to reject them outright. Neither paradigm is all bad, so I only take what I need and leave the rest, letting the divine settle accounts in the long run. "So if I don't fit there, where do I fit" is the question that plagues my soul at this point. If I look at the myth of Nyale, I recognize an innate and god given ability to create a world out of word (the ways in which I define myself) and the ways in which I try to meet my own very human needs in this world that says I should not even exist. Like Nyale spanning the cosmos, I search the larger community amongst my brothers and sisters looking for a common thread of thought, an affirming touch, conversation that makes my soul soar and that doesn't wrap itself up in religiosity and prejudice. Unlike Nyale I had to recognize fast that I can't live in this world alone. I need companions and long for them. I'm not trying to be the sole proprietor of divinity in this life.

The original deity had made all and all existed within it. The cosmos was made to be shared, to multiply and be abundant. The thing Nyale recognized after many years was that we can only create, not destroy. But what worlds will we create? Worlds made of war and hatred of difference? Or will we create worlds where difference is embraced with as much zeal as sameness? The Bambara creation myth set me on a path to recovering the human in my life (not just my sexuality) and in this world, an unfinished task at best and one that has pushed far beyond the limits of my sexuality without denying it.

The Bambara creation myth taught me that community is not the stuff of isolation, but is made of meeting basic human needs--my own and those of others. To love and nurture one another to become our best selves is the goal of community, not to battle against the natural divine connection we all share, as Nyale tried to do in being rid of Faro. She had to learn that the divine is never an isolated issue and never just about the self. The divine belongs to no one group or person. It belongs to us all. Creating worlds of hatred or worlds of love and compassion are always a communal effort begun from the heart. A heart that understands that it is divine to connect and create knows such great responsibility and yearns for the greatest intimacies of community. When we don't understand our divinity, the result is violence. Unloved flesh, unloved spirit always seek revenge upon the community one way or the other.

The Bambara myth made me more empathic and vulnerable to my own human need for affirmation and affirming the needs of others. This is what it means for the Word of God to manifest itself within the realm of the human. It's the quality of our human interactions that is important. When we meet do we bless or curse? So now when I meet people my spirit lurches forward in a silent, unseen dance to embrace the spirit of the other. This embrace is like an umbilical cord , soul-to-soul, through which we exchange our unique stories, our joys, our hurts so as to create something more than any of us could call forth on our own. This is the essence of community. It is the Bambara story of creation all over again in our everyday meetings and greetings. Sometimes the other dancers cannot release their spirits to join mine (or vice versa) in the dance of life for fear or because they may sense a difference they can't embrace because it doesn't fit the standards of their religion or value system. These losses are not just theirs; they are ours, everybody's loss in the long run. No new worlds of nurture are created in which to thrive as human beings.

The sad thing is that not everyone is ready to let the depths of who they are shine forth in the vulnerable space that is authentic community. Many of us would rather hide behind the labels by which we live in our careers, gender roles, and positions of power, or settle (un)comfortably into our limited religious views. To step outside of these confines would make us more vulnerable than many of us care to become publicly or privately. So we hide behind the singularity that is our own deep isolation, rarely creating systems of human worth in the world.

The Bambara myth pushed me beyond such a sad existence and is still pushing me with each day's encounter of other human beings to find ties that bind us one to another. I am sometimes left to dance across the cosmic floor alone, but I live by the faith that having the courage to take to the dance floor of life creates the possibility for a better world to spin into being.

Work Cited

Gleason, Judith. Oya: *In Praise of an African Goddess.* 1987. San Francisco: Harper, 1992.

When I fell in love, I surprisingly did not feel conflicted about whether or not it was wrong. I knew immediately that the amazing and intensely spiritual love I shared with another woman was not, and could not, be a sin.

On My Journey Now...
By Scarab

During my teen years, the pianist/director of the youth choir was a well-known dyke in the community. During one rehearsal, she walked over to the choir stand to talk to us. She leaned against the banister where my hand rested. She pressed her breast against the back of my hand. I remember feeling she knew exactly what she was doing; feeling like I was being tested somehow. I dared not move my hand.

I grew up in a religious home. My father is a Baptist minister and pastor in the South. My mother is referred to as "The First Lady." I have been a PK (preacher's kid) all my life. I grew up in the church. For this I am thankful. It provided a foundation for me. I grew up hearing and watching my grandparents, on both sides, praying, singing and leading devotion in church. My grandparents' rural Southern church even bears my family name (imagine a church where just about everyone is related to you).

Up until eight years ago, when I moved away from home, my father had always been my pastor as well. I went to, and sometimes held offices in, Sunday school, district Sunday school congresses, vacation Bible school, Baptist training union, choir rehearsal, youth meetings, district youth meetings, Wednesday night prayer meetings/Bible studies, New Year's Eve midnight watch services, pastor's conferences, baptisms, weddings, funerals, and on and on.

It still amazes me when I mention, in passing, a Bible story to an acquaintance and they have no idea what I'm talking about! Moses, Noah, Abraham, Isaac, Jacob, Daniel and the lions' den, David and Goliath, Cain and Abel, Naomi and Ruth are all an ingrained part of my childhood. Sometimes I have to remind myself that not everyone was raised the way I was. Not everyone knows these ancient stories. I'm thankful for the kind of childhood I had.

I did not come out to myself until age twenty-three, when I fell in love for the first time with a woman. This period of my life was a huge awakening for me on many levels. But most importantly, it was the beginning, the birth of my spirituality and consequently the rebirth of my religion, my faith.

As a child, I was surrounded by the doctrines and beliefs of the Baptist denomination. At age nine I accepted Christ as my Savior, and I have no doubts about my salvation. But Baptists, as do many denominations, believe homosexuality is a sin. At age twenty-three I could no longer deny my lesbianism, and it caused me to question my religious beliefs. Did I believe because I was raised that way, or was it because I truly had faith in the Baptist teachings? I realized it was a little of both.

When I fell in love, I surprisingly did not feel conflicted about whether or not it was wrong. I knew immediately that the amazing and intensely spiritual love I shared with another woman was not, and *could not,* be a sin. I am not talking about the old saying, "if it feels good, do it." I believe everyone is born with an innate sixth sense that helps one differentiate between right and wrong. Our gut feeling, intuition, inner voice tells us. It's just up to us, should we have the mental, emotional and spiritual capacity, to listen. I listened and in my listening, in my connection with this woman, with this other spirit, I experienced the divinity within myself, the God in me, around me. My spiritual and religious journey as an independent adult woman was beginning.

❧❧❧

Study to show thyself approved unto God,
a workman that needeth not be ashamed,
rightly dividing the word of truth.
—II Timothy 2:15

Once I *knew* I was not sinning, I thought: How do I back it up to my parents with scripture? I grew up in the church. I'll get words like "abomination," "sin" and "perversion" tossed at me. Leviticus, Romans, I Corinthians, I Timothy, Adam and Eve, and, of course, Sodom and Gomorrah will be thrown in my face. How do I face that? How do I combat it? II Timothy 2:15 gave me my answer. I had to study, understand God's word for myself; find my own truth. And not just in regards to homosexuality, but in regards to all my religious and spiritual beliefs

I began my own investigation. I picked up a couple of pamphlets on homosexuality and religion distributed by a gay-friendly denomination. I began re-reading the Bible, starting with Genesis. I was particularly enlightened and encouraged by Linda Villarosa's "Revelations," in *Afrekete,* an anthology of Black lesbian writing edited by Catherine E. McKinley and L. Joyce DeLaney (Anchor Books). It made me realize that I had to search and research deeper. But perhaps the most insightful reading by far has been Daniel A. Helminiak's book, *What the Bible Really Says About Homosexuality* (Alamo Square Press). It is a must-read for anyone seeking to reconcile their sexuality with their religious beliefs. This book provided me with the scriptural ammunition I need to fight the homophobia—guised as Christian love—of ignorant people.

For years the Bible has been misquoted, misrepresented, mistranslated and misinterpreted. Scripture passages have been taken out of context scripturally, historically, culturally and anthropologically and used (abused) to support, condone and instill racism, slavery, misogyny and homophobia. In one word: HATRED. "Whoever does not love does not know God, because God is love" (I John 4:8). Therefore, when ignorant religious zealots—who have either been spoon-fed the Word without reading it themselves, or have only *read* the Bible, not studied it—claim to damn us to hell in the name of Jesus Christ and out of love, they lie. And, worst of all, they blaspheme!

> It is, in fact, a sad irony that the overwhelmingly white Christian Right movement is capitalizing on homophobia in Black communities. Groups like the Moral Majority and the Christian Coalition have never marched side by side with or fought for issues affecting people of color. In fact, the Christian Right has actively lobbied against issues such as voting rights and affirmative action. But now they're recruiting our people [hello, Reggie White], taking advantage of the deep spiritual commitment of the African-American community and distorting Christianity to pass anti-gay and lesbian initiatives and turn straight Blacks against gays—similar to the way their ancestors distorted Christianity to justify slavery.
> —Linda Villarosa, "Revelations"

My reading and studying, which is an ongoing process, has just proved what I already knew in my heart. The Bible does NOT condemn homosexuality. Actually, once I examined closely the scriptures often used against us—the original Hebrew and Greek texts and the original cultural, historical context in which they were written, instead of a Twentieth Century context—I found the Bible is not preaching that homosexuality is a sin! There are even possible homosexual relationships in the Bible: Jonathan and David in I and II Samuel, and Ruth and Naomi in the book of Ruth.

All that being said, one could get bogged down and maybe even discouraged by the daunting task of serious anthropological/historical biblical research and study. Gays and heterosexuals seem to be caught up in unimportant details: ritual and tradition. Like the Pharisees and Sadducees of old, we are caught up in the letter of the law. "One of the reasons Jesus was killed was because he challenged the real importance of the Law," says Helminiak. Jesus himself did things while on Earth that were against Jewish law, the Old Testament. And the Pharisees and Sadducees tried to kill Him on these "infractions." Jesus was not, and is not, concerned with religious rituals for the sake of doing them, for tradition. There is no salvation in religion. Jesus is concerned with a person's heart. "Blessed are the pure in heart, for they shall see God" (Matthew 5:8).

"Where's pop?" I asked on the phone.
"Oh, he's doing some dyke's father's funeral," mama answered.

I grew up hearing the jokes and derogatory comments my parents made about homosexuals.

J.T. is a choir member at my dad's church. Beautiful voice, and very effeminate. At home, after a service when J.T. had a solo, mama and daddy both commented that the "He" J.T. was lovingly singing about probably wasn't God at all, but "some punk." (cue the laugh track)

I still hear them. Then, I laughed. Now, I want to cry or scream in anger and frustration. My parents have no idea that each joke and demeaning remark against homosexuality cuts me like a knife. The way my mama talked about my lesbian sister— my mother stripped this poor bereft woman of her humanity, her personhood! Is that what my parents would think of me? Less than human; not deserving of respect; "some dyke"? My mother denied reverence, respect for the religious ritual of a funeral for the woman's father because she's gay. I know, by my parents' comments over the years, that they consider people like me to be sick, perverted, gross and unnatural. Maybe one of my purposes in life is to educate them, and others like them, as to just how wrong they are.

I still have some hurdles to cross. I am, at age thirty-one, not out to my parents. I want to tell them. I know there is nothing I could say or do that would make them stop loving me. But who I am flies in the face of my parents' religious beliefs. They will be hurt, disappointed and probably angry.

I am not out at the church at which I am currently a member. In my own small ways, though, I've been out at my church. I've worn my rainbow bracelet, and my *Out on Film* T-shirt to choir rehearsal. And I always park my rainbow-covered car (a heart, peace sign and yin-yang symbol, thank you very much) close to the church, daring somebody to say *something* to me about them. The thing is, even if someone recognized my multicolored paraphernalia as gay pride symbols and not religious symbols, I doubt they'd say one word to me.

I am out in other aspects of my life—at work, in the community, with friends. I love my church and my preachin'/teachin' pastor. It has been a great source of spiritual guidance and fellowship for me. The spirit-filled, clapping, rocking, expressive worship service is what I am used to and find comfortable. It is familiar and ancient. When I come on Sunday I know I'll hear a sermon to feed my spirit, not some dull, laid-back emotionless lecture. It *is* the Black worship experience. We are a spirited people. The choir I am a part of is an anointed ministry of which I am proud to be a member. The Holy Ghost high (if you've never had one, it's amazing) I get while singing with them is truly a blessing. I am comfortable with every aspect of my church home, except one: in the Baptist tradition, they believe homosexuality is a sin. It is rarely mentioned. So rarely that I've deluded myself into thinking it's a non-issue. But then I am reminded.

At choir rehearsal we always have a period before, and after, to voice praises and ask for prayer. At one rehearsal, a fellow choir member asked for prayer for pro football player Reggie White because he was being attacked for his anti-gay stance. I cringed as soon as she said the man's name. Her remark sparked a ripple effect throughout the choir. People were commenting on gays, how we should stand, like Reggie, for God. Even my choir director commented on the plethora of multicolored symbols she'd seen on "their" cars. I sat still, not saying a word, realizing I was getting angrier by the second. I wanted with all my heart to just stand up, grab my things, and storm out of there. But I didn't. I sat there… silent.

Even though I rarely socialize with them outside of church, my fellow choir members are my family—my church family. Coming out to them would alienate me from them and eventually that church–the church I love. They would probably believe my homosexuality to be something from which I needed to be delivered. The irony is that I'm sure I'm not the only homo in that church, or in that choir. We've always been in the church, from the usher board and the choir to the pulpit *(oh say it ain't so)*.

"Do any of your friends go to church?" mama asked.

I wish more of my close friends went to church and had the same beliefs as I do. A couple of them—literally—go to church occasionally. But the rest do not. All of my friends, lesbians of color, believe in God. Some were raised Baptist, others Catholic, one Jehovah's Witness. But for varied reasons, not just lesbianism, they left the church. The main reason is, I believe, that they just do not share or agree with some of the beliefs of their particular church/denomination. However, my friends' search for their religious freedom and individuality has made them some of the most spiritual people I know—even more so than some people who go to church every Sunday. In a way they have formed their own *personal* religions. The term "religion" does not have to mean an organized doctrine. My friends and I share some of the same spiritual beliefs and ideas. Still, I wish we shared more of the same *religious* beliefs. I want the same fellowship I have with my church family with my chosen family.

> For where two or three come together in my name,
> there am I with them.
> —Matthew 18:20

There is definitely truth in the saying "there are no accidents." There really are no such things as coincidences. I agree with Patti LaBelle in that "coincidences" are the everyday miracles of our lives. Everyday blessings. 'Coincidences' are just God's way of staying invisible," Patti Labelle says in her book *Don't Block the Blessings*. Truly, they are Divine Guidance. It is no accident that I am writing these words at this time. It's a part of my life journey; my spiritual path.

It is also no accident that I am connecting with Julie (not her real name). Julie is a part of my past, the most painful part. She and I were in love with the same woman at the same time. We couldn't stand each other. The whole drama was ugly, hurtful and painful for all involved. I wouldn't wish what I went thought on my worst enemy. I know that only God got me through that time. And because of God all three of us are now friends.

It had been over a year since I had last seen Julie. I saw her at a panel discussion on Black gay and lesbian literature. Our running into each other was definitely no "coincidence." After the panel she and I lost ourselves, for a moment, in a discussion on the mistranslation and misinterpretation of homosexuality in the Bible. Since then we've been trying to hook up to discuss scriptures, but have been playing phone tag. But I know we'll talk when, as Julie says, it's "ordained" for us to do so.

Like myself, Julie is a religious *and* spiritual person. In her last phone message Julie mentioned the idea of coordinating, with one of her fellow church members, a Bible study for gays and lesbians in order "to be empowered by God's truth" and "put an end to all the deception as well as have a fellowship [with] Christians who are gay and who are believers."

The idea of joining with other Christians *in the life* to study the Bible is so exciting to me. It is something I've never experienced. I can only imagine how empowering and spiritually uplifting this could be. Julie asked me to pray for its manifestation. I will.

"On my journey now… Lord, I wouldn't take nothin' …"
—Negro spiritual

For me, religion without the spirituality to back it up is empty, void, nothing. I once had a girlfriend who was amazed that I was spiritual *and* religious. She couldn't understand the coexistence of the two, so she wanted to "learn everything" about me. I believe some gays take their frustration with, and hatred of, organized religion and religious dogma out on God, which is a dangerous thing. Because it has been used against us, some of us have this animosity toward religion (even the word itself) and Christianity. Homosexuality and Christianity are not antithetical to each other. Religion and spirituality do not have to be antithetical to each other either. My religious upbringing, for which I am truly thankful, provided me with a foundation, a framework. Now, as an adult, my spiritual growth is filling in the spaces of that framework. Like my friends, I am forming my own personal religion. Although I consider my basic beliefs to be Baptist, some of my beliefs are clearly non-Baptist. I'm sure my thoughts and feelings about spirituality, gem stone energy and the Yoruba Orisa, to name a few, would shock my father and my fellow church members. My fellow Christians' fear of the supernatural amazes me, considering God is a supernatural being who performs supernatural acts. The supernatural, the metaphysical, the natural (I use that term loosely), the Big Bang, creationism, evolution—I believe it's all related. I'm learning the connectedness of *everything* and the Divine in everything.

God is sending the people and situations to me to help me grow. And so my investigation continues. My spiritual path is a part of my life journey and therefore an ongoing process. I will continue to delve further into the Bible, biblical history/society,

Christianity and Baptist doctrine/theology and spirituality. Why? Because I must. I need to be sure about what I believe. And when I speak of my beliefs, I need to speak with conviction and with courage. I need to be ready. Especially for my parents. Right now they do not know the whole me. There is so much I will share with them, about my lesbianism and how it co-exists with my faith/religion, my spirituality. I will shed the pseudonym and move on to continued growth. There's business I need to tend to.

She listened intently, not knowing me from Adam, to all of the story I have just disclosed to you. When I was done, she took my hands and told me to pray, right then and right there. Then she told me to go home and pray, and that she would pray for me on her own.

From Here to Eternity
By H.L. Sudler

My road to salvation was not an easy one. I am a man constantly at odds with his past. My mother has been banished from my life, my brother and I are estranged, my father is dead, and I have considered suicide three times. How do I find the strength to keep on living, you ask? One word: God.

I am a walking contradiction.

I always have been, really. A ball of fire seen as an ice cream cone. A little guy too big for his britches. A ballsy, if insubordinate, war horse terrified who grew up terrified of *The Exorcist*. A bossy independent in desperate need of human affection. Too black for whites, too white for blacks. An honorary Jew named Hassan, says one friend. A white man in black skin, says a relative. A Catholic who was once deeply engaged in a homosexual love with a Baptist, says me.

To fully understand the following narrative, my complicated relationship with God, there is something that you will first have to comprehend about this affair, and that is me. Because in understanding me, you will better understand God. And while that may sound immediately presumptuous, it is merely to illustrate how big He is, how beautiful He is, and how forgiving The Creator can be. For even after years of rebuking Him in the typical, hypocritical fashion that has been raised to an art form by humans, He saw me as worthwhile enough to send a messenger to save me from a hellish existence that nearly ended in my suicide. The messenger: a handsome young man at a birthday party that would change my life, and the way I looked at it, forever.

He would arrive not a minute too soon.

He knoweth our frame;
He remembereth that we are dust.
—Psalm 103:14

Childhood Woes

I am a walking contradiction. I always have been, really. Born equal parts of diverse parents, my life was and remains a constant struggle between the good and bad parts of each. My mother: adopted, Puerto Rican, crafty both in nature and in spirit, is also extremely intelligent, complex, volatile, formidable, talented, untrustworthy, duplicitous, and heinous. My father, born in Union, S.C., one of six children, was an alcoholic, a simple man, very well-loved by friends and family, a hard worker; also volatile, stubborn, a tale spinner, and habitually depressed.

I grew up in Philadelphia, Pa., no more tragic than any other child who is the product of a broken home. I am the eldest of four: two boys and two girls. My earliest childhood memory is of me in a crib as my father argued furiously with my mother: an omen to our future family dynamics. By the time I was five years old my parents were separated; by the time I was eight they were divorced. My father remarried quickly, and had two daughters by that union. My brother and I stayed with my mother.

The battleground that was to be my childhood, that definitively shaped me into who I am today, was fatherless and filled with child abuses both physical and mental. At the age of seven, as a punishment, my mother made me watch *The Exorcist* in full; I don't think I have yet recovered from the trauma of that betrayal. I was also slapped, punched, and beaten for very little or any reason until I left home for college. I have had hot tea thrown on me, books slapped on top of my head, spit drizzling down my face. I have been humiliated in front of people that I did not know. I was told that I was a fag, that I was weak and stupid, that I, like my father, laughed too much, was too friendly with people. As a teenager, I was made to strip nude in the living room, in front of my brother, for an impromptu, pointless, and fruitless drug search. I was told by my brother that he was her favorite son because that is what our mother had told him. In addition, my mother vindictively did not allow anyone in my family to attend my high school graduation, where I received a full four-year paid scholarship to Temple University, among other honors. She did, however, manage to cash a check from a synagogue intended for me. It was a book scholarship awarded for being the best male writer in my school. I never saw any of that money, nor any of the other money she subsequently stole. Nor my childhood, which I also felt had been robbed from me.

> If any man among you seem to be religious,
> and bridleth not his tongue,
> but deceiveth his own heart,
> this man's religion is vain.
> —James 1:26

God as a Distant Planet

I reveal my past not for pity or sympathy, but to point out to you unadorned, no frills, my background and to make a direct correlation to the type of person I would later become: bitter and insecure, defensive and lacking in trust and faith, full of wrath, a lightning rod for arguments that I sought to win at any cost. I, too, humiliated and degraded people in my circle, bullying them into accepting whatever I wanted. I, too, became a tale spinner, making up stories about my childhood: that it was better than it actually was. Anything to rewrite the past, to distance myself away from my mother and everything that she had done to me.

By the time I left home for undergrad, religion was to me then as it had always been during my childhood, something remote yet mandatory. Catholicism teaches you order and repetition, and that was the only thing I retained: order and repetition. My relationship with God was as impersonal, as hypocritical, as third-party as one could get. The only thing that I liked about the religion was that, unlike Baptist services, the masses were short and to the point, and you could attend in any style of dress, any time of day, seven days a week.

Catholicism has been long labeled a "beautiful" and "rich" religion. And it was that beauty—the sunlight pouring in through the large, stained-glass church; its quiet sanctuary away from the world; the melodic chanting; the ornate candles; the order of the service; the all-powerful, ominous organ—to which I was attracted. Not necessarily God. Not necessarily His message. And like many children of the Catholic faith, all the problems that had plagued me, that continued to haunt me—including chronic depressions, low self-esteem, bitterness, self-loathing, unexplained anger at innocent bystanders, that I should have given up to God, laid at His altar—stayed with me, governing all of my actions, causing irreversible and instantly regrettable mistakes. Mistakes that I would repeat over and over and over, until I began to hate everything that I was, everything that I was becoming, everything that I did. Until I began to contemplate suicide as the answer to the question that was my life: why go on living if you despise yourself so much? Better: why go on living if the person who gave you life despises you so much?

Not once, but three times during the course of my life would I consider suicide—each time coming dangerously close to the final act.

> Train up a child in the way he should go:
> and when he is old, he will not depart from it.
> —Proverbs 22:6

The Darkest Hours

Between the ages of seventeen and twenty-five, my life darkened blacker than any midnight sky. My relationship with my mother deteriorated to nothing after many unsuccessful attempts to make peace with my past and trust her again—feeling that was the only way I was going to lay to rest the growing dissatisfaction in myself. At every turn, every time, she proved me wrong. My brother, caught in the middle of this family dysfunction, moved away to Japan to begin his own family. I have seen him only once in the past five years—and that was at our father's funeral. My father and I, despite spending a great deal of our lives apart from one another, came to a truce, much of which is chronicled in my essay, "The Acceptance Speech," which depicts our troubled relationship and its repair surrounding the admission that I was gay.

Nevertheless, my life seemed a waste, traveling quickly from bad to worse. Every valuable relationship I had, I destroyed. For every weak person that crossed my path, I served as a bear trap. I kept people at arm's length, never seeing fit to trust anyone. And then it dawned on me, only after I had gotten the wonderful job with the wonderful money and the wonderful apartment, that I was alone. The one person I did not want to become, I became anyway—my mother. I developed into what she had molded: a defensive, angry human being, unresponsive to compliments, unable to return a compliment, inept at affection, cold, distant, and aloof. Or, the most stinging of assessments from any lover: "You're just not a giving person, Hassan. Face it."

If he only knew, contrary to my outward behavior, that inside I was screaming to give, needing to be loved, and unable to force myself to relax and be the man I always wanted to be. And so I fell into a hole called depression. It started off with me reconfiguring my past in my mind. If this one thing had been different, if only this hadn't happened, I'd be different, I'd be better. But soon enough, after these flights of fantasy came to an end, I'd come crashing down to the hard reality that nothing had changed. The depression eventually crippled me. I could not go outside, could not eat; I'd call out from work for days at a time, would not speak to anyone, could not stand the sight of myself. I'd slap my own face, pull my hair. Despondent, I'd ask myself: What's wrong with me? And in my mind I'd hear her voice say that I was weak, that I was just like my father, that I was good for nothing.

It is true what they say about suicide: It's not about causing pain, but ending it. Despite therapy, three times I came to that conclusion. Once, one evening, I opened the window to my penthouse apartment and nearly jumped six stories to street level. I remember that night, feeling all alone, feeling strangely still, as if the entire world—birds, people, the universe—was holding its breath, waiting to see if I had the guts to go through with it. True to my upbringing, I second-guessed myself, thinking that I might be wrong about all this. I sat at the sill, crying for hours. Later, in the middle of the night, I was so disgusted with myself that I went down to the kitchen and almost slit my wrists with a knife. Another time, I nearly swallowed thirty tablets of Demerol, which would surely have killed me.

Where was God all this time? Not with me, not in my eyes. But He was—only I couldn't see it. One night after the Demerol incident, I could not stand to be in the house any longer and went for a long walk. I found myself in downtown Philadelphia, in its gay neighborhood. It was there that a black transsexual stopped me on the street.

She said, "Honey, what's wrong?"

I looked up at her, not wanting any trouble, not wanting to talk or be bothered. I lamely laughed her off. "Do I look that bad?"

She replied, deadpan: "You look that bad."

If I was willing to talk, she said, she was willing to listen. And with no place to be or go, we found ourselves in a bar having tea.

She listened intently, not knowing me from Adam, to all of the story I have just disclosed to you. When I was done, she took my hands and told me to pray, right then and right there. Then she told me to go home and pray, and that she would pray for me on her own. To this day, I credit her with saving my life. And whenever I see her, in a club or on the street in broad daylight, I march myself over to her, and hug, kiss and thank her for being my friend.

After our talk, we stood and she hugged me tightly, as if she knew that was what my soul was craving. She told me to seek her out if I found myself in trouble again. The club kids knew where to find her.

And thus was the miracle of God working for me. I prayed then, I prayed when I got home, I prayed the next day. For strength, for guidance, for an answer. And I got what I prayed for. I found the strength to phone my friends, what few I had. I reached out to them, basking in humility, no longer melodramatically playing the role of I-can-go-it-alone. And soon, after days, weeks, months, I felt renewed, a wholly different person, stronger, clearer headed. I realized that, to a degree, I could leave my awful past in the past and start again, making changes in myself, becoming the person that I wanted to be.

I took the good aspects of my father and put them to work. No longer did I heed my mother's words that I was too friendly with people. I went out of my way to make friends and build relationships. I no longer concentrated on the negative aspects of myself. I worked hard on my reinvention, delving seriously into my writing, into publishing, into work, into charity.

But in hindsight it was all an act. For as soon as I was better, I forgot all about God. Sending kisses up to Him with thanks, I proceeded on with my life, pretty much without Him.

But God said unto him,
Thou fool, this night thy soul shall be required of thee...
—Luke 12:20

Losing My Religion

One Sunday back in 1992, I was invited to a birthday party in a Philadelphia bar that I nearly did not attend. And there, whether you believe in kismet or not, I fell in love at first sight with a handsome young man named Dana. He was the friend of a friend, from a very religious family I was told, a twin, very sweet and very nice. Under instruction, my friends set out to put us together.

Sitting here typing this, I realize now that what happened to Dana and I was nothing short of a miracle: a love story, a religious awakening, the final chapter in my old life, the first chapter in my new life. I was reborn. Dana and I dated for the summer months, but the relationship was not to last. He was not out to his very religious family, not serious about his life, and he was an alcoholic. I think I pushed him too far and too fast for a serious relationship, and he fled without a note or a call. This burned me, needless to say, because I loved him very much and knew I had from the moment I laid eyes on him. Subsequently, I moved on to a series of less than satisfying relationships and sexual encounters that left me exhausted and feeling somewhat cheapened. Finally, in lieu of seeking out a mate, I decided that I'd just have sex when I needed it, and that I'd concentrate fully on work.

When I saw Dana again, seven years later, I was a very different person. I was no-nonsense and very committed to work. I had a network of friends. I was well-respected. I was an uncle, a published author, and was at the beginning of my journey as a magazine publisher.

He came into the bookstore where I worked and initially, never forgetting a past hurt, I was chilly toward him. He asked me to join him and a friend at the club where we first met. I started not to go, and only went because another friend said I needed to get out. Once there, he was determined to talk with me. And so he talked and I listened; he talked and I listened; he talked and I listened. And eventually my feelings for him resurfaced, and I thawed enough so that by the end of the night I conceded that he could call me.

Our road to a new relationship was tough. It was difficult for me to get beyond being abandoned by him, as I had come to realize abandonment was a recurring theme in my life. But he held on fast despite my typical boasts of independence; held on like no other lover. And this marked quality struck a chord in me. It was this loyalty to which I was unaccustomed, but I surely welcomed it.

This could not have come a minute too soon. For more than a year, I had this strong urge to do this magazine, which I felt would be good for the LGBT community. A little voice inside my head kept telling me: This is good, this is needed, what you are doing is important. Also, playing devil's advocate, was my mother's voice telling me once again that I could not do this; that I, like my father, was weak and a failure.

In January, under God's hands, I crashed. For months, I had been preparing to debut my magazine, working endless hours on top of my law profession. This meant ceaseless phone calls, visiting clients, managing the staff, editing articles, choosing the cover, writing the opening and closing essays, and so on. Doing all of this while working, while in a new relationship, while getting very little sleep, I soon came to realize that I was running on empty. And then one day I cracked and suffered a physical and emotional breakdown. Simply put, I burned out.

On the same day that I suffered that meltdown, Dana stopped by the law firm unannounced. He said that he came by just to see me and say hello, but looking at me he knew something was wrong. I told him that I could not go on, that I was under so much pressure to do this, to get this right, that I did not think that I had the strength to publish this magazine. He asked me if I had talked to God, if I had prayed to Him for strength and guidance. I said no. He said that I should.

He said to me, and I shall never forget, that this was not about me and failure; that this was God's way of showing me that I needed Him, that without Him there would be no way that I could proceed or succeed with this project. That this project did not rest on my strength but His, and His will, and that I needed to acknowledge that He was in control, and to rest my burdens with Him. He was leaving me with no other choice but to turn to Him for strength and guidance. No human could help me now, nor any amount of money. Passage lay squarely with Him. And this urge that I had was Him talking to me, telling me that I could do this project, but only with Him, only with His blessing, only with His permission.

It was a revelation, a fountain. And I stood there, at once both lost and found, and thoroughly convinced that I had a choice to make and a lifestyle to amend.

> Though he fall, he shall not be utterly cast down:
> for the Lord upholdeth him with his hand.
> —Psalm 37:24

God's Unchanging Hand

To see one's life pass before one's eyes is a scary thing. To see it with such clarity, from the moment you are born to this very minute, is awesome. To have that sight funneled through spiritual awakening, without the assistance of a near-death experience, is simply divine. All at once, you realize your place in the world. All at once, you can look over your life and see everything that has brought you to the point where you now exist. All at once, you understand God's perfect timing. All at once, you understand your function in God's plan. And you realize through all your hypocrisies where God was concerned that He loved you anyway, that He was there with you anyway, that He spared you, was patient with you, and engineered the perfect plan to bring you right to His doorstep.

So it was with me. Sitting and mulling over Dana's words, I realized all that and more. Finally, I could see why my life had been so difficult. It was more than just the building of character; it was a transition to ready me for God's plan, for God's work.

Finally, I could chart my life, my evolution, through incidents that would lead me to this moment, that would mature me and bring me closer to Him than I realized I could ever be. Finally, I realized that He had spared me from suicide and depression, from abuse and self-loathing, so that I could turn and rest in His arms, so that I could be empowered through Him. Finally, I realized that I had someone who understood me better than anyone else, who knew my troubles, who had seen me through them, to whom I could have been talking, but had chosen not to.

I went on to publish that magazine. And I went on to realize the publication would not be the most important thing I would do. There would be more, God willing. And that experience, which felt as difficult as childbirth, was to prepare me for future work.

As like Saul on the road to Damascus, the scales fell from my eyes and I was able to see and enjoy all of God's blessings around me. My health, my home, my job, my man, my talent, my friends, my family. Everything became a blessing. God had given me all I ever wanted in my life, had given what fuels me more and better than anger: love.

Over time, my understanding of God has deepened and continues to grow rich. And although I remain imperfect, it is the striving in His name that I enjoy. It is the realization that I have been blessed, and as such, I have a responsibility to be unselfish, and pass on my blessings, pass on His word, His lessons to be learned: not to lecture or pontificate or judge. It is the realization that His word is not meant to be a guide for what you should not do, but what you can do. With His love, with His strength, and with His guidance.

But I have prayed for thee, that thy faith fail not:
and when thou art converted, strengthen thy brethren.
—Luke 22:32

His Eyes on a Sparrow

When the day comes that I stand before God, I shall be at the crossroads of gratitude. Whom do I have to thank more, thank first: The Message or The Messenger? Do I thank first God for having brought me a man that I will love forever, who still knows me better than any other human being--even though we are no longer together, and who inspired me and was there at the beginning of my new life? Or do I thank Dana for bringing me to God, and a peace and purpose and belonging that I think all humans crave and should experience?

Only I know the answer. And maybe now you do, too. No matter what, on that day, at that hour, at that minute, I will surely be a very lucky man. No, scratch that. I will surely be a very blessed man.

And I am, I think. I am. Amen for that.

Amen for that.

If I wanted to stay a part of the church, I would have to leave my lesbian self at the door. Could I? Did I want to do that? Am I really in spiritual fellowship with people if I can't be my true, one hundred percent self? If my church family doesn't accept me fully and completely, is it really my family?

Sufficient As I Am
By Tawanna Sullivan

Born and raised a Baptist, I was deeply involved with the church for the first nineteen years of my life. I spent an average of three days a week there: regular Sunday services, Wednesday night Bible Study, and youth/young adult activities on Saturday.

I was a Christian by rote. I could recite the books of the Bible and had memorized lots of verses, but didn't really think about what I was learning. That began to change one Sunday morning with a discussion in Young Adult Sunday School class. Rev. Sam, the Youth/Young Adult pastor, asked, "What would you do if you were or had gotten someone else pregnant?"

There were about fifteen of us in the room and, like Stepford children, all of us just recited the correct answer. "Well, the right thing to do is marry the mother/father of my child."

Then, the reverend threw us a curve ball. "What if you didn't love or even like the mother/father of the baby? What if getting married to this person would be like entering a living hell?"

I thought about it for a moment. "Don't you still have to get married? If it's a bad marriage aren't you just suffering the consequences of your own sin?" Even as I said it, I knew it was a weak argument.

Rev. Sam drove his point home. "Do you really believe that a kind, loving God would want you to enter a loveless, lifeless marriage? Can you fix a situation by creating a worse one? Would that be good for you? For the baby? What society, your parents, or even your pastor tells you to do does not always reflect God's will for your life."

Those words rocked the foundation of my sixteen-year-old existence. It was the first time anyone had ever challenged me to examine my beliefs. Before when I encountered doctrine that I thought was strange, I glossed over it. After this Sunday School lesson I stopped mindlessly absorbing sermons and religious teachings and started really thinking about what I was hearing. I began sorting through my own thoughts and ideas. "Do I believe this because I really believe it or because it's been drilled into my head as the truth?"

I started reading books about religion and spirituality. I began to understand the difference between trying to "be good" because you don't want to go to Hell and doing the right thing solely because you genuinely believe it is right. When you are motivated by fear (of God, Hell, etc.), it's easy to feel insecure and miserable. (If I slip and fall on a patch of ice, is it because God is getting me back for some recent, perhaps unintentional, sin?)

If I were in a relationship with a human being that was controlling and manipulative, I would be trying to find a way out. It is definitely not the kind of relationship I wanted to have with God. I continued reading about other religious beliefs. I was not looking to convert to a completely new ideology, but I wanted to explore how others viewed their relationship with God.

At nineteen, when I finally realized that I was a lesbian, I had already figured out that gays and lesbians were not horrible creatures despised by God. Two facts led me to this conclusion. I had re-examined the Sodom and Gomorrah story and couldn't see how anyone could use it as an argument against homosexuality. When the people of the village demanded to have Lot's visitors turned over to them, Lot's response was, "Leave those men alone, but you can sexually molest my daughters if you want." Yes, this is the only righteous man in town. Lot gets away free while his wife is turned into a pillar of salt for daring to look back. So God hates homosexuals but Lot's treatment of his daughters is fine—the story just does not sound right to me.

Also, though my pastor preached that homosexuality was unnatural, I never thought of it that way. Unnatural means something that is forced, something that did not occur normally. My attraction to women is something that developed naturally and normally. It's not as if I was attracted to men but had somehow "trained" myself to want women. Loving women is just as normal as having brown skin. It's not something that I chose but part of who I am. In short, I didn't have a problem with being gay and God didn't have a problem with it either.

Though I was growing more secure with my relationship with God, I was not sure about my relationship with the church. The most visible gay people there were in the choir. Though people whispered about them, no one would come right out and accuse them of being gay. At the same time, these men, no matter how many gaydar alarms they set off, pretended to be straight. They dare not acknowledge a lover inside the church. Once in a while, one would bring a female friend to church and introduce her as a "fiancee"; I wouldn't hold my breath waiting for a wedding. When the pastor or some other church member started talking about "those people," they pretended not to hear.

If I wanted to stay a part of the church, I would have to leave my lesbian self at the door. Could I? Did I want to do that? Am I really in spiritual fellowship with people if I can't be my true, one hundred percent self? If my church family doesn't accept me fully and completely, is it really my family?

At the time I was pondering this, I came across Walt Whitman's "One Hour to Madness and Joy." This poem really resonated with me. It talks about escaping from the molds that other people cast for you and realizing that you are sufficient as you are. Forget the expectations of others and live your life. If I wanted to be happy (and I did), there was only one choice: I had to let the church go.

Most of my friends and social activities had been through the church, but it was not hard to fill that void. I found new friends, started learning more about myself, and exploring the world around me. I had a new life and, after a few more years, a completely new concept of God.

For me, God is a positive, life-affirming spiritual force that we all have a link to via our souls. Think of an octopus-like creature but with an infinite number of arms, each arm attached to one of us. God is not concerned about your religious affiliation, but about the content of your heart. Since you can control the content of your heart, you ultimately are the one who determines the degree and intensity of that relationship. For example, if you are filled with rage and hatred, how can you then be open to receiving that life-affirming, loving spirit? You have to be willing to let go of negative, soul-sapping obstacles.

This spiritual link to God also links us to each other. I can't cut myself off from you and not somehow obstruct my relationship with God. This doesn't mean that we have to love or like each other, but I have to respect you as a fellow being and treat you with compassion.

In my view, it does not matter what religious beliefs you hold—as long as those beliefs do not actually put stumbling blocks in your spiritual path. More importantly, you can't let other people dictate what your relationship with God is going to be.

That, in my opinion, is an African religion once removed. The dancing, the singing, the backbeat… and vodao leaders, like old-fashioned gospel preachers, led revolutions.

Vodao: a short interview of Patrice Suncircle
By Ethel Ligon, Grandmother
(The first shaper of her life returns, briefly, to interview her.)

Ethel Ligon: Remember I used to always talk to you about your soul?

Patrice Suncircle: Yes. Everyone else was concerned that I got enough food, clean clothes and a good education. You cared about all that, too, but you were the only one who actively cared about my soul. It was a good while down the road before I realized that.

EL: You don't go to church anymore. I always took you to church every Sunday. Can you even remember a Sunday we missed?

PS: I can't remember, though there must have been at least one. Every Sunday Uncle Lawrence and Aunt Mae would pick us up and we would all drive to the Bell Eagle Church of God in Christ.

I remember the music. I remember when the preacher's wife would sing solo. Years later I heard another woman whose voice reminded me of Sister Chandler. That woman was Mahalia Jackson. Sister Chandler never made any records (as far as I know), but I'll never forget her voice.

No, ma'am, I don't attend a church, but I'm still a seeker. Your attention to my soul saw to that.

EL: Well, Pat, who are you seeking?
PS: I'm seeking not someone, but to evolve. I don't mean that to sound fancy. When I say "evolve," I mean getting closer to and more like the Creator, God.

EL: I followed Jesus to do that.
PS: I know. I remember how I never heard you curse, ever. That sounds strange to hear about someone nowadays.

EL: I can't believe the wickedness back here now. I'd be scared to live outside the church.
PS: But I believe Divine Love is everywhere, Gran'ma. That's something that comes from growing up the way that I did. I found a strong community in our church. Other times I would go out and play by myself in the woods and fields and find something just as powerful. Different, but as holy. That land and the teachings made me what I am now.

EL: What you call yourself? What religion are you now?
PS: Storytelling.

EL: Telling stories!
PS: I am a writer. The Creator gave me that gift. That's fortunate, because I have many "windows" to look through. My windows are woman, African-American, Cherokee, queer, Irish. These things that make up me enrich my stories, expand my spirit.

The windows bring questions and I look to my spiritual path to answer them. This is the path that I find in my heart through meditating, reading teachers such as Luisah Teish, Credo Mutwa, Lao Tzu, Rumi, Yeshua, Audre Lorde and others. And I am especially taught and touched by Nature.

EL: Who are the people on this—path, you call it? God is everywhere, but it's good to have godly people around you. I always liked to be with the Saints.

PS: I don't belong to any congregation. I do have friendships that are very, very important to me. Two gay men who share my connection to African-based religions. A straight woman who I regularly go hiking with.

EL: Gay is what we used to call "funny."
PS: Yes, ma'am. Women are my love life. I didn't realize this until I was in my twenties. I had already moved away from the religion that I was raised in. I was as secular as at any point in my life. When I remembered that earlier religion at all, I remembered the music, the people and the Bible stories. With me, the dogma never sank in. I don't ever remember homosexuality being mentioned.

When I came out the closest I was to a spiritual path was writing. I wrote a lot of poetry at that time.

EL: I won't get on you about all that. Where I am now, a lot of things have come clear to me. Go on about your path.
PS: Well, there's vodao.

EL: Who?
PS: Northern California is like a raging wild garden when it comes to cultures and ideas. You have to be very careful. You could end up bouncing like a Ping-Pong ball for years. But I had spiritual goals, the ones I formed growing up down there with you. They might have faded for a while but they never left. Two paths come together in me again and again. The "Watercourse Way" of Taoism. Water is giving enough to seep and be diverted through any crack. It is powerful enough to wear down and to shape to its own flow the hardest rock. It is the philosophy of Taoism that I follow. The path which diverges with this one is vodao... Now wait a minute, Gran'ma, I'm not talking about the movie picture stuff with pins stuck into dolls and all that. The real vodao is a way to train your mind. It is a way to access other dimensions. It's a way to meet the spirits and it is a path that I'm still learning. Both are Nature paths.

There is a deep meditative state to vodao and a dancing shamanic side to Taoism. The characters in my stories practice both. In my home I have altars for both.

EL: Voodoo, huh?
PS: Gran'ma, we had possession in the Sanctified Church, though you all would not have called it that. Remember that time at Missionary Burke's revival service when that woman leaned so far back that she was almost parallel to the floor and nobody could see what was holding her up? I remember the expressions I've seen on people's faces. That, in my opinion, is an African religion once removed. The dancing, the singing, the backbeat… and vodao leaders, like old-fashioned gospel preachers, led revolutions.

EL: All right. You seem to be doing well.
PS: Like grass pushing up through pavement. And I am an Aries, after all. I have a certain Joy that has stayed with me all of my life.

EL: I always did pray for you.
PS: I know. I remember when I was reading some of the Bhakti yoga teachers I realized that I had heard before some of the things they were writing. I'd had those feelings before. Some of those words were yours in a different language and time. So I tell people that my black Cherokee grandmother was my first guru, a true one.

EL: You are known through your works, Pat. How are you helping?
PS: I try to overcome my fears (always trying to overcome my fears), enough to help people who need it. Giving what I can and really listening to people when they talk. These are things everyone can do. But I've been given a gift and I want to raise the dead. Nothing less.

I believe that the greatest miracle of Yeshua was not calling back the physical body of Lazarus from the tomb. Instead it was the Sermon on the Mount and the other teachings. A physical body will only die again after a number of years. If, however, you raise a dead or dying spirit then you give life back to something that will evolve across the years and life spans and incarnations.

The world is full of people whose spirits seem DOA—dead on arrival. Artists—who are storytellers—writers, poets, musicians, dancers, actors, painters can raise the dead. With their messages they can give the spirit back life. Given these gifts by the Creator, that is our challenge. The future of the world depends on it. That is not a grandiose statement; only true.

EL: I taught Sunday school classes for forty years…
PS: Because your church wouldn't allow women preachers…

EL: Well, but I still believe I helped a lot of spirits along.
PS: Yesterday I went to church. A simple service with complex messages. My friend and I drove out to the seashore at Pt. Reyes and walked along the cliffs, then down to the beach. I carried my small statue of Quanyin. I listened to the wind and the surf. I felt blessed.

What I felt was acceptance.

I could never fall in love with a Path that questioned the greatest thing that I have to give, which is my love. Because that is my connection to Divine Love.

EL: Keep on keeping on, Pat.

—Mrs. Ethel Williams Ligon, 1895-1991

I believed that we should live as we are called to live. Her coming out came later and was impacted by mine. Our spirituality and sexuality affected and informed one another. Our decisions changed the lives we lived. We never saw it coming.

Walking in Love and Truth
By Rev. Karen G. Thompson

"Hey Ma, how ya doin'?" *she said when I answered the phone. She sounded a bit hesitant, as if she had something on her mind. This call was a little earlier than most. I knew though that she wanted to talk.*

"I'm good baby girl. What's going on with you?" *She would get to IT eventually, whatever IT was. After some silence it came.*

"Well Ma, I just wanted to call and tell you that I am a lesbian!" *There it was. All in one breath. One shoe had dropped. I knew it was coming. I was glad she was at a point where she could handle and live her truth.*

"I know."

"You know? Whaddya mean you know? If you knew why didn't YOU tell ME?" *We laughed.*

"A mother knows these things. All those conversations about sex and sexuality, what did you think, that I didn't hear you? I knew you were seeking and searching. I was just a place for you to process through. I figured when you were ready YOU would let me know. So what took you so long to tell me?"

"Ma, I just figured, since you are a minister and all, that you would just damn me to hell if you knew I was a lesbian." *There was the other shoe dropping.*

I was angry that she would think that of me. After all our conversations, all we'd shared… I am her mother. How could she see me that way?

"I love you." *I said simply.* "You are my child. I always said you should *be honest in who you are and need to be. I don't love you any less than before because I know you are a lesbian. I am proud of you. I love you and God loves you for who you are."*

She is not my birth child. I am not even her legally adoptive mother, or even a close relative. But mother and daughter we are. We met when she was fourteen years old. She was a very outgoing personality who would call and stop by to see me at work. She was born and raised in Burlington, N.C., where I worked. She was a part of one of the programs our agency operated. She would not go away.

She would talk with me. There was the afternoon she came to my office and told me of her plans to go out of town for the weekend. I asked the standard parental questions: who and why. She provided the information and I told her she was not going. She obeyed. She lived with her grandmother and great-grandmother who had no control over her. She had too much independence for a fourteen-year-old. The pattern started there. She would tell me what she was up to and somewhere in there I became the parental voice offering advice and discipline. I think she adopted me first and I gave in because of her persistence. When I left my job a year and a half later we stayed in touch.

She would call to check on me occasionally or I would call to check in on her. Her grandparents knew who I was and they were quite happy to know that somebody was "keeping her straight." Three years later, it was time for college. I helped her with her essays over the phone. We discussed where she would apply and what she wanted to do with her life. She called for a letter of recommendation, which I was happy to provide. The responses came, as did her decision to go to school in the city in which I lived. At the time, I was employed at the university she chose. That took our relationship to a new level.

When she was sick, she called and I showed up with soup and medication. She would spend weekends at my home. She took care of my son—her little brother. Whatever she needed I was happy to help with. She started calling me Ma, with pride. There

I was all of thirty-one years old with a nineteen-year-old calling me Ma in public, much to the questions of all around. She was my daughter. My parents knew of her. I took her home with me to meet them. They became "Grandma and Grandpa" to her. My sister and brother were politely "Aunt and Uncle." We were a family. She knew all my friends or knew of them. Men I dated knew I had two children.

A part of the growth in our relationship came through our nightly conversations while she was in college. These were usually late, sometimes after midnight. She would call. "Hey Ma, how ya doin'?" That usually meant she wanted to talk and there was something on her mind. I would start listening for IT. Our conversations were about any and everything. Her relationships. Her concerns. School. What she should do with her life. Where she would go for the summer. This also included shooting down many a scheme which usually began with, "So Ma, let me tell you what I'm gonna do…" Like me, she always had a plan. We knew each other so well that conversation came easy. Our roles were clear. Parent and child. Mother and daughter. Friend and friend to the end.

Two of our more frequent topics of conversation were sexuality and spirituality. She would call in the quiet of her midnight hours when schoolwork and the tasks of life were complete and we would end up on one of those two roads. She had a lot of questions. I also heard what she would not ask. We talked about relationships, about homosexuality, heterosexuality and about bisexuality. We talked about what it meant to be in an intimate relationship with someone else. We never talked in specifics, however. Like all children, there was the occasional, "Ugh, Ma. Let's not go there." She always knew whatever the problem or situation I was there for her.

I heard and listened to her questions about sexuality. She was working through her issues. I never pushed, never asked what was going on with her. I let her know she needed to be herself. She was always to be herself, not what people wanted her to be, but the best authentic representation of herself, and that included her sexuality. If she was going to be a heterosexual, she should be open and honest in it. If she was going to be a homosexual, she should be open and honest in that too. In my opinion, the worst place to live was in a lie. That could only be miserable and unhappy. I wanted her to be happy.

At the same time as we discussed sexuality, we also talked about spirituality. Years after having left the church, I was attending and participating in church once again. We both had our issues with church and the institution of religion. To both of us, organized religion represented another repressive institution in many ways, but I was determined to deal with my spirituality. Even as a recovering fundamentalist Christian, I knew of and talked freely about how church and spirit connected. I was recovering from years of oppressive interpretations of the Bible and Christianity in the Baptist church, my place of choice. She had been a Baptist all her life and was starting to question where the church fit on her faith journey.

Over the years we had talked about my deepening faith and love for God, even as we talked about her being hesitant to go to church. I recommitted my life to serving God and became a member of a church, which I once vowed never to do. I saw where my life and experiences of God could help others on their faith journey in exploring their spirituality and connectedness to the Divine. We talked through many issues, hers and mine, around spirituality. I made a decision to become a minister. I answered the call to ministry. She answered the call to come out of the closet and we started down a new road.

Our coming out happened in 1997. I came out first. I acknowledged the call to be a minister. I started serving differently in our church, which she attended occasionally. I started preaching and teaching Bible study. We still had our late night talks about spirituality and sexuality. My resolve was the same: I believed there had to be honesty in sexuality and spirituality. I believed neither should be repressed. I believed that we should live as we are called to live. Her coming out came later and was impacted by mine. Our spirituality and sexuality affected and informed one another. Our decisions changed the lives we lived. We never saw it coming.

"Ma, I just figured since you are a minister and all, that you would just damn me to hell." I was put out by her concern that our relationship would change if she came out to me. I was bothered by her implication that my call as a minister changed our relationship and all that we discussed over the years. Her coming out was not a problem. Her admission and desire to walk as a lesbian was a wonderful thing in my opinion. I was bothered, annoyed, concerned and put out by her hesitation. It had nothing to do with who she knew me to be, but was fueled by her own encounters and understanding of church, specifically the conservative nature of the Baptist church.

Her belief that homosexuality and spirituality (more specifically Christianity as a means of dealing with spirituality) were at odds with each other was not far-fetched, though. Nor was it a personal indictment of me, I realized. After dealing with my emotions I started pondering the church and sexuality. The church and homosexuality. The church and heterosexuality. My knowledge of church helped me realize that there was much to what she said, and hadn't said.

I remembered what I was taught when I attended fundamentalist churches and more conservative churches. I also knew how various parts of the Bible were interpreted as being in opposition to and condemning of homosexuals and homosexuality. In my reading of the Bible, the themes of love and forgiveness are primary.

I'd had the Bible thrown at me when I was getting divorced. My husband and I went to counseling because our marriage was not working. I was ready to leave the marriage. The counselor we went to see was also a minister in the fundamentalist Christian denomination in which we were both raised. He showed us from the Bible where it says that God hates divorce. He told me in the presence of my husband that God would kill me if I left my husband. A year later, I left my husband and the church. If God were going to kill me, I would not be in a church waiting for this judgment to come. Needless to say, I got divorced, I am still alive, I rediscovered God away from the fundamentalist Christians, and I am a witness that it does not take much to interpret scripture to the detriment of others.

I was firm in my belief that gays and lesbians had a place in the church. These things were in my heart but were never challenged. Whatever anyone or I believed, it was a non-issue in my life with my daughter. She was out. I was a minister and her mother. Life carried on for us, as did our conversations about everything, including sexuality, relationships, life and Spirit.

The following year, she graduated from college and I left for seminary in New York City. I arrived at Union Theological Seminary after a year of seminary in North Carolina at Shaw Divinity, a Baptist seminary. Union reopened my thoughts on the issue of gays and the church. There were gays on faculty, on staff and in the classroom. For the first time in my life, I was around people who walked boldly in their sexual preference, while fully engaged in living out their spiritual lives as Christians. They were ministers and theologians. They became my friends and colleagues over the next two years. They influenced the formulation of my concrete gay and lesbian theology.

At Union I read gay theology by various theologians. I read and read. It was one thing to love my daughter for who she was, but another to embrace a broader gay theology as I came to grips with the call to pastor. What kind of pastor did I want to be? What did I want to teach about God's love that was given to us through Jesus Christ? The answer was that I wanted to teach love. The Bible is clear on this, as is Jesus. The greatest commandment is love. Love your neighbor as your self.

Sexual orientation did not matter to me. Though I too had been ostracized in the church and had a finger wagged in my face because of choices I'd made in my life, I learned about and embraced God's love, forgiveness and mercy for myself and wanted others to feel and know that joy. Gays and lesbians needed to know that they were included at the table. Union opened my eyes to gay theology. More than that, Union brought me to a place of accountability for my theological beliefs. They were no longer what I thought. They were my *beliefs* and what I wanted to live. I didn't want anyone to ever see my call to minister as a damning experience. I wanted my life as a minister to be about inviting all to the table. My church would be a church where all were welcome.

My daughter and I talked while I was at Union. I told her how much she would like Union. I passed on to her books on gay and lesbian theology. This was a new world for us. I was glad to show her that I was not the only person who affirmed gays and lesbians in the Christian church. I saw these authors as places from which she could begin to affirm her own identity as a Christian and begin to explore where she was heading with her spiritual life. It bothered me that she no longer went to church. It bothered me that she was not comfortable enough to find a place for her. It bothered me, as a minister, that so many like her walked away from the church and their relationship with God because of their sexual preference.

I was ordained in the Baptist church while in seminary and I worked part-time as Director of Christian Education at a Congregational Church in New York. After graduating from seminary I was offered a full time position, which added duties of Assistant Pastor. Though far more liberal than the Baptist church, the subject never came up in church. No one ever asked and I saw no reason for me to pronounce my theological beliefs on homosexuality and the church.

One year after seminary, however, the inevitable happened: controversy in the church. We all imagined that there could be gays and lesbians in our church. It had not been an issue. All were welcome. We prided ourselves on being a multicultural church. We spoke of diversity and how to attract more people to our church. There was some of everybody there. We had former Catholics and former Baptists, former fundamentalists and former Episcopalians. We had interracial marriages and interfaith marriages. We were a progressive church.

Then a gay couple started attending our church. They were a

wonderful couple and family. Two men who loved and were committed to each other, along with their two children from one of the men's former marriage, arrived at our church one cold January morning. They came to love us and we loved them. They joined the church and jumped in with both feet. Well, all four feet. They were a wonderful addition to our church. Their children came to Sunday School. They were in church every Sunday and eager to help in any way they could.

They were there to be active participants and active they were. One day, though, it seemed that someone noticed their gayness in the context of their increasing involvement in the church. They were on boards and committees. We loved them and were happy to have them. They cooked and they cleaned. We loved them more.

But when one of them started to assist in teaching a Sunday School class and wanted to lead congregational singing in the contemporary Sunday morning worship service people started frowning. Why then the displeasure, I wondered. If they could join the church, participate in the church, come every week and be loved, then why were we up in arms and having ongoing conversations about the place for homosexuals in our church?

People made their opinions known. Suddenly, our liberal church was looking quite conservative. The Bible was put on the table. The usual scriptures were opened. We all had the right to interpret those scriptures according to the bylaws and beliefs of the church. Now some were accused of having the "wrong" interpretation. The question of these men's membership in our church and what their membership in our church meant was discussed. I heard my daughter's voice once again: *"Ma, I just figured since you are a minister and all, that you would just damn me to hell if you knew I was a lesbian."*

I said my piece and took my stand. I believe in the Bible as the word of God, but I don't believe that the Bible is inerrant; ordinary men and women translated it. The scriptures are to be interpreted by all—but I believe they first have to be inspected and examined in the historical context and time in which they were written. Who wrote the Bible, why it was written and to whom it was written are questions to be answered before the text can be brought forward for today. The Bible is to be studied and interpreted in context. It is not to be taken out of context to fuel our prejudices against what we choose not to understand.

Since these men professed their love for Jesus Christ when they joined the church, why was there a problem? Who were we to stand in judgment or sit in condemnation? The church leaders looked at the issue through Bible study and discussions trying to answer the questions of those who brought the issue to us. Eventually the topic died down and we were left at the same place where we'd started.

Our stance on the Bible was the same. All had the right to interpret the Bible as led by the Holy Spirit. The church's opinion on these men's right to membership had not changed. All are welcome in the church to live out their life in Christ. The difference was that now people knew where each other stood on the issue of homosexuality and the church. A few opted to leave the church. Most stayed. We affirmed our belief that all had a place in the church. We were changed.

The following year I decided to leave my job there. I was at a crossroads on several issues. I wanted to pastor and I needed to do so in a place that was clear on where it stood on the most potent issues challenging the Church. I did some research, spoke to a few friends and began to seriously consider what the next few years of my life in ministry would look like, and where I could live out my call to pastor and to love.

I am a female minister. I am a black minister. I have a gay daughter and a teenage son, both of whom need a place wherever I am in ministry. I would betray neither in my call as a minister. I am also unwilling to compromise on certain issues. We love or we don't. I desired to be in a denomination that was affirming of all people and their place in the Christian church and in ministry. I did not want to be affiliated or associated with ambiguous beliefs. I was ordained Baptist, was serving in another denomination and was satisfied with neither. I chose to become a minister in the

United Church of Christ (UCC), a denomination where I could, in good conscience, live out my call to be a minister.

The UCC as a denomination is not perfect. However, where others are stuck in their exclusive interpretations of the gospel (Good News) of Christ and in what they see as inerrant interpretations of the Bible that promote ostracizing, isolating and expelling people from the Church, the United Church of Christ chooses to be unique in its openness and affirmation of all people. It is a church of firsts, daring to make a difference and have a voice that calls the mainstream to a higher order. It is a church that is active in the world, committed to social justice and committed to making change. In 1972, the UCC was the first church in history to ordain an openly gay person and six years later ordained the first openly lesbian minister.

We are a church committed to letting the world know that church is a safe place to live a life of faith and walk the spiritual journey. Gay, lesbian, bisexual and transgender people are welcome at the table. Black, white, brown and red are invited to the feast. We are a multicultural, multiracial, open and affirming church. I, too, sit at that table, welcoming and inviting all who come to sit with Christ.

I was very happy to call my daughter and tell her all about the UCC and my decision to change denominations. It was a learning process and an eye-opening experience to find a church that was making strides in demonstrating God's love and care for gay, lesbian, bisexual and transgender persons. As I spoke to my daughter she wanted to know why I was making the change. I reminded her of our conversation of seven years earlier when she came out to me. She was vague on the details, so I reminded her of her words.

Those few words have informed who I am as a minister. My expression of love and encouragement is not a closet expression to my lesbian child and her lesbian and gay friends. It is a broad and open love and welcome as a woman and Christian minister to all people who seek to live out their spirituality as a Christian and within the Christian church.

Months after getting married, my new husband and I joined our first church together. It was a UCC church. I am a member as well as a clergy person. Our church in St. Petersburg, Fla., is a wonderful example of what church can be. We are black, we are white, we are gay, we are lesbian and we are Christian living out God's love together.

I encouraged my daughter to find a UCC church that works for her. All UCC churches are not like ours in St. Pete; one has to look. She went to her first UCC service one Sunday morning and called to report: *"Hey Ma, that was cool!"* The church she attended was small. She met a lesbian couple there who are raising their daughter together. No one blinked or batted an eye at her very butch look. They were just happy she was there and invited her back. She plans to go back, but she also plans to visit a few more UCC churches in her area.

We still talk. The topics are the same. Spirituality, sexuality, sex, relationships, careers and what we want to do with our lives. We continue on our spiritual journey together, each committed to walking in the truth we have declared to each other.

long time ago i learned that every woman who sleeps with women has a coming out *story. longer ago still i learned that every woman who discovers new spirits she didn't know existed has a* conversion *story. but here are mine all mixed together and neither seem to have a plot.*

summers & the seven paths of yemaya
By Natasha Tinsley

millennial may: this can only have happened in may, the millennium, month of multiracial politics for a new america. one monday mid-month

i've just gotten home, sweaty, from a hip-hop class. tara, home sick from work, is in bed under our new soft cotton sheets. someone unexpectedly knocks at our door (even though no one knocks at our door unexpectedly, ever). a stained-fingered clipboard-armed census taker is outside and i invite him in, flustered. tara comes out and the clipboard is on the candle-cluttered table, askew under the weave of guatemalan quetzales and the haitian ironwork vévé. gender. age. race. i can have him check as many as apply and i tell him, african-american and nothing else. tara has a whole question which asks her if she is of hispanic origin—yes—but there's no box for her under the race question. relationship: we're roommates, right? he asks, pen poised over that box. wait, what are our choices? i ask. finally he gets to the one i want: unmarried domestic partner. yes, yes, that one, i say. uncomfortable or surprised he looks away to the window where he meets the eyes of our lady of sorrow—staring red and hearts from a pearl cross-covered candle on the altar— and he marks that box, too. and there it is, we have been counted, two cohabiting colored lesbians, lucky to have found an apartment we can afford in berkeley, california, east bay of america's mixed-race and lgbt holy land.

it's funny how summers blend together relentlessly crosscurrenting in and out of each other like a crazy-colored multilayered weave. springs don't do that or autumns or winters; only summers. i've spent many summers many places partly staying in graduate school for travel funding. you can tell me that's all part of my mixed-race identity search if you want, but then you also better tell me which triangle-traded spirits i'm looking for across these oceans in the first place. now i could open my eyes from a blink and the rose-gardened church i pass every day on my triangular walks between the apartment, the campus (where i pretend to be a student) and the studio (where i pretend to dance hip hop) could become the rose-gardened church i passed every morning in antigua, guatemala, fueled on endless cups of brown-sugar sweetened black coffee and talking to the woman who sold pearl string crosses about curses and countermagic, and i wouldn't miss two steps, i don't think. but that's a false start; no, that's not the summer i wanted to begin talking about. the summer i'm thinking of is the one between the time i lived in jamaica and the time i started graduate school. between the time i met yemaya and the time i met angelia. *that* one.

the night before i left jamaica i lost the charm bracelet gift from christmas before. i had been out on the porch until almost five that morning with miss ann's son richie. i liked very much the way he sucked on my breasts and this, this pre-dawn necking, this was something i was doing, my thought-eyes floating above outside my body looking on watching the spectacle except when his mouth came back to my breast. flirting with richie made me part of the neighborhood and this proved it was real. he apologized for not being able to fuck me out on the porch and didn't understand that i didn't care. the next morning (which was three hours later) i looked everywhere for that charm bracelet before i had to leave for norman manley international, but i never found it.

the apartment where i live now has a deck which looks across to our neighbor's garden where they hired landscapers to put in roses and camellias and morning glory and even things like rocks. sometimes the unhappy-looking blond house owner comes outside to smoke a cigarette or drink wine.

i used to have a photograph of the house where i lived in kingston, that year between undergrad and grad, yemaya and angelia, that i would hang on refrigerator doors wherever i lived after i got back. i don't know what happened to that, either; i've moved too many times. in the picture the house is bright white whitewashed white with a big brown iron gate and two front facing windows and bloomed bougainvillea twisting and draping. i'd look at it and it was like a magic screen and underneath i'd see the oceans of bodies whirling by that were where i lived then. miss ann and miss cutie and miss sandra and her baby and little sandra and jennifer coming by auntie v's dropping in watching young and the restless telling stories about the other miss valerie and her disappeared husband or asking for help on their daughter's maths or coming for church or hanging laundry or anything. renata's move through the door with her hips and sandals and mouth-cornered smile. kesia with breasts like weapons and patrice proud of her dreds and family thighs. imani bringing honey and pawpaw and mango when my brother was in the hospital and i was sad because i couldn't go visit him. i lived with so many women then.

there was another photograph renata sent me that i would tape on the wall in my room. this one was of a yard not like my neighbor's now. me and patrice, faces framed by bamboo, watch kumina queenie in long red and blue plaid dress and matching headwrap stare squint-eyed at a white clothed table, bright with bottles of orange crush, banana and pineapple, while musicians twist bodies to play on her left. queenie is famous, carrying spirits for seventy years, and we went there on the advice of imani but were never sure if this was a ceremony for foreigners or not. but i was confirmed catholic and had never been to a ceremony where a woman was in charge before and so i liked it: she talked language i did know and language i didn't, sounding like gathering to her mouth invisible africa dusts swirling at ankles in her yard so unlike our neighbors' now. yes, i lived with many women then.

one saturday, after a bus ride from halfway tree where a man put his hand up my dress on a packed number 36, i came back to auntie v's and sat on the cement living room floor for four hours and had my hair braided up by a woman who did that in her off hours from the lingerie-sewing factory. i was tired of my hair frizzing up by noon and i was tired of not looking like people not because of my skin color but because of my hair texture (i wanted to be unmarked for once) and after four hours of twisting my neck i was just tired. just before i came back to the states i sat on a different floor undoing those braids which were already slipping out. after i got back i decided to let my hair grow natural (like queenie's yard i think today): no more relaxers, and no more braids.

this story is still the wrong story. long time ago i learned that every woman who sleeps with women has a *coming out* story. longer ago still i learned that every woman who discovers new spirits she didn't know existed has a *conversion* story. but here are mine all mixed together and neither seem to have a plot: only a collection of circumstances and feelings and words more muddled than honey far away and here.

in jamaica i learned yemaya. her, well, her i must have met my second day there standing at port royal dehydrated despite two kola champagnes in my turquoise dress looking across the waters at lime cay, and thinking that i could look on forever and ever and ever. but i also learned her name here. the virgin mary has a story, one story, that makes her famous: you know what it is. yemaya doesn't have that kind of story; you don't know her for just one story. ocean waters, remember, ocean waters. she is everywhere seascape meets sand blue around your ankles, not somewhere, anywhere currents like junes and there she is and you know her. i met her many times, and she was always more blue.

here, too, i meet brown women who burn blue candles with her white outline and i wonder.

i wrote letters about some of these things to my work friend angelia in oakland. she wrote me back on lined paper, with blocky girl-like handwriting, that she loved my stories about the valeries and was very unhappy with her boyfriend.

i left jamaica in may, 1995. i don't remember the plane ride back; seeing the bay as i landed which i always remember; i don't remember who picked me up at the airport; i don't remember who i called when i got home. only before and after.

one saturday, i asked tara what she was doing five years ago. i don't know, she says first, before i prod her to tell me more. i've seen her pictures in san diego; red-dyed hair, artistically shopped clothes, almost-white boyfriend she's too pretty for, always. i try to imagine her at the beaches she misses. i try to imagine her nights he was out with the boys and she went out without him, liquid eyes in the dim gold lights of bars, laughing and flirting with her girlfriends. sometimes i imagine she looks like yemaya too.

i will never forget five years ago and never remember it. from may until september every day that summer i could feel the blood rushing just under my skin pulsing its beneath side and i glowed, glassly i was moving constantly, conscientiously, losing weight, exuberantly. something was trying to come out of my body and i didn't understand yet couldn't understand that it wasn't hip or stomach or thighs that wanted to dissolve, brilliantly, that that was not how a body took itself to itself. i woke up, climbed ghost stairs, showered with incense burning, rubbed myself with honeysuckle oil because imani used to rub herself with flower-made oils every morning. i made up my first altars, partly remembered and partly invented, with candles and waters and flowers and incense and oils and my table altars got confused with my body altars. angelia at work loved the smell of me.

the summer i was waking up my brother was waking up too, more painfully. one night he threatened to kill himself in the house with our sister nicole and me. i remember making phone calls at the top of the stairs; i remember riding to the hospital after him; not being able to see him; riding home; staying up all night watching tv afterward because we were too somewhere to sleep, reruns flashing until the sun rose and we finally went to bed. we did that for days afterward, living parenthesed in our own time. no one ever told us this but we were very brave together.

i danced then, too. tuesdays, wednesdays and saturdays i went to samba classes in the mission. i met yemaya there too and learned her dances imagining brasil in the mission cultural center. sometimes weekends angelia and i would go to ashkenaz after drinking honey wine at the blue nile and hear reggae and samba bands and dance and then talk until night blurred against nicole's tv in her foggy windowed car delaying going home to the boyfriend she complained about ceaselessly, unthinkingly.

i asked tara what she was doing five years ago. at first she doesn't tell me. i think she must have known, before i did, that she had a body that did beautiful things. she asked me once, propped up against the green and red couch pillows spilling on the floor, why eclectically traveled me is with a ghetto child like herself. as if you have to travel to see things, i say and i think the thing is not to travel to meet the santas but to be there to receive them when the they come.

one night what had to happen happened. after a night of drinks and dancing angelia and i stayed overnight in san francisco at a friend's house in her picture-windowed blue-couched living room. angelia kissed me and kissed me again. and then i felt breasts and hips and stomachs women's together pressed together like yemaya and oshun and my body was made for this; like for the water; and i knew this, and i knew this and

angelia promised, soon, to leave her boyfriend. she didn't. i was left alone with this thing that i had discovered was my skin.

that month renata sent me a brightly drawn card and pictures of me with braids and patrice and queenie in jamaica. i wrote her a long letter about angelia. she never wrote back.

in september nicole drove me and my boxes to palo alto to start stanford. i came to study caribbean women's literature at a golden-tiled open-spaced campus where women of color were rarer than pearls before swine. the famous church front there was gold-plated and hollowed-out. it's hard for me to remember people i liked there. i do remember someone i envied: a beautiful woman in spanish class who was so visibly *a black lesbian* in all corners of her skin. the grids *lesbian straight bisexual* and *black white other* never fit me; me, brown woman who loves women; sometimes i wish they would.

i missed renata that month. and wished for angelia.

i learned to do many things alone. learned to live in my skin alone. to take myself to dance classes alone. to light candles alone. walk, looking at the ground or the hills or the sky, alone. jamaica was the only time that i ever was surrounded by women.

at stanford i lived in the multicultural block of student suites. at stanford my mind became a two-room suite. one room was bright: many windowed; dizzy with sun; honey-floored; edged in white and blue and green. the other was dark: carpeted, walled; ceilingless, but capped with a choke of grey clouds; the windows small and high and unbreathable. both were my rooms. both growing shabbier, the passage between more routine. i didn't know how to unlock the door or where the exit was. i didn't know

where to put the altar there. some days i was choking in doorways.
i watched a lot of young and the restless there.

one saturday i took the train up the peninsula with vylinh, a
beautiful woman i met in a coming out group, to go to a different
light bookstore in the castro. we went and were so excited to be
around other dykes; we stayed much later than we meant to. we
went to a café which i remember was bathed in light like gold
dust. i was so happy and had the best salad and coffee i'd ever had
and we went out for a drink from a woman bartender with biceps
i wanted to wrap ribbons around and before we went dancing
stopped to get our fortunes read. the psychic got everything
wrong: she seemed nervous and i guessed was new at this. i
pretended to believe her to be nice. she got everything wrong but
she reminded me of some things i was forgetting, about queenie
and women who read the cards in jamaica.

now i ask tara what she was doing four years ago. nothing,
she says. going out, dating stupid guys i guess. are you writing
about me are you still writing?

the first summer came after the summer with angelia and i
had department funding to go to haiti (in hurricane season). the
program was called haiti today: people, culture, and politics,
summer institute in les cayes and i was there with other graduate
students and one famous writer. one night when the power was
out, leaning against yellow cement walls i asked the writer about
lesbians in haiti (imagining bars). her hands reminded me of my
best friend's in high school. she smiled and told me that many
many mambos loved other women and i should go to ceremonies,
not bars, if i wanted to see.

now i ask tara what she was doing four years ago. this time
she remembers that summer she went to mexico. she talks about
what it was like to wake up and walk down to the water that she'd
slept by and she talks about what it was like to be, for the first

time, in a place where everybody is brown like her. how powerful it is to be somewhere where you're comfortable in your skin and comfortable sharing it.

one night what had to happen, happened.

in les cayes august 15th is the feast of the assumption which is also a feast for erzulie who is also yemaya. mosquito pinned skin stretched tighter to fit me, i went to the fete at gelee beach. the mountains behind were surrounded by hibiscus and cactus. there was fresh fried fish and plantains and rum and coke for sale on the beach and bands playing and i had never heard mizik rasin before. i was dancing on the beach with sofia and we liked the music. i had never heard mizik rasin before and i didn't know it brought spirits; i was dancing on the beach with sofia and my heart was like a drum against my throat and then it wasn't me it wasn't me in my body yemaya my hands moved in waves blue under my eyelids conch in my thighs my body wasn't mine and i knew i knew it was made for this this is what was trying to fly out from under my skin made to pass on to santas but i didn't know how and sofia held me and walked me to the car when yemaya didn't want to cross the water and chanted *nou pa vini pou rete no* telling the spirit she couldn't come to stay i wasn't ready yet nou pa vini pou rete no—

when i got back to oakland i went to a mambo who told me i should set up a new altar. angelia yelled, screamed, she hated the idea of the altar, how could i be taken in by all that, how could i give myself to someone invisible when she needs me to make her real life bearable. i realized that to me wanting to love yemaya and wanting to love women is the same but it won't be to everybody and even to people trying to love me too. two months later i walked out of angelia's house and never saw her again.

back in oakland i ate organic salads and fresh breads and smoothies and then more than that. my hips and thighs came back and my flesh collected itself to itself and at first i was afraid. that it weighed me down. that whatever santas i was looking for couldn't find their way through it. but, after all, a body is good for dancing.

when i went back to my mambo in january she was happy to see me and gave me a bath to help open my skin to take in good things and not be so afraid of them. i bought a new santa clara candle and a chango.

the seasons change. tara is

my autumn love. i met her on white seas of fog surrounding my then-house, convincing her to stay the night there. (i told her afterward that fog means the spirits are nearby.) i met her on white seas of cotton sheets, laying brown face to colorless morning windows. we vacationed that november without traveling in our bodies. when the rain shattered against the window spilling the ground up to meet us her voice is like, is like ocean waters—

that fall tara asked me about the candles on my altar. that fall she asked me how i came to love women. she asked me, in that white sea of november sheets, for my coming out story. for my conversion story. hoping for stories that would make sense to her.

i did not have that kind of line-to-line story for her, then. i don't have it now. this is all i have to give her.

this is how i became the colored lesbian who lights candles to our lady of sorrows and checks the boxes on the census and has nothing to offer her but my skin, and blood, and sometimes flowers.

some spiritual terms as i understand them:
kumina: Yoruba-based religion practiced in Jamaica, recognizing a pantheon of ancestral and nature spirits; related to Santeria, Vodoun, and Candomble
santas: spirits of the Yoruba pantheon are often called "santos" by Caribbean practitioners; "santas" is feminine

Yemaya: Yoruba diasporic female spirit of seas and oceans recognized in much of the Spanish-, English-, and Portuguese-speaking Caribbean and South America. Yemaya has seven principle manifestations or *paths;* as Yemaya Okuti she is linked to lesbian women and sometimes said to love female river spirit Oshun.
Oshun: Yoruba diasporic female spirit of rivers said to love Yemaya
Chango: Yoruba diasporic warrior spirit who carries a labyris and is associated with dance
mambo: Haitian Vodoun priestess
Erzulie: Yoruba diasporic spirit in Haitian Vodoun, counterpart to both Yemaya and Oshun and patroness of same-gender loving practitioners

The challenge had been made, and I felt that all of the young, gay people there expected me to defend us all with authority. My voice shook with anger and a little bit of fear that I wouldn't be able to meet this challenge. "Listen, you don't love me, you don't know me, you don't understand me," I said, barely able to remain composed and keep from crying.

Revelations
By Linda Villarosa

In the May 1991 issue of *Essence* magazine, my mother and I wrote about my coming out as a lesbian. That article received a tremendous reception—most of it positive—and it remains the most responded-to article in the history of the magazine. Due to the avalanche of mail, my mother and I followed up with "Readers Respond to Coming Out," which ran later that year in the October issue. This article was much more political, allowing me to speak out directly against homophobia in Black communities. Almost overnight, I was unexpectedly catapulted into the public arena, which began a wave of national speaking engagements that left me to cope with both adulation and condemnation.

Before I came out in print, I never had someone tell me I was going to hell. Now people say it regularly. When my mother and I addressed a conference of Black social workers about how families may confront homophobia and accept lesbian and gay children, a sad-eyed man, round-shouldered in a baggy suit, approached me. "I enjoyed hearing what you had to say," he offered, his hand extended. "But you're a sinner. You're going to hell." He said this casually, through a half-smile, as though ready to add, "Have a nice day."

Some people put their condemnation in writing, spitting angry religion-like curse words. These are two of the several letters I received at *Essence*.

> *From Smyrna, Georgia:* [Your] behavior is a sin against God that can be forgiven by sincere repentance and turning away from the sin of homosexuality. In fact, the word of God is very clear on the immorality of homosexuality. Read 1 Corinthians 6:9. Homosexuals and the homosexual lifestyle will never be accepted. I believe that sharing the Word with those individuals afflicted with the sin of homosexuality and imparting love and patience, they can receive the loving salvation of Jesus Christ. This is the only way you, and other homosexuals, can become normal, saved persons.

> *From Winchester, New York:* [Essence] should be ashamed of itself for having a woman like Linda Villarosa on your staff. Lesbian *[sic]* is not a sickness, it's a sin, and if that woman does not repent, she is going to perish. She should read Mathew *[sic]* chapter 19 verses 4 and 5. Read it and see what it says. Linda, no one wants to know who you are!

The worst verbal attack came at Oregon State University, where I was to address a large group of students about being Black, lesbian, and out. The trouble started before I arrived. I had requested that the organizers contact African-American student groups about coming to my lecture, because I believe that it's extremely important for Blacks—gay and straight—to know that Black lesbians exist and can be happy and out and secure in their identities. A member of the school's Black Women's Alliance (BWA), who was also friendly with the gay group on campus, agreed to make an announcement at BWA's next meeting to garner support and ensure a strong Black presence at the lecture. At the end of the meeting she told the other sisters that an editor from *Essence* would be speaking the following evening. Several women clapped and nodded. "She'll be talking about what it's like to be a Black lesbian," the young woman continued. At that point, the room fell silent. Finally, one woman stood up and said, "Lesbianism is nastiness and they should get a vaccine to make them normal." Spurred on, another declared, "Gays are against God, and because of my religion, I can't hear this woman speak." In the end, another exasperated sister said, "Can we please stop talking about this, I'm getting physically ill."

Thankfully, I didn't know about this backlash or I would've been too freaked to do the lecture. Expressions of homophobia hurt deeply, but coming from other Black women the pain is particularly acute. Knowing that I would be facing such resistance in what was already a largely white audience on a conservative college campus may well have paralyzed me.

The lecture went fine. The question-and-answer period was particularly long with interested students—gay, straight, and of many races and ethnicities—hungry for answers and information. After awhile I became tired and announced that I'd answer one final question. A clean-cut white guy wearing a baseball cap waved his hand frantically from the balcony. And there it was: "You and all gays are going to hell. I'm telling you this because God taught me to love you." Then he cited a Bible passage: "Read Leviticus 20:13."

Bedlam broke out in the room. After several minutes, I got things quieted down and looked out into the expectant faces of the audience. The challenge had been made, and I felt that all of the young, gay people there expected me to defend us all with authority. My voice shook with anger and a little bit of fear that I wouldn't be able to meet this challenge. "Listen, you don't love me, you don't know me, you don't understand me," I said, barely able to remain composed and keep from crying. "You're using religion to cloak your horrible message in the language of love. People like you have used religion to suppress everything you find offensive. In the past the Bible was used to justify slavery and now you're using it to justify your fear and hatred of those of us who are living our lives as gays and lesbians."

The tension broke and the crowd began to applaud, but I felt empty. Even the reporters covering the event saw through my strong front and brave smile. The next day's edition of the *Corvallis (Ore.) Gazette-Times* reported that as I stepped from the podium, I had seemed stunned. It was true: I was stunned. And sad. My words had sounded hollow to me, as though I had been reading from a textbook. I hadn't felt them. My reaction had been a knee-jerk response to being attacked in public; but deep within me, I knew I wasn't so sure about myself. Where do I really stand spiritually? That heckler knew exactly how he felt and where he stands, why didn't I?

Nothing in my own religious upbringing prepared me for these attacks. My family attended an integrated, "progressive" Episcopal church. There were a handful of families of color like us and lots of groovy white people, interracial couples, and aging hippies with their adopted children of color in tow. Our choir didn't sing gospel music, but folky spiritual ballads accompanied by the organ, guitar, and African and Native drumming.

I don't remember learning many specific religious lessons from our minister. With his long hair flowing over his Roman collar, Father Hammond preached through sleepy eyes, as though he'd been out late drinking the night before. His words were inspirational and easy to understand, filled with references to pop culture. A quote from *Playboy* magazine could seamlessly segue into biblical verse. My mother taught my fourth-grade Sunday school class, stressing discipline and openmindedness. One Saturday morning the group of us gathered for a field trip to a nearby synagogue. We looked like a bunch of "We Are the World" poster children. "It's important to learn about the way other people worship," my mother explained, looking over our group to make sure our two lines were straight and orderly and no noses were running.

To further my religious studies, I attended weeks and weeks of confirmation classes every Thursday night. On confirmation day, I walked down the church aisle, clutching a white prayer book in white-gloved hands. I was wearing a white dress, white lace socks, white patent-leather shoes, and had a white handkerchief pinned to my head. I looked like a brown-skinned vestal virgin awaiting sacrifice. I don't remember one spiritual lesson from that time, but I do remember how hard it was to try to stay clean in all those bleached-white clothes.

We also visited St. John's, my grandmother's Baptist church, on trips back to Chicago, where I was born. Getting dressed for service was a major production. My grandmother had to decide which of her many wigs and hats to wear and whether or not to put on her fur, a decision that had little to do with the temperature outside. After the frenzied preparations, we'd all pile into my grandfather's Electra 225 and float to church in the boat-sized car.

Once inside, I'd always scrunch into my grandmother's side and maneuver a way to sit by her. I knew she was important in this community from the way heads would turn as she led the family—straight-backed—down the aisle to our pew, and I wanted a little of that limelight.

The service really wasn't as fun as the preparation, mainly because of its three-hour length. Until someone got the Spirit. I'd hold my breath as the organ pounded out the same repetitive note and the singing rang louder, rising to more and more tremerous shouts. Inevitably, some well-dressed woman would take to the aisle, chanting and skipping. Then two strong, well-practiced sisters, dressed in white gloves and nurse's uniforms, would walk briskly over and efficiently bring the saved soul back to this world and dispatch her into the care of family members. I would tug at Grandmother's sleeve asking questions about the moment of high drama, but she would slap my Vaselined knees together and hiss into my ear, "Stop-staring-close-your-lips-don't-bite-your-cuticles-put-your-gloves-back-on." The only thing I knew for certain was that no one in our family would ever get the spirit, because my grandmother would die of embarrassment.

From my parents' church I learned about respect for difference and community across seemingly unbridgeable differences, and through my grandmother's church I connected with my Southern Baptist roots. But nothing from my religious past had prepared me to deal with the continued abuse I was receiving from so-called religious people. It was time for me to begin studying the Bible, but, more importantly, it was time to discover my own spiritual core.

First, I dug out the dusty copy of the Revised Standard Version of the Bible left over from my days in confirmation classes, and I looked up the passages that had been thrown in my face. I started with 1 Corinthians 6:9 and 10, which read: "Do not be deceived; neither the immoral, nor idolaters, nor adulterers, nor homosexuals, nor thieves, nor the greedy, nor drunkards, nor revilers, nor robbers will inherit the kingdom of God."

I felt skeptical; had the authors of the Bible really used the word "homosexual" two thousand years ago? No, they had not. The New Testament had been written in Greek and then translated into Hebrew. In 1382 the Bible was first translated into English, and in 1611 came the King James (or authorized) Version. The Bible I was reading had been revised 335 years later. I purchased a paperback copy of the King James Version and looked up 1 Corinthians 6:9 and 10. This earlier version never used the word "homosexual" but listed the "effeminate" and "abusers of themselves with mankind" in its inventory of the "unrighteous," and that had been translated to mean "homosexual" in the revised version. Something had been lost—or gained—in translation.

I decided not to spend much more time trying to sort out what the authors meant and what lessons they were trying to teach about homosexuality—if that's even what they were talking about—in the context of social systems from twenty centuries past. In fact, even after reading Genesis 19 many times, I still didn't see how the story of Sodom had anything to do with gay sex. In that story, Lot, a holy man and resident of the evil city of Sodom, is visited by two angels. Genesis 19:4-8 reads:

> ... the men of the city, the men of Sodom, both young and old, all the people to the last man, surrounded the house; and they called to Lot, "Where are the men who came to you tonight [i.e., the angels]? Bring them out to us, that we may know them." Lot went out of the door to the men, shut the door after him, and said, "I beg you, my brothers, do not act so wickedly. Behold, I have two daughters who have not known man; let me bring them to you, and do them as you please; only do nothing to these men..."

Eventually, the angels strike the men blind, and God rains fire and brimstone down on the city and burns it down. From this story comes the word "sodomy"—a pejorative term for gay sex. And now, when a city like New York is described as a modern-day Sodom, the underlying assumption is that it's full of sin and sex and gays. Even assuming that the word "know" refers to sex, it seems a stretch to use it to condemn gays and lesbians. Why isn't anyone questioning Lot for offering to turn over his virginal daughters to the mob of men, which is the most obvious aberrance relayed there?

Moving on, I looked up Matthew 19:4 and 5, which says: "He answered, 'Have you not read that he who made them from the beginning made them male and female,'" and said, 'For this reason a man shall leave his father and mother and be joined to his wife, and the two shall become one flesh.'"

Upon further reading, it was easy to see that the letter writer from Westchester, New York, had taken these verses completely out of context. The passage had nothing to do with lesbians and gay men but was clearly a condemnation of divorce. In fact, the verses she cited were an answer to the question "Is it lawful to divorce one's wife for any cause?" (Matthew 19:3). Verse 9 says that "whoever divorces his wife, except for unchastity, and marries another, commits adultery." In case there's any question about the seriousness of adultery, Leviticus 20:10 spells it out clearly: "If a man commits adultery with the wife of his neighbor, both the adulterer and the adulteress shall be put to death." What does this have to do with queerness?

Next I looked up Leviticus 20:13: "If a man lies with a male as with a woman, both of them have committed an abomination; they shall be put to death, their blood is upon them." I guess they could be murdered along with the divorced remarried couple from earlier Leviticus verses. At this point, I started getting angry.

It doesn't take a biblical scholar to figure out that people use the Bible selectively. The people who write me letters are not sending hate mail to people who are divorced or to those who have cheated on their spouses. The man who lashed out at me in Oregon is not condemning people who eat pork ("And the swine, because it parts the hoof and is cloven-footed but does not chew the cud, is unclean to you. Of their flesh you shall not eat, and their carcasses you shall not touch; they are unclean to you": Leviticus 11:7-8) or shellfish ("...anything in the seas or the rivers that has not fins and scales, of the swarming creatures in the waters and of the living creatures that are in the waters, is an abomination to you": Leviticus 11:10).

Neither is he cursing or carrying on about cattle breeders, farmers who grow two different crops, or anyone who wears a poly-cotton blend of clothing despite Leviticus 19:19: "You shall not let your cattle breed with a different kind; you shall not sow your field with two different kinds of seed; nor shall there come upon you a garment of cloth made of two kinds of stuff."

These people are also overlooking beautiful, lyrical passages in the Bible that celebrate same-sex love. In Ruth 1:16-17 of the Old Testament, Ruth says to Naomi: "Entreat me not to leave you or to return from following you; for where you go I will go, and where you lodge I will lodge; your people shall be my people, and your God my God; where you die I will die, and there will I be buried."

David and Jonathan of the Old Testament seem to be deeply in love: "...the soul of Jonathan was knit to the soul of David, and Jonathan loved him as his own soul" (1 Samuel 18:1). When Jonathan dies in the war, David writes: "...your love to me was wonderful, passing the love of women" (2 Samuel 1:26).

Many so-called righteous people are taking the Bible literally when it suits them, ignoring anything that doesn't easily support their narrow condemnations or calls into question their own lifestyles. And many Black people are using the Bible against their lesbian and gay sisters and brothers just as whites used the scriptures against our ancestors when they interpreted passages such as Ephesians 6:5-6— "Slaves, be obedient to those who are your earthly masters, with fear and trembling, in singleness of heart, as to Christ; not in the way of eyeservice, as men-pleasers, but as servants of Christ" — to mean that our people should remain enslaved.

It is, in fact, a sad irony that the overwhelmingly white Christian Right movement is capitalizing on homophobia in Black communities. Groups like the Moral Majority and the Christian Coalition have never marched side by side with or fought for issues affecting people of color. In fact, the Christian Right has actively lobbied against issues such as voting rights and affirmative action. But now they're recruiting our people, taking advantage of the deep spiritual commitment of the African-American community and distorting Christianity to pass anti-gay and lesbian legal initiatives and turn straight Blacks against gays—similar to the way their ancestors distorted Christianity to justify slavery.

My Bible studies behind me, I felt fortified intellectually but still on shaky ground spiritually. But I knew exactly what I needed to do. I had heard about Unity Fellowship Church and its lively congregation of hundreds of mostly Black lesbians and gay men that worshiped on Sundays at New York City's Lesbian and Gay Community Services Center. Although I had always found excuses to avoid going, now it was time.

When I arrived that first Sunday, the room at the Center was packed with people; in fact, close to one hundred latecomers had to be turned away. The service began with testimonials. Person after person stood up and testified to what had happened over the week: breakups, gay bashing, rejections by parents, eviction from apartments, illness, sadness, loneliness, addiction, sorrow, seemed to silence the news of triumphs and causes for celebration. Pain filled the room, Black pain, gay pain. But when the pastor, Elder Zachary Jones, marched into the room to the tune of "We've come this far by faith... ," the mood in the room changed to one of joy.

"It doesn't have nothing to do with who you sleep with, but what's in your heart," Rev. Zach shouted over the low hum of the choir. "Who says God doesn't love gay people? There's love in this room." And there was. A measure of healing had begun. His simple words struck a chord in me, and I felt relieved and then cleansed. As I looked around at the hundreds of other Black lesbian and gay people in the room—who like me had been searching for a spiritual home—I knew I had found a place where I could be comfortable and explore my own spirituality.

Fortified in mind and spirit, from my connection with this community, I felt ready to face the world. And an opportunity presented itself while I was giving a talk at a Black cultural center on the West Coast. After going through my usual song and dance about how it felt to be Black and a lesbian, I began fielding questions. I noticed a woman raising her hand tentatively. She was a sister in her mid-thirties, turned out in an expensive, corporate-looking suit and bright gold jewelry, with her hair freshly done in braided extensions. "You seem like a really nice woman and I enjoyed hearing your story," she began slowly. "But as a Christian woman I need to share this with you. I went through a period in my life when I thought I was attracted to women. But then I discovered Jesus Christ. By reading the Bible, I realized that homosexuality was unnatural and that I was a sinner. If I continued in the life, I would be condemned."

"Where does the Bible say that?" I asked.

Opening her purse, she pulled out a small, worn copy of the New Testament and began to read from a marked passage. "'For this reason God gave them up to dishonorable passions. Their women exchanged natural relations for unnatural, and the men likewise gave up natural relations with women and were consumed with passion for one another, men committing shameless acts with men and receiving in their own persons the due penalty for their error.' Romans 1, verses 26 and 27."

I listened politely as she read. When she had finished, I reached into my backpack and pulled out my own copy of the Bible. "'In like manner that the women adorn themselves in modest apparel with propriety and moderation, not with braided hair or gold or pearls or costly clothing,' 1 Timothy, chapter 2, verse 9," I read. "And 1 Timothy 2:11 and 12 say, 'Let a woman learn in silence with all submissiveness. I permit no woman to teach or to have authority over men; she is to keep silent.' I'm sure in your work you have had to supervise men. I know I have. And even by standing up and speaking out today, I guess we're both sinning."

"Wait, that's not fair," she said, her face looking at once confused and angry. "It's not right to take the Bible out of context like that."

"Why?" I countered. "That's what you're doing."

Even as I hit her close to home, I felt sorry for this woman. She was obviously confused and probably a closet case, and I knew I was preying on that, attacking her with scriptures almost as I had been attacked. I was aiming at a place she had only recently uncovered—where she was still vulnerable.

"Listen," I said softly. "I don't want to do this. All of us need to stop taking the Bible so literally, and begin to read it critically and intelligently. You know, there are some important messages that we can understand and agree on." I opened my Bible to Leviticus 19:17 and read in a clear voice, "You shall not hate your brother in your heart, but you shall reason with your neighbor, lest you bear sin because of him. You shall not take vengeance or bear any grudge against the sons of your own people, but you shall love your neighbor as yourself." And this time my words sounded strong and confident, and were definitely my own.

As a counselor, I see the deep damage that internalized homophobia has done within the black gay and lesbian community. I have seen us kept from our full potential as humans, lovers and contributors to our local and world communities due to the fear that we carry. …Many times this damage is directly traceable to our experiences in African-American churches.

In Broad Daylight
By Rev. Jim Webb

I attended a drag ball several years ago, during which the emcee kept asking the girls "Can you walk the daylight?"—meaning "Do you have the skill and courage to do drag by the light of day, where it might become more apparent that you are a drag? Can you 'pass' as a woman?" "Walking the daylight" was seen as the "acid test" of being a fully evolved drag queen.

In the African American LGBT community, we may want to ask ourselves a similar question. In this instance, "walking the daylight" may mean refusing to cower to the homophobia that has been an inherent part of the African-American community, including many African-American churches.

For example, when the minister of the largest African-American church in the Washington, D.C. area recently made derogatory remarks about "dykes and fags" from the pulpit, equating homosexuals with prostitutes and drug addicts, an "openly gay" member of his congregation (who ironically refused to give his name) had an interesting comment: He stated that although he disagreed with the pastor's homophobia, he attended the church because of the fellowship it offered. I'm sure he had his reasons for attending a homophobic church and withholding his name, but in my humble opinion, his comment seemed like internalized homophobia masquerading as a true rationale. His logic is akin to that of an African American attending a Ku Klux Klan gathering because the Klan serves good hush puppies.

Internalized homophobia is so insidious precisely because it can "pass" for logical rationale—even in the daylight of scrutiny. As a counselor, I see the deep damage that internalized homophobia has done within the black gay and lesbian community. I have seen us kept from our full potential as humans, lovers and contributors to our local and world communities due to the fear that we carry. I have seen this fear translated into the pain of isolation. Many times this damage is directly traceable to our experiences in African-American churches.

My own experience with a traditional African-American church was similarly negative. On one of my rare adult appearances (as a tribute to my mother), I heard the same diatribe that I had heard countless times while growing up. Howww-mowww-SEX-u-ALLS, drug dealers and murderers were all castigated in the same breath. However, the minister had known me from childhood, and knew that I was a Howww-mowww-SEX-u-ALL. Though only tacitly, I felt that he and the church had long ago accepted my homosexuality. He was aware of my partner and my mother sitting among the congregation, yet there was the same stance regarding homosexuality. The rationale for my silence was that I didn't want to disrupt the service or call undue attention or controversy to my mother. I had to keep asking myself, however, "Is this rationale valid, or is it fear?"

Any logic to this rationale ended when my mother died. I took my next steps by vocally declining to make a substantial contribution to the church in my mother's memory, despite the fact that it was widely expected that I would. I have evolved past the place where tacit acceptance (the way a disruptive child is tolerated) is enough. So have many others. We do more now than "tolerate" ourselves: We embrace ourselves—and we expect to receive the Church's embrace. If churches are not ready to embrace us, then they are not ready to embrace our money.

For me, taking this stance was an important "baby step" in my process of development. Coming out is a series of evolutionary steps tied, in part, to the level of social, economic and emotional empowerment we have achieved. We must all evolve at our own pace, and in a way that is wise. However, we should also always ask ourselves, "Am I living in fear, and is this fear masquerading as a logical rationale? Am I ready to break the pattern of silence caused by my fear?" We can ask ourselves if our pattern of silence is helping us or hurting us by limiting and isolating us. Is it hurting us by subtly undermining our self-esteem and instilling an insidious form of internalized homophobia in our hearts and minds? We should also ask if this silence is helping or hurting someone else, such as the gay, potentially suicidal teen out there who needs to see an affirming role model. This thought process can be a guide to how we take our next steps.

Those next steps, as they relate to our traditional African-American churches, are quite personal. We can all ask ourselves whether we should continue to support organizations that don't support us, or whether we should find organizations that do. We may even consider opening a dialogue regarding homosexuality in our current churches. No matter what next steps we take, however, we can be assured that we are not alone. With every passing day, there are many more courageous spirits who are there to lock arms and embrace us as we "walk the daylight" of our own spiritual and self-acceptance together.

I tried to fit my conflicted and fidgety boy body into those Kingdom Hall seats, and just as I was getting comfortable the JWs predicted the end of the world. There had been so many things snatched from under me: boyhood, dignity and hope—and now this. …What a bummer. … How do you pack for doom?

Who Say Amen Over Me?
By Marvin K. White

I wouldn't call what I'm on a spiritual path. Where I come from we don't have paths. Paths are in fairy tales. Little Red Riding Hood was on a path. Hansel and Gretel were on a path. Oakland, for a poor black child, doesn't have paths; it has streets, very, very, mean streets. Streets paved in trouble and disappointment. Streets so bleak… Okay, you get it: mean streets. There were no moss-covered stepping-stones to Jesus, quaint bridges to Buddha or familiar avenues to Allah. To call my spiritual journey a path is too polite for what god and I put each other through. God was never where he said he was going to be, waiting for me on said path. He surely picked up his things and left when I didn't show up. I have spent a lifetime duckin' and dodgin' god, showing him that I didn't need him, and it has been no easy feat. As a child my relationship with god was strained, exhausting even, but as an adult the knot that is my spirituality is beginning to come undone and in its undoing is where I am finding the god of my dreams.

When we were growing up my mother, bless her heart, never said a bad word about Curley Joseph White, my dad. She easily could have. She could have looked at us, saw him and turned her hate for him toward us. We knew this was a possibility. She could have stood in every doorway to our lives and kept him out. She didn't. She allowed us a curtain, window, door-sized crack of hope for his return.

We in turn never praised him or made him a mythic or heroic figure—at least not in front of her. He was not perfect, was never perfect. From his side of the family, my paternal grandmother would look at us with a distant eye. Embarrassed for the son of hers who left a wife with five babies, she did not know how to reach out to us. His distance became hers, as evidenced by the four pairs of Spiderman pajamas in one size for his four boys of varying height that we received one Christmas. They were too small—and to top it off, we didn't even celebrate Christmas. His brothers and sisters, my uncles and aunts, would commiserate with my mother over his scoundrel and doglike ways and even offered on occasion monetary help or emotional support. One of his brothers, my uncle Edmund, a bus driver, would allow us to sit at the front of his bus and ride the entire bus route of his shift. My younger brother convinced me that this was fun and we fought for the privilege of watching him in the coach's commander's chair, charming the work-wearied women and disarming the barely bread-winning men.

We dared not ask for much more. My mother would never allow us to ask of people not descended of Dorcas, her grandmother, and my great-grandmother. If she or the women she came from could not provide what we needed, then we understood it was not needed. My mother didn't need help. She, along with her mother, my grandmother, took fierce care of us. She could even stomach him, my dad, poking his head into our lives on some random graduation day or football game to claim some part, some credit for our milestones, her hard work.

We, along with all of the other fatherless children who lived in the Oakland Housing Authority apartments, traded stories about our fathers like the baseball cards of our bubble gum-packed youth. It was rare that a father would show up in these apartments. This meant that none of the boys could ever say, "at least I see my daddy" or "you don't even know who your daddy is." Father figures were few and mother figures plentiful.

Unfortunately, we were not growing up to be or could choose to be mothers. Our mothers gave us what they could of their masculine selves and let us piece together the rest. We were awestruck by television, singing and movie stars. We worshiped the holy trinity of masculinity, The Jameses: Evans, Brown and Earl Jones. Mixed in with some of the random preaching of the rare teacher, the coach, the reoccurring wise janitor, the mailman, the liquor store owner or security officer, we pieced ourselves together into athletes, womanizers, drug dealers, crackheads, thieves, and in one odd case—mine—gay.

Growing up in those apartments we were all still black, girls/young ladies, boys/thugs or ruffians and homosexuals/punks. To everyone who examined the boys it was clear into which category they fell. I was clear. I heard what they called me and I knew that everything I was called was everything that kept me out: teacher's pet, mama's boy, spoiled, bookworm. Softness was ridiculed. I learned to keep quiet and sink into the worlds that the books I found revealed—my mother's romance novels, then her *Watchtowers* and *Awakes*, my grandmother's dream book, *National Enquirers,* then the Bible and my uncle's girlie magazines. Worlds so clearly written about that I leaped into the pages, became characters and became excited by them.

I also read my sister's books. Girls had books that dealt with bodies blossoming, love and rejection, not the train yard, basketball court or gang fight where boys in books found themselves. Girls in girls' books asked questions like the heroine of the Judy Blume novel, *Are You There God? It's Me, Margaret.* I didn't like her at first. She was able to question god and demand a little blonde-headed petite revelation. I wasn't. White girls get to do everything. For me god was there. God was watching. God was waiting. God was coming to get us. We had been taught early on that yes, there was a god there. And whatever world I escaped to, he was watching. So I lived hunched over my life, protecting it from whoever was reading over my shoulder.

For a while there was no mention of gods or fathers until somewhere during my elementary school years, when my mom became involved with the Jehovah's Witnesses. This meant we were JWs too. There were many women in my family who were JWs. My great-grandmother studied "the truth" as did my grandmother and now my mom. In between the trips to Reno, the all-night poker parties, the gathering and cooking for the holidays that we were not supposed to be celebrating, including birthdays and Christmases, my mom still studied. There were many Saturdays when we sat for what seemed like six hours in a fidgety Bible study. There were also Tuesday and Thursday night book studies and then Sunday services—no more and no less than any other devoted Christians.

But what made the experience so confusing was the way in which people looked at us. We were embarrassed by this religion. We didn't clap or get loud. We didn't fall out or shout. We didn't receive blood transfusions. We didn't do anything fun. I think that's how my mother liked it. Raising five children by herself she chose a god who was in control of things and who could ultimately control her children, children that were growing with weed like speed into adulthood. This father figure left no doubt about what he wanted from us. We should expect punishment if we did not listen to him and heavenly rewards if we did. There's this image that appears on one of the many thousands of books that JWs publish that showed a lion laying down with a lamb; it was what heaven was supposed to be like. It was confusing. I had watched Mutual of Omaha's *Wild Kingdom*. I knew what lions did to lambs. But in that heaven, lions were vegetarians, friends with lambs, and everyone milled about happy and smiling. This image terrified me.

This god, Jehovah, was strict. He taught us to fear other gods. To this day, I believe that I am the only one of my mother's children who has developed a belief system about god that is different from hers. We weren't prepared for the questions and taunts of the other kids. We grew up ashamed of god and our relationship with him. My mother did not choose wisely. This god would soon disappoint me as much as my real father did.

I tried to fit my conflicted and fidgety boy body into those Kingdom Hall seats, and just as I was getting comfortable the JWs predicted the end of the world. There had been so many things snatched from under me: boyhood, dignity and hope—and now this. It was my understanding that the end of the world was coming the summer between my fourth and fifth grade years. What a bummer. I started saying goodbye to everybody. I told them that I would be leaving. I imagined being beamed up to heaven during some made-for-TV rapture. I didn't know what it meant—fire, brimstone; what do I know from apocalypse? How do you pack for doom? I was just getting started here. It felt like I was switching schools just when I was getting popular. Twice. It's fucked up and fucked me up for years. It was such a disappointment to show up at sixth grade, still poor, still ashy, still awkward-looking, having to explain to other kids why I was still there, explaining my god away like I had done my dad on many occasions. Dang god. But like I said, I had been there before. I had waited for longer than summers for my dad to come and get me and he never did.

It may sound like a leap of Dr. Phil proportions, but a lot of my self-worth was formed by how these two—my mother's choices, my dad and my god—treated me. Neither one wanted me. Neither one came for me. The knot tightened as I grew more and more mad at them both. My ex-lover believes that I have "abandonment issues." When my two father figures, the two who were supposed to mean the most to me, don't keep their promises, isn't it understandable? Between Curley Joseph White, my dad, and Jehovah, my god, I began to devalue all the things in me that should have pleased them. Eventually my "good boy" image was just a front to hide the war waging inside my body, a war of, well, biblical proportions. Good and evil fought as fiercely as the boys in my neighborhood did. I confused men and gods all the time and confused sex for love. The knot of emotions that is my relationship with men and gods was tied tight inside of me.

After the requisite failed attempts at coupling with someone of the opposite sex, I only had dates with girls as I needed them, for proms. I listen to some of the stories that my male friends have about their boyhood sexual encounters with other boys and wonder with envy why there was no one my age within radar range to touch me. I remember looking at my sexuality not so much as a reconciling, but an interrogation. Who are you, Marvin? Why are you different? You know this is wrong. "This" being a feeling toward men that I never wanted to get caught exhibiting. I was already ashamed that I wasn't ashamed.

I was relieved, actually, when my sister finally called me a faggot. I became less worried about who called my difference by some nasty name. I was actually freed by her betrayal. She offered the proof I needed. Called me something that scared and thrilled me both. It's like finding out that sometimes what we call "gon' crazy" might be called Alzheimer's disease. I had a name for this condition. But it's not a name that fathers or gods like. I was very clear that how and whom I loved was not pleasing to my fathers. So I hid it like Adam once he found out he was naked. Okay, that's my last Bible reference.

When boys, boys in men's bodies, and men finally met me where I was sexually, it was both tragic and explosive. Let me say that again, clearly. When I started having sex… When I started fucking and sucking—there, I said it—there was a way in which I knew that men needed me. Unless I was a really awful lay, they stayed, at least until we were both spent. In bed I tried my hardest not to disappoint, to not be disappointing. All my attention was focused on what I was doing wrong or right sexually. What my partner was doing, unless it clued me in to how they needed me to behave, was irrelevant. I excused feelings of being used just to hear someone comment on how flawless my skin was, so brown, so smooth. I drank it all in.

I took this hyper-exoticized glory to my head. I was intoxicated by these compliments. If someone looked me in the face and said I was cute or handsome, I would discount it; I didn't need to feel beautiful. Sex became a way to feel close to men and to feel wanted. It validated me. Sex informed me that my partner wanted to be there, in that bed, in that park or in that booth. No one told me that this knot of feelings would have to be unwound. No one told me about sex, low self-esteem, objectification, bad self-image, and abandonment issues: the Jehovah's Witness Values Meal.

Oh—and AIDS. Yeah, I heard the right-wingers say that it was god's wrath. I didn't realize that I hadn't deflected all of the churches full of preachers who were preaching abomination sermons in front of my gay brothers' faces. I thought I was strong enough to withstand these attacks. I stayed away from church because I couldn't handle hearing this message of hopelessness. I wasn't a turn-or-burn kind of guy. But as much as we were told that we were to blame for AIDS, I blamed god. He took away more men out of my life, men who should have been here to share their stories. He took men who were the first to tell me that I am connected to them because I am telling stories. These were men who I didn't have to put out for or put up with. While my familial lineage was blurred with hurt, my literary lineage flowered from a huge fruit tree. I don't blame god for AIDS; I blame him for being in collusion with the forces that drive broken boys like me into the damaged arms, beds and throats of other dispirited and unhealthy men.

I blame him for allowing me to think that I needed to save my brothers, both my biological and universal ones, from my sex. Even today when I am visiting my mother's, our family center, it is not uncommon to only greet my brothers with the requisite head-nodding "what's up?" There is an unwritten and unspoken code amongst the men in our family. We are men, masculine, and play out these roles down to the back slapping, cursing, burping, farting and spitting. Rarely do I bring up gay-specific anecdotes, nor rock anyone's comfort boat. I remain at a safe distance. I am reduced to a twelve-year-old boy, awkward and desperate not to be different.

Once, my sister told me that my brother Marc was displeased with me when he saw me kissing a man on the lips. I was embarrassed, for him. I disappoint everyone. Fall short of everyone's expectations. I remain in collusion with the ideas of masculinity in my family. I couldn't dare imagine him not speaking to me. I want to keep my family. I often feel like I am granted or afforded a place in our family, a place guaranteed to the straight members.

I have played along with the idea that I had to prove myself a man, even if I was gay. I didn't even brag when I performed on national television, albeit in drag, or performed on stage at Lincoln Center in New York, even though I was in a group called the Pomo Afro Homos. I keep the same relationship with my mother. Only it goes further to the core of what I believe about myself—that if I am totally honest with her, she will have to choose between me and her god and surely I would lose. God made us make these choices. God kept them from me.

So this knot, my spirituality, is where I am finding god. Inherent in being a Jehovah's Witness is the witness part. There is a way in which being a "Witness" happens to you. I like a real god now, one that I have to find, and one that I have to discover. My god should reflect how I live in and move through this world. I like a high/low god. I love the "on high-ness" of god but I love the god of the "bless the child who got his own-ness" too. I like my god to come and visit me on the dance floor, speak to me from burning bush speaker boxes in my favorite night club where I have often found myself in the middle of the gyrating boys, eyes closed, unaware of who is looking, what I have worn to attract who, how fat or skinny I am, dancing with an imagined partner, dipped and spun like I have always dreamt I was light enough to be. I have imagined myself very far from home on the dance floor. I have welled up with tears thinking of who has danced on the floor beneath me, before me. I have had my mind so cleared of clutter that I receive words that feel like they are being given to me because I am freeing myself in the music. I am a Whirling Dervish. I am divine. And I'm only as far away as closed eyes can take me. There; I like a god there. Just someplace that's only as far as closed eyes. Not as mystic as Hinduism.

I like a god that reminds me that I am not the only good child in whatever den of iniquity I happen to be in; that there are other children here on their way to or coming back from someplace spiritually. I like a god who still visits with the spirit boys who I attract now. The ones whose pants I pull down and I Ching. The ones who re-read my misfortune as calling. The ones who spill their tea leaves onto my belly. I like a god of conjuring children, the bold juju boys and magic queens. I like a god that still lets the children lay hands and heal.

I like the god who said something so sweet to my grandmother that it woke her up singing "Amazing Grace." I like the smite god, who don't like ugly. And I've been ugly. I have done some things so self-destructive that I am amazed that I am still standing. I like a god that can withstand a test. I have put myself in harm's way as if to say, "Is this where you will save me?"—even when I lost all hope that someone could save me. I like a god who can fail a test, let me believe all the hype about him, then when I am disappointed have me understand that he would not be the last man that would disappoint me. I have learned to not be disappointed in men or gods. I have a god now that will love me no more than I love myself. I like that.

It occurs to me that no one that we grew up with was singled out as the one who was going to be a preacher. I thought that in every black neighborhood there was one overachieving Sunday school student, who read Bible passages with such passion that everyone knew that he had to be a P.I.T. (Preacher In Training). While no one had such a lofty calling where I grew up, more than one person—actually, most people—either under their welfared breaths or to my sissified face, called me a punk and recognized my "peculiar ways." I like a god who took thirty-seven years to reveal to me what to do with this calling, a god who I cursed when there was no honor to this calling, particularly when it seemed more curse than anything else. I like a god who made me switch when I walked so everyone could see me coming and knew how to treat me once I had arrived. More than one mama saw the pink light shining through the cracks in my boyhood and shielded her eyes, tried to warn the others to watch how their children played with me. I knew in ways that the other children could not imagine that I was different.

There is a way in which I was run out. I believe now that that's the gifts of broken communities, families, fathers and gods. They run you out and don't allow you back in. They force you out into the world, a world where they know you belong. They call you so many things and you think it shame. It works; you never go back completely. You arrive at thirty-seven in the pages of an anthology for gay and lesbian black folks talking about spirit stuff. Your calling, your casting out, exists then.

I remember clearly my mother shielding us from the Hare Krishnas with their freakish, shaved bald white heads, tambourines and incense, dancing wildly on Telegraph Avenue in Berkeley or at the co-op grocery store near our North Oakland home. I also remember the Jehovah's Witnesses within feet, quiet and unassuming, taking up far less space for their god. Who are these people that sing and dance and chant for their god? I think about them today because Karma and Yoga are a part of my lexicon. I think about reincarnation and the release from the cycles of life and death without feelings of retribution, betrayal or guilt. I no longer feel like I couldn't handle being abandoned again by family. I think about the many ways one makes his way to "the divine," so different from the one quiet and steady way of being a Jehovah's Witness. I now dance my way to divinity, chant my way to higher consciousness and meditate my way to full actualization. I have gone from being a Witness to being something to witness.

My god never kept his word; others did. And I listened to their misinterpretations. He was never where he said he was going to be. So I learned to ask myself "What am I doing here?" And "Who am I waiting for?" I like a god and a spirituality that says I am saved because I create something that will last longer than my body. I create stories and speak them.

And the only who I need to say amen over me is me.

That summer, I hid particularly apropos New Testament quotes on slips of paper all over the apartment for my mother to find. She got the message but was too thrown off guard by the bizarre nature of this tactic to fly into a rage. Nevertheless, she put her foot down. She didn't like being preached to about her attitudes and behaviors, and she was right.

What I Did With My Summer Vocation
By Eva Yaa Asantewaa

To the God of many names and one Spirit...
—Rosemary L. Bray

*I do not think I will ever reach a stage when I will say,
'This is what I believe. Finished.'
What I believe is alive... and open to growth...*
—Madeleine L'Engle

When I was a kid in Catholic elementary school in my largely Italian neighborhood, there were no Black nuns. No Black nuns, no Black nun role models. No Black nun role models, no vocation for little Black girls like me to grow up to be the Bride of Christ. A blessing in disguise—but not in the disguise of a habit.

Of course, there was that Black sister—I mean nun, of course, but she was a *sistah,* too—who sat in the Times Square subway station begging for donations. She was always there. Whenever my two Bajan aunts would hustle me off to see my adopted aunties and surrogate grandparents—their Jewish and Puerto Rican ILGWU co-workers in the garment district—we'd see Sistah and pass her pretty hurriedly without comment. And definitely without spare change. I felt sorry for her draped in that old black habit (got her in a spell) in the sweltering subway underground. Even as a child, I thought she must be the most misguided individual I'd ever seen.

The bright working-class and lower middle-class Black girls in my school didn't yearn to be nuns. They wanted to be doctors, dentists, lawyers, teachers. Their parents took them to piano, violin, and tap dance lessons on Saturday mornings. I didn't know what I wanted to be, but I could dance up a storm; write up a storm, too.

The idea of being covered in black, head to toe, was too closely associated with family funerals or with crazy nuns wielding wooden rulers like police batons. (I liked the rosary beads, though. Still think they're cool.) Obviously, this was before black became the New York City Thing, particularly in the East Village where I now make my home. (Time was, I'd leave my apartment, wondering if I should have worn a slip under my skirt. Now, East Village women are wearing just black slips, no skirts!) I didn't want to be like Subway Sistah, abandoned in the airless underground, forced to beg money for some dubious cause.

Still, I had a certain inexplicable attraction toward God. Not Jesus. God. Today, I would call it Spirit or Great Mystery, as indigenous people do, and regard it as beyond gender and description, as Kabbalists do. It was a full-blown, mystical, Nusrat Fateh Ali Khan kind of thing even then, and I had no idea where it came from. Certainly not from my maternal aunts who flirted with the Black church—more fun than those boring, droning priests and more social. Nor from my mother with her unshakable allegiance to the Pope, her conservative politics and racial self-hatred. Nor from my Anglican-raised father who seemed privately skeptical about religion though publicly polite about it. Now I know it probably came from my aged maternal grandfather whose early history with theosophy, astrology, hypnosis, and yogic mind science and healing was carefully concealed by my family until his death two summers after I graduated college.

Is it possible, then, that given a Black nun role model, this mystical little Black girl could have heard the call to convent life?

What you need to know about my childhood summers is that they were generally lonely. My possessive, emotionally unstable mother restricted contact with other children. She was forced to turn me loose just long enough each school day for the outside world to work its dread influence. Cultivation of my friendships outside of school was, therefore, minimal. Summer removed neighborhood children even further from my reach.

And yet summers would stretch out long and broad like fields of wildflowers; I loved them. A summer-born child, I felt healthier in the warmth. As an only child, I knew well how to make my own fun. Outdoors, I'd ride my bike and skate. Indoors, I'd shut myself off in the basement or my room, watching television, writing stories and poetry, reading books, books, books. Mostly, I'd be off in an intricate fantasy, a cinematic extravaganza. Summer was my time to have the full run of my mind—without having to cram it with grammar, spelling, history, math. I excelled in school, but I was even greater at thinking things through on my own. Summer gave me time and space for deep reflection.

Maybe Mrs. Clarke's daughter had a wee bit too much unstructured time one pre-teen summer. I assigned myself the challenge of reading the Bible, cover to cover. I don't recall how far I got, or just when I tired of all the begatting and skipped to the good parts, but I became a Bible belter. That summer, I hid particularly apropos New Testament quotes on slips of paper all over the apartment for my mother to find. She got the message but was too thrown off guard by the bizarre nature of this tactic to fly into a rage. Nevertheless, she put her foot down. She didn't like being preached to about her attitudes and behaviors, and she was right. Today, when the Christian Right throws selective Bible passages at queer people, I don't like it any better than my mother had. It was a pretty extreme thing to do. In my quiet way, I was a pretty intense kid.

Basically a good kid—at least, one too traumatized by the triple threat of Jehovah ("Love me—or I'll damn you to hell!"), his squadron of ruler-wielding nuns, and my mother to be anything but good. In the Church, we sopped up a culture built around duty, judgment, and punishment, the futile quest for perfection, perfection as defined by people who did not know us and whom we did not know. How many other children, I wonder now, made up sins just to have something to say to the confessional priest, the representative of an institution that assumes we're all sinners from the git-go?

Religion offered me and my classmates a "safe," codified sense of right and wrong, a two-dimensional sense of self, a predigested reaction to the complexities of life and of people. Almighty God, too, was helplessly frozen in place—and a very remote place, at that.

I remember, with pleasure, another of my childhood summers. That year, I accidentally discovered the sheer gorgeousness of the approach of dawn. Thereafter, I had to have it every day. I'd wake up very early and watch the sky lighten and blush. I never shared it with anyone, my sun-worshipping, pagan summer—a harbinger of future experiences with nature-based, feminist spirituality. When the Church spoke of grace—that outpouring of blessings from the Divine—it was an abstract force, a doctrine to be taken on faith. For me, the beauty of the natural world reflected the living presence of grace, this richness close to hand, visible to the eye, delicious on the tongue.

My childhood summers were filled with the cawing of crows, the nose-tingling aroma of magenta roses. I lived in a part of the city where one could appreciate Nature's way with greenery, her giving and her taking. My bedroom window afforded me a good view of the sky over my mother's unkempt garden. I could bay at the full moon or train my telescope at the stars: There was always something to engage both brain hemispheres.

That essential magic box, television, brought me *The Outer Limits, The Twilight Zone,* suburban witches with twitchy noses, avuncular Martians, even talking cars and horses! In its dopey way, television declared that, for better or for worse, the world pulsed with life far stranger, more wonderful, more unpredictable and malleable—more *queer,* if you will—than anything I'd been taught to expect. Little did I know, as a kid, that the Western definition of reality was relatively new and local; that, over vast areas of this planet, people still embraced older, richer understandings of the universe. When other people fret over the possibility of life after death or question whether one can really commune with departed ancestors, it is very useful to remember I am the descendant of Africans.

I grew older but no less spiritually sensitive, enriched by a good Catholic girls' high school with liberal nuns who marched in solidarity with the Berrigan brothers and, later, by my university's more adventurous Jesuits and lay teachers. Having long since left Catholic identity and practice somewhere among the kneeling benches and confession booths of St. Gabriel's, I now sought out books on myth, mysticism, world religions, Jungian and humanistic psychology, parapsychology, early mind-body-spirit stuff. It wasn't hard, then, to find support for these interests in my academic environment. Professors eagerly brought us the latest experiments from Esalen and turned classes into encounter groups. Hell—we all wanted to break free of the mindset that created and sustained the Vietnam War.

Feminism interested me, too, and the gay rights movement, though these struggles seemed far away: The concerns of my fellow Black students, the anxiety of draft-eligible classmates, were much more part of my everyday life. Still, I read about feminism with excitement, with a sense of a world about to be turned on its head. How I longed for that upheaval! Clueless, I nevertheless devoured everything I could find on gay and lesbian issues, sitting on the sidelines and cheering on a burgeoning movement that would not become my own until my mid-thirties.

Religion, as ruled by the mainstream powers-that-be, held no attraction for me. My clear pattern of skepticism (of religious authority), resistance (to rigid dogma and practice), and desire (for direct experience of the sacred) persisted into young adulthood. One of my first forays into queer community involved a lesbian-only, Goddess-focused ritual group—a setting I now find smugly limited and limiting, in its own way, as a patriarchal church. If there is a Great Goddess, she is trans(beyond)gender and decidedly nonseparatist, welcoming and *queer* in the very best sense of that controversial word.

Don't misunderstand. I *do* love goddesses (with a small g). They explain and reclaim for me aspects of myself, of consciousness, and of reality that Christianity and heterocentric society have ignored or covered in shame. Sekhmet is a favorite example—the Egyptian lionheaded goddess widely defamed as vengeful and bloodthirsty. Powerful goddesses have been maligned throughout the history of religion and myth. In truth, Sekhmet was once considered the very oldest, the virtual mother of all gods!

Bast—the well-known Egyptian cat goddess—may have been a lionheaded deity once, her characteristics muted and tamed over time. Sekhmet retained her reputation for fierceness and for bringing illness but, paradoxically, also being the great patron of healers. In the story of these two goddesses, we see the typical patriarchal interpretation of female strength as terrifying evil and the campaign to diminish that strength. Goddess scholar Patricia Monaghan has said that the Greek Aphrodite, far from being the inoffensive Barbie doll of the ancient world, was so threatening to the Church that her surviving statues are almost all battered and broken, deliberate acts of vandalism.

Yet Bast—who appears to me to be an aspect of Sekhmet, an energy on a continuum with her—retains an intriguing power. We may think of her as the small feline who, even when "domesticated," still bears the instincts and soul of a feral animal. She belongs to the realm of mystery and nighttime: She's lunar. Her night vision, innate sensitivity and uncommon agility are survival skills that she will share with and use on behalf of those she passionately cares about.

Sekhmet is a solar goddess who brings strength, purification and protection to those who love her. She demands honesty and integrity, and she raises confidence. She does not tolerate bull and does not allow those who she loves to put up with it either. Her healing way is to strengthen the body—especially the bones, muscle and posture.

As befits a solar goddess, Sekhmet wants things to grow—not remain small, constricted, cramped, repressed. She does not like to see a person diminished. When you work with Sekhmet, you find yourself moving into big spaces, big roles and having a bigger voice—which interestingly does not preclude humility and simplicity. Grounding is essential. Her energy can overwhelm if you are spacy and ungrounded. A good vessel carries her energy well.

Today, my exploration continues; as the folks in recovery say, I take what I like and leave the rest. I like spiritual ideas and practices that unchain the human mind and spirit, that reconnect us to the sacred, cherishable world, that transform and heal. My nourishing sources may range as widely as Kabbalah and Luisah Teish, shamanic practices and Buddhist meditation. I welcome both Jesus (clearly a bisexual Jewish shaman) and Kwan Yin (bodhisattva and goddess of compassion) as my two main healing mentors. If an idea or practice makes sense to my mind, heart and gut, I know I have something worth keeping and sharing. If it doesn't, even if its source appears politically correct, then it does not become part of my life. Bottom line is: I belong to no religion. I belong to God.

The little girl who had no recognizable role models and no road map for her spiritual journey did have, nevertheless, a strong instinct to make her path by walking. Rather than a convent, she found a multitude of worlds. As my colleague Donna Henes declares, "I practice spirituality the way our ancestors did: I make it up as I go along."

I respect those progressive Catholics who have been ridiculed for practicing "supermarket Catholicism"—that is, accepting some Church teachings and rules while rejecting others. We all really do live in a supermarket—Catholics and non-Catholics alike—a Grand Union even bigger than the Catholic Church. Bigger than patriarchy. Bigger than cultural and religious xenophobia. *And open all night!*

Contributors' Notes

Beverly Saunders Biddle was ordained as a minister of Spiritual Consciousness in 2003 by the Inner Visions Institute for Spiritual Development (IVISD) in Silver Spring, Md. As a master teacher and spiritual life coach, Rev. Beve serves on the IVISD faculty, conducts classes and workshops, and maintains a coaching practice in Washington, D.C. She is the founder and spiritual director of World Epiphany (WE) Ministries and also serves her church home at Unity of Washington, D.C. as director of spiritual programs. Rev. Beve and her life partner of twelve years share a home in Washington, D.C.

Amina M. Binta (née Donna M. Butts), an ordained minister, is a native of Washington, D.C., and currently resides in Takoma Park, Md. She is a graduate of the Howard University School of Divinity and obtained a doctorate degree from Wesley Theological Seminary. The title of her dissertation is "The Quest for Intentional Inclusion in a Black Baptist Church." Rev. Dr. Donna M. Butts is a member of the Covenant Baptist Church in Washington, D.C.

A man of eclectic interests, integrity, variegated talents and abilities, **Alaric Wendell Blair** remains a committed member of the black gay literati. He has contributed to the *Harvard Gay and Lesbian Review* and *Lambda Book Report*. He has also served as resident literary critic and book reviewer for *Venus Magazine*. Blair's literary career was catapulted with the publishing of his first novel, *The End of Innocence: a journey into the life,* a novel chronicling the joys and pains of growing up gay in Chicago. Currently, Blair resides in Brooklyn, N.Y., where he is working on the second installation to his first novel and a nonfiction (independent) study of black gay men and religion/spirituality and relationships.

Sharon Bridgforth is a proud RedBone press author/the Lambda Literary Award-winning author of *the bull-jean stories* and the Lambda Literary Award-nominated *love conjure/blues*. Bridgforth is the anchor artist for the Austin Project (sponsored by the Center for African and African American Studies at the University of Texas at Austin). Her work is available in many anthologies/and has received support from the National Endowment for the Arts Commissioning Program; the National Endowment for the Arts/Theatre Communications Group Playwright in Residence Program; and the Rockefeller Foundation Multi-Arts Production Fund Award. For more information check out www.sharonbridgforth.com.

C.C. Carter earned her M.A. in creative writing from Queens College in New York. She received her B.A. in English literature from Spelman College in Atlanta. Carter is the author of the Lambda Literary Award-nominated collection of poetry, *Body Language* (Kings Crossing Publishing). Her work has been anthologized in *Best Black Women's Erotica* and *Best Lesbian Erotica* (Cleis Press).

Tonda S. Clarke is a writer, seeker of spiritual elevation and daughter of the Creator. Her work has been published in various newspapers, magazines and anthologies, including a previous RedBone Press title, *does your mama know?*. She has performed her poetry in venues from Seattle, Wash., to Charlotte, N.C., where she currently resides.

Herndon L. Davis is author of the inspirational/spirituality book, *Black, Gay and Christian,* as well as the forthcoming follow-up, "Black Gay Spiritual Warfare." He is also the TV host/executive producer of "The Herndon Davis Reports," the world's first black gay/lesbian focused weekly TV news talk show on satellite/cable. Davis can be reached directly at http://herndondavis.com.

Mona de Vestel's work explores the expression of marginalized voices in American society. Mona is of Tutsi (Burundi) and Belgian ancestry; she grew up in Brussels, Belgium. Her completed works include a memoir, "The Color of Exile," and a screenplay, "Kali's Ashes." She is currently at work on a novel, "Voices," about the effects of genocide on Tutsi and Lakota cultures. De Vestel teaches writing and new media at the SUNY Institute of Technology; she lives in Utica, N.Y. with her partner, Celia.

Elisa Durrette is a freelance writer living in Dallas, Texas. Her writing, spanning everything from original short stories to articles on HIV/AIDS, has appeared in a number of national and international publications. Durrette is a graduate of Princeton University, where she studied creative writing with Toni Morrison, Joyce Carol Oates and A.J. Verdelle.

Anthony Farmer, a spiritual life coach, Usui Reiki Master Teacher/Practitioner and shamanic healer, inspires people to their greatness. Through his practice, Visions of the Heart, Heart-Centered Coaching, Teaching and Healing, he supports people in transforming and healing their lives. He recently joined the faculty of Inner Visions Institute for Spiritual Development. His essay, "Who Stole Your Passion: Rekindling Your Inner Fire," is included in the book *A Guide to Getting It: Purpose and Passion*. He is the author of the e-newsletter *Wisdom from the Coach's Corner* and is currently working on his next book, "The Tree Whisperer: Notes and Meditations." He believes that "to connect passionately to your heart is to connect to life."

Kenyon Farrow is a writer and activist living in Brooklyn, N.Y. He is the new culture editor for *Clamor Magazine,* and co-editor of *Letters from Young Activists: Today's Rebels Speak Out* (Nation Books). His essays have appeared at www.BlackAIDS.org and www.Popandpolitics.com, *Bay Windows, City Limits, The Objector* and *Between the Lines*. Farrow is the communications and public education coordinator for New York State Black Gay Network.

Rev. Wanda Y. Floyd founded Imani Metropolitan Community Church (MCC) of Durham, N.C. in 1997. Imani MCC provides a place of safety for many who continue to struggle with their sexuality and spirituality; the congregation is comprised of predominately African-American Christian lesbians, gays, bisexuals and transgendered people. Rev. Floyd has served on numerous boards of gay organizations in the North Carolina area, and co-chaired WOW 2003, an ecumenical conference for the Welcoming Church Movement within the United States and Canada. Currently she is on the steering committee for the North Carolina Religious Coalition for Marriage Equality, a fellow in the Wildacres Leadership Initiative, and a participant in the Sustaining Pastoral Excellence two-year program. She resides in North Carolina with Sheryl Griffin, her life partner of ten years.

A talented writer and gifted mind, **Clarence J. Fluker** is a native of East Cleveland, Ohio, and holds degrees from Morgan State University and American University. His work has appeared in a variety of publications, including the *Cleveland Bar Journal, The Journal of Intergroup Relations* and *ARISE* magazine, where he served as Next Generation Editor. As an engaging speaker on the topic of race and sexual orientation, he has spoken to campus groups at universities throughout the United States, including Columbia University, Case Western Reserve University and Ohio University. In August of 2003, Fluker was the youngest speaker to address a rally to commemorate the life and work of Bayard Rustin preceding the fortieth anniversary of the March on Washington.

Tracee Ford was born and raised in Columbus, Ga. She attended Spelman College where she studied religion. Since then, Ford has been extremely active in the nonprofit sector, working with various youth organizations and educating the public about HIV prevention. She is involved with the Gay and Lesbian Community Center in Baltimore, Md., where she sat on the Board of Directors for two years. Ford is currently working with Community Mediation Program, a grassroots nonprofit peacemaking organization in Baltimore.

Diane Foster graduated from the University of Alabama with a master's degree in medical social work. Foster was a Fulbright scholar in Ghana, West Africa, conducting research on the psychosocial implications of vaginal vesicular fistula. She recently retired from the University of Alabama where she worked as a senior computer operator while operating a computer service business; Foster also taught computer skills to youth expelled from the public school system. Her zest for spiritual knowledge of God came one day in church when she heard these words coming from the pulpit: "For God so loved the world that He gave His only begotten son, that whosoever believed in Him shall not perish but have everlasting life." These words took on new meaning, and she began to ponder this meaning in terms of her sexual orientation. Her enlightenment led her to write on the subject. She recently finished writing "Escape into Reality: Breaking Biblical Psychological Chains of Homosexual (and other) Enslavements." Foster currently resides in Albuquerque, N. Mex. with her wife Ellen. Foster can be reached at broide1@hotmail.com.

Steven G. Fullwood is an archivist at the Schomburg Center for Research in Black Culture in New York City. He founded the Black Gay and Lesbian Archive to aid in the preservation of black lesbian, gay, bisexual, transgender, Same Gender Loving, queer, questioning and in the life history and culture. Fullwood is also the author of *Funny,* and a freelance writer whose work has appeared in Africana.com, *Black Issues Book Review, Lambda Book Report, Vibe* and other publications. www.stevengfullwood.org.

Anthony R.G. Hardaway was educated in Mississippi; he has earned an AA and BA in speech and dramatic arts. For the past fifteen years, Hardaway has worked for a privately owned black theater company; in his spare time he travels, educating the black gay village about our history while collecting and seeking out nationally known same-gender loving celebrities in order to connect them to the South. Hardaway works with the International Federation of Black Prides, Fire & Ink: A Writers Festival for GLBT People of African Descent, and Brothers United Network of Tennessee.

Dorothy Harris is a deacon candidate at Unity Fellowship Church Baltimore, where she is also the president of the women's ministry. She and her partner reside in Columbia, Md.

Michaela Harrison swam to Earth during a total eclipse of the sun in Washington, D.C. Pisces, poet, prophet, singer, scholar, silly girl, she has a master's degree in Africana studies from New York University. A writer and a singer since the age of five, she is also a community health educator and an aspiring mambo with intentions of healing the world. Until recently, she lived in New Orleans, where she wrote, cared for children and stray cats, and sold seashell jewelry.

G. Winston James is a Jamaican-born poet and short fiction writer. He holds an MFA in fiction from Brooklyn College, City University of New York, and is the author of the Lambda Literary Award-nominated poetry collection *Lyric: Poems Along a Broken Road*. He is co-editor of *Spirited: Affirming the Soul and Black Gay/Lesbian Identity*.

Lynwoodt Jenkins' credits include writing and performing his one-man stage play, *Faggot,* which ran at the San Francisco Queer Arts Festival and the National Black Theatre Festival; voice-overs in local (Atlanta) and national commercials; and teaching "The Meisner (acting) Technique" at Actors Express, Spelman College and Georgia Ensemble Theatre. He is working on a novel and a play depicting the truth and stereotypes of black, same-gender-loving men.

American Theatre Magazine named interdisciplinary artist **Daniel Alexander Jones** one of fifteen up-and-coming artists whose work will be transforming America's stages for decades to come. His preoccupation with the spaces between and beyond absolutes inspires his new work for theater as a writer, director and performer. His plays and performance texts include *Blood:Shock:Boogie, Earthbirths/The Blackbird Cipher, La Chanteuse Nubienne* and *clayangels*. His play *Bel Canto* was developed at the Sundance Theatre Lab and premiered in 2003 under the direction of Robbie McCauley. Jones holds a bachelor's degree in Africana studies from Vassar College and a master's degree in theater from Brown University. In the last ten years of professional practice, Daniel has been a company member with Frontera @ Hyde Park Theatre in Austin and Penumbra Theatre Company in St. Paul; has toured the U.S. and U.K. as a performer; and he has maintained active collaborations with several artists including Sharon Bridgforth, Helga Davis, Joni L. Jones and Erik Ehn. A resident of Manhattan, Daniel is a member of New Dramatists, and is at work on his first book project.

Kaija Langley is an MFA candidate in creative writing at St. Mary's College (of California). She is currently at work on a novel and a collection of short stories. Her prose has appeared in *The Baltimore Sun, Girlfriends* and *Poetry Midwest*. She is a recent East Coast transplant to the San Francisco Bay area.

Earthlyn Marselean Manuel is an author and visual artist living in northern California. She is the author and illustrator of the *Black Angel Cards: A Soul Revival Guide for Black Women* (Harper San Francisco, 1999) and author of *Seeking Enchantment: a Spiritual Journey of Healing from Oppression* (Kasai River Press, 2002).

The work of **Bahíyyih Maroon** appears in numerous places including *Spirit and Flame: An Anthology of Young Black Poets, Free Mumia, Bint el Nas* and *The New York Times*. As an author, performance art director and architectural anthropologist, she regularly engages with questions of Belief and Dwelling in cultural space and advocates the ongoing creation of emancipatory places in our everyday life. She is a founding member of the Constellationist Movement, a participant in the Neo-Soul Black Language Brigade, and an ardent supporter of decadent communism, the black rock coalition and Supra Dadaist interventions. Bahíyyih writes under the sign of mother, warrior, poet and seeker of motion. She lives according to the belief that language is among the last remaining gifts in humanity's contemporary possession. She believes in the use of language to bring about daily resurrection, salvation, redemption and yes, Joy.

Jorhán Mbonisi is a writer-teacher-student living in Silver Spring, Md. The recipient of a number of awards in theater, television, and music, Mbonisi looks forward to creating change through art.

Rev. Dyan "Abena" McCray is the founding pastor of Unity Fellowship Church, Washington, D.C., an affiliate of the Unity Fellowship Church Movement. Rev. McCray served for three years on the board of directors of DC Black Gay & Lesbian Pride Inc., and presently serves on the executive board of directors of the Mautner Project (a national agency that serves lesbians, their families and caregivers challenged with cancer). In an article in the August 2002 issue of *ARISE* magazine, Rev. McCray states, "My mission is to be the voice of those whose voices are not heard." Rev. McCray is presently studying at Virginia Theological Seminary.

Monique Meadows is a witchy blueswoman who hails from the Midwest. Coming out in her early twenties in Washington, D.C. as a fiercely proud black femme dyke led Meadows to pivotal activist roles in the black lesbian and feminist spirituality communities. Now moving joyfully through her thirties, Meadows is preparing for initiation as a priestess of Yemaya, expanding her work as a Reiki master, and exploring the sacred sexuality of submission.

Rev. Irene Monroe is a professor of religion and associate director of multicultural and spiritual programming at Pine Manor College. She is a Ford Fellow completing her doctorate in the Religion, Gender and Culture Program at Harvard Divinity School. Monroe is a religion columnist who writes "Queer Take" for the online publication *The Witness,* a progressive Episcopal magazine, and "The Religion Thang" for *In Newsweekly,* the largest lesbian, gay, bisexual and transgender newspaper in New England.

Kathleen E. Morris, author of *Speaking in Whispers: African-American Lesbian Erotica,* is a personal freedom advocate living in Maryland. Her widely published fiction, personal essays, nonfiction and literary reviews and critiques provide "a mirror in which readers can see their own beauty, power and potentials reflected." As founder of The Erotic Pen workshops, Morris offers her services as editor, book doctor, writing coach and workshop facilitator to those who seek development of self-expression and personal voice through writing. Current projects include the continued development of her book manuscript, "Without Exception or Limitation."

Tonya Parker, a native Virginian, is a trainer, counselor, massage therapist and writer. You can find her work in *Testimonies: Lesbian Coming Out Stories* (3rd edition) and *Biting the Apple: First Taste.*

Conrad R. Pegues is a writer living in Memphis, Tenn. He has been published in several anthologies. He believes writing should be a process of revelation, not only for the writer but for the reader as well.

Scarab... justified, ancient, sacred. All praise and glory to God! I'm not only a Christian, but a disciple of Christ who strives to live a life of ministry in every area of my life. I reside in Atlanta, Ga. where my ministry carries over into my career as marketing manager for a nonprofit that fights hunger. I'm also very active in my church. A writer since my youth, my essay here marks my first publication. My prayer for you all is a life filled with the love of Christ, the power of the Holy Spirit, and the peace of God which surpasses all understanding. In all your ways acknowledge Him, and He shall direct your paths. Proverbs 3:6

H.L. Sudler is a board member of the National Lesbian and Gay Journalists Association. He was the publisher of *Café Magazine,* and is the president of Archer Enterprises, which produces *Page & Author.* He has just completed work on his first novel, "Summerville," and is at work on its sequel, "Return to Summerville." He is a native of Philadelphia who now resides in Washington, D.C. www.pageandauthor.com.

Tawanna Sullivan is the owner/webmaster of Kuma2.net, a Web site that encourages black lesbians to explore their sensuality and sexuality through writing erotica. The twenty-nine-year-old has given up on organized religion. Although she has attended many church services in her lifetime, she has found greater spiritual uplift simply from surrounding herself with loving, caring people. Tawanna lives in New Jersey with her life partner, Martina.

Born in west Tennessee, **Patrice Suncircle** has lived various places, from Florida to Hawaii. She now makes her home in northern California. She has been writing much of her life, mostly writing dark fantasy and erotica; her work has been published under the pseudonym Pat Williams in Susie Bright's erotic anthologies. Suncircle is currently writing a novel about a vampire who strolls the streets of New York during the Harlem Renaissance, rubbing shoulders with Miss Hurston, Mr. Hughes, Mr. Nugent and all.

Rev. Karen Georgia Thompson is a Black, heterosexual, female, pastor, poet, writer and teacher who was born in Jamaica. She is the proud mother of two wonderful children, Catilla and Patrick. She is the pastor of an open and affirming United

Church of Christ congregation in Florida. She is a graduate of Union Theological Seminary in New York City.

Natasha Tinsley is a native of the San Francisco Bay Area, where she was deeply fed and inspired by family, friends, and the colors and presences of the bay. Her studies have given her the opportunity to do research and learn in unexpected ways in Jamaica, Haiti, the Dominican Republic and Puerto Rico, while collecting materials for a dissertation on the writing of Caribbean women who love women. Currently she lives in Chicago with her cat Dulce, teaches Caribbean literature at the University of Chicago, and is thankful for the daily beauty of Lake Michigan.

Linda Villarosa is a former executive editor of *Essence* magazine. She is a well-known author, freelance journalist, and full-time mother of two.

Rev. Jim Webb is an ordained interfaith minister, and author of *Pathways to Inner Peace: Life-saving Processes for Healing Heart, Mind, and Soul.*

Marvin K. White, author of the Lambda Literary Award-nominated collection of poetry *last rights* and *nothin' ugly fly* (RedBone Press), is a poet, performer, playwright, visual artist as well as a community arts organizer. His poetry has been anthologized in *The Road Before Us: 100 Black Gay Poets; My Brothers Keeper; Gents, Bad Boys and Barbarians: New Gay Writing; Things Shaped in Passing; Sojourner: Writing in the Age of AIDS; Bum Rush the Page; Role Call;* and *Think Again*, as well as other local and national publications. A former member of the critically acclaimed Pomo Afro Homos, he has led creative arts and writing workshops from inner city elementary schools to youth centers for runaway kids to black gay youth support groups. He is co-founder of B/GLAM (Black Gay Letters and Arts Movement), an organization whose goal is to preserve, present and incubate black gay artistic expressions. www.marvinkwhite.com.

Native New Yorker **Eva Yaa Asantewaa** draws upon lifelong interests in both the spirit and the natural world, cross-cultural symbols and imagery, words of power, and "radical magick." She maintains a private practice in Tarot, meditation coaching, dreamwork, Therapeutic Touch and other holistic modalities. She has produced and facilitated workshops and special events sponsored by over fifty health, social service, spiritual, feminist, people of color and GLBT organizations including the Audre Lorde Project, GMAD, GMHC, Housing Works, Healing Works, New York Open Center, Staten Island HIV Care Network, and the Women's Rites Center. Eva is also a published poet, a dance journalist, and a former producer/host at Pacifica Radio's WBAI (1987089), including work with the Women's Radio Collective, the Gay and Lesbian Independent Broadcasters, and "The Tuesday Arts Magazine."

Permissions

About the Editors

G. Winston James is a Jamaican-born poet and short fiction writer. He holds an MFA in fiction from Brooklyn College, City University of New York, and is the author of the Lambda Literary Award-nominated poetry collection *Lyric: Poems Along a Broken Road.* His poetry also appears in numerous anthologies and publications, including *Black Ivy: A Literary and Visual Arts Magazine; Bloom Magazine: Queer Fiction, Art, Poetry and More; Freedom in This Village: Twenty-Five Years of Black Gay Men's Writing; Kuumba: A Poetry Journal for Black People in the Life; Milking Black Bull; The Nubian Gallery; Role Call: A Generational Anthology of Social and Political Black Literature and Art;* and the Lambda Literary Award-winning anthologies, *Sojourner: Black Gay Voices in the Age of AIDS* and *The Road Before Us.* His fiction and essays can also be found in *Brooklyn Review; Callaloo: A Journal of African-American and African Arts and Letters; Fighting Words: Personal Essays by Black Gay Men; His 2: Brilliant New Fiction by Gay Writers; The Mammoth Book of Gay Erotica; Shade: An Anthology of Short Fiction by Gay Men of African Descent; Think Again;* and *Waves: An Anthology of New Gay Fiction.* A former executive director of the Other Countries Black Gay Expression artists collective, he was a founding organizer of Fire & Ink: A Writers Festival for GLBT People of African Descent. James is co-editor of the historic anthology *Spirited: Affirming the Soul and Black Gay/Lesbian Identity.*

Lisa C. Moore is the founder and editor of RedBone Press, which publishes work that celebrates the culture of black lesbians and gay men and further promotes understanding between black gays and lesbians and the black mainstream. RedBone's first book, *does your mama know? An Anthology of Black Lesbian Coming Out Stories,* won two 1997 Lambda Literary Awards, for Small Press and Lesbian Studies. The second title, *the bull-jean stories* by Sharon Bridgforth, won the 1998 Lambda Literary Award for Small Press. RedBone has also published *love conjure/blues,* a novel by Sharon Bridgforth; *last rights* and *nothin' ugly fly*, both books of poetry by Marvin K. White (all published 2004); and *Where the Apple Falls*, poetry by Samiya Bashir (2005). Moore is currently in production for "sassy b. gonn: Searching for Black Lesbian Elders," a video documentary stemming from her master's research in anthropology (University of Texas, 2000). Moore was also lead organizer of the Fire & Ink writers festival for GLBT people of African descent held at the University of Illinois-Chicago in September 2002; she is currently board president of Fire & Ink (www.fireandink.org). Moore is co-editor of *Spirited: Affirming the Soul and Black Gay/Lesbian Identity*.